COLLAPSIBLE BASKET PATTERNS

by Rick and Karen Longabaugh

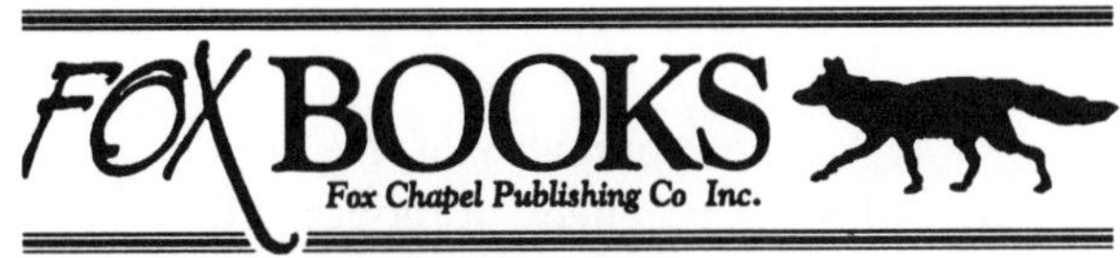

Fox Chapel Publishing Co., Inc.
PO Box 7948
Lancaster, PA 17604-7948

In Appreciation

We wish to thank all those who have had a part in the creation of this book – for their ideas, encouragement, and support.

Acknowledgements / Credits

Pattern Designs
Rick Longabaugh
Ardis Longabaugh
Tana Althauser
Lorna Smith

Graphic Design
Lorna Smith Graphic Design
Chehalis, Washington

Photography
Greg Krogstad Photography
Seattle, Washington

ISBN # 1-56523-087-6

To order your copy of this book,
please send check or money order
for $12.95 plus $2.50 postage to:
Fox Chapel Book Orders
Box 7948
Lancaster, PA 17604-7948

Try your favorite book supplier first!

Contents

Instructions

Introduction

All patterns in this book can be cut on either the bandsaw or scrollsaw. See page 5 for specific bandsaw instructions and page 6 for specific scrollsaw intructions.

Materials

Saw Blades
- Bandsaw - 1/8" Standard gauge blade (.020 thickness)
- Scrollsaw - #9 blade

3/4 " Hardwood: ash, walnut, mahogany, cherry, maple, oak, etc.
Clamps
Double - sided tape or spray adhesive

6/32 Machine screws
- Flathead or
- Roundhead

Small drum or pad sander
Oil (Danish, Tung or Min-Wax)
1/8" Drill bit
Wood glue

General Instructions

To use this pattern book most effectively, we suggest making photo copies of the patterns you wish to cut out. An advantage to the copier is that you can enlarge or reduce the pattern to fit the size wood you choose to use. Use double-sided tape or a spray adhesive to adhere the pattern to the wood. Spray adhesives can be purchased at most arts & crafts, photography, and department stores. Pay special attention to purchase one that states "temporary bond" or "repositionable". Lightly spray the back of the pattern, not the wood, then position the pattern onto the work piece.

Two factors will determine how deep the basket will fold out, the thickness of the blade, and the bevel of the table when cutting. A thicker blade produces a deeper basket, as does the 4° bevel over the 5°. Therefore, we recommend practicing with an inexpensive grade of wood until you determine the proper bevel for the thickness of the blade you are using. In the materials listed above we have recommended blade sizes for the bandsaw and scrollsaw, and have given bevels on each pattern to get you started. **Note:** If you use a bandsaw blade other than the thickness listed above, you may need to put some weight in the basket for a few hours until it will remain open on its own.

We have stated a drill bit size and corresponding machine screw size in the materials listed above. If, however, you choose to use a size other than what is listed, use a drill bit one size smaller than the machine screws you are using. This will ensure that the screws will fit snugly, providing enough resistance so the basket does not swing freely. You can determine the length of the machine screw you need for any given pivot point by measuring the length of its dotted line on the pattern. If you wish to counter sink the screw, keep in mind that you will need a shorter length of screw than what the dotted line measured.

Sand any rough edges on the outer shape and the first rung of the basket. If the basket or foot catches on any edges when pivoted, try sanding a little more. For a more refined look use a roundover router bit on the edges.

When the basket is completed, soak it in oil according to the manufactures' instructions.

Bandsaw Instructions

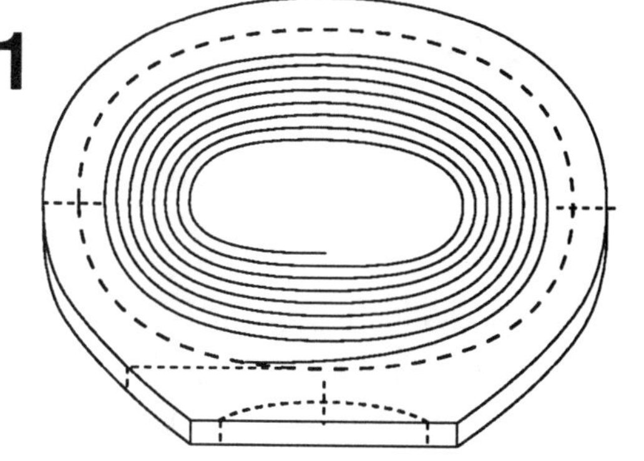

Step 1 Adhere pattern to work piece. Cut outer shape of basket.

Step 2 Mark the drill points using a hammer and center punch. Drill basket and foot pivot points the length of their dotted lines.

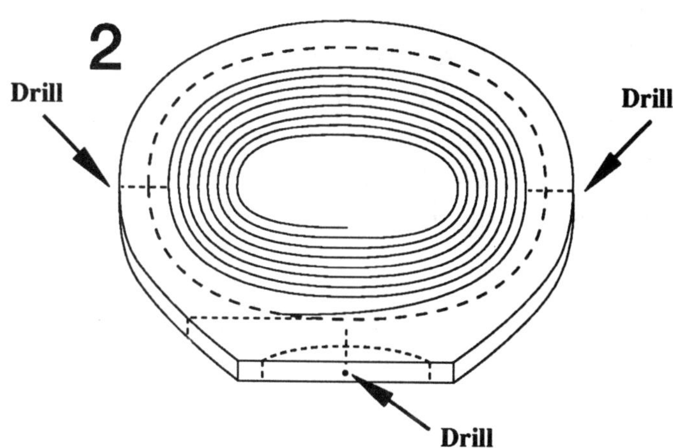

Step 3 Cut along dashed lines (with table flat) to separate inner basket and foot. Glue outer shape where cut was made, and clamp.

Step 4 Using the bevel indicated on the pattern, cut basket rungs following the solid line, shut off saw and back out blade. Glue 1"-2" at start of cut, and clamp.

Step 5 Assemble basket and foot with screws at drilled pivot points.

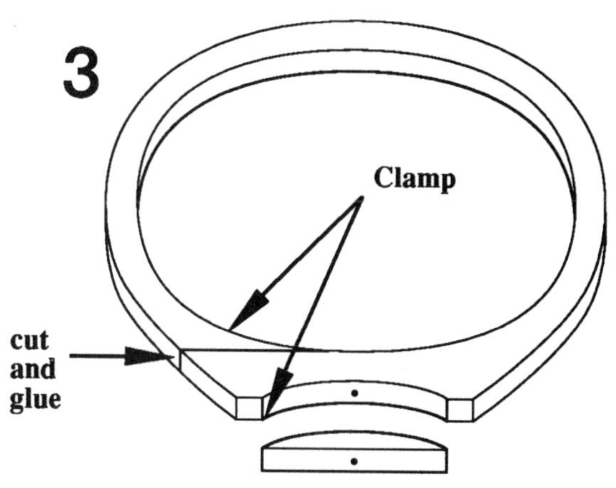

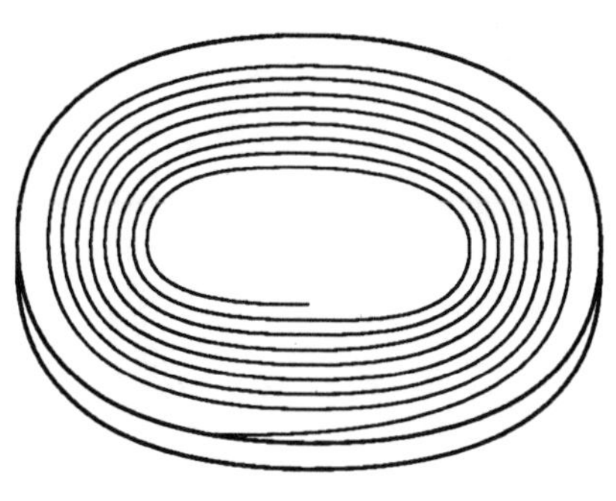

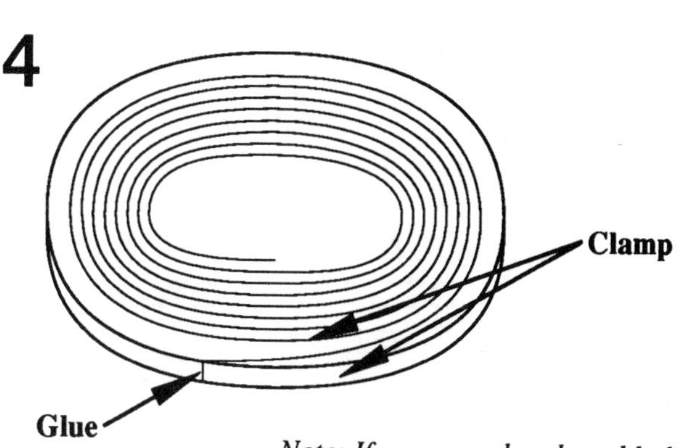

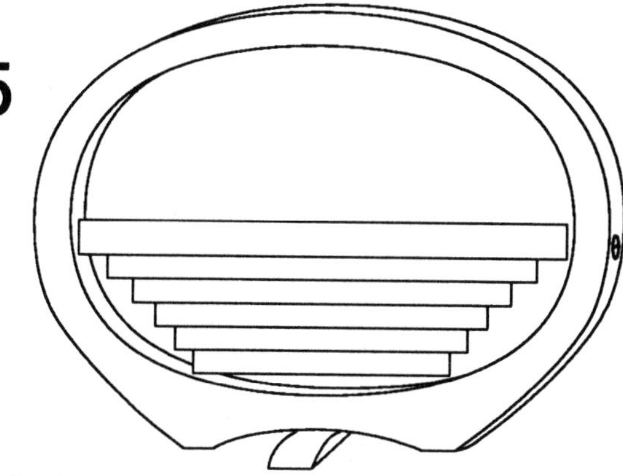

Note: If you use a bandsaw blade other than the thickness listed above, you may need to put some weight in the basket for a few hours until it will remain open on its own.

Scrollsaw Instructions

Step 1 Adhere pattern to work piece. Cut outer shape of basket.

Step 2 Mark the drill points using a hammer and center punch. Drill basket and foot pivot points the length of their dotted lines.

Step 3 With table flat, cut along dashed lines to separate foot. Drill at points A, B, C using a 1/16" drill bit. Beginning at Point A, cut along dashed lines (with table flat) to separate inner basket from the outer shape.

Step 4 Using the bevel indicated on the pattern, cut basket rungs following the solid line. If your table tilts to the left begin your cut at Point C and finish at Point B. If your table tilts to the right begin your cut at Point B and finish at Point C. **Note**: It is easier to begin at Point C and end at Point B.

Step 5 Assemble basket and foot with screws at drilled pivot points.

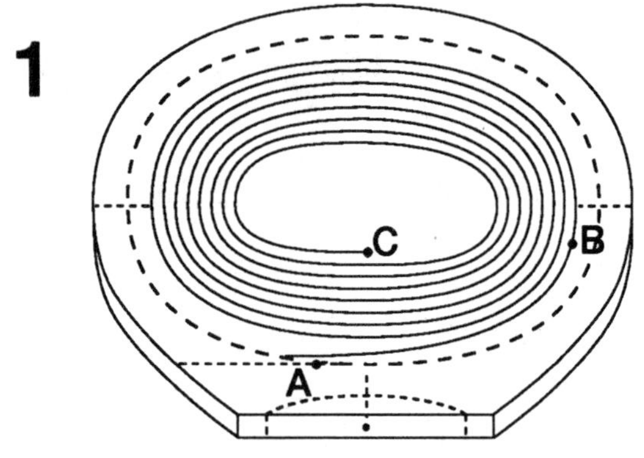

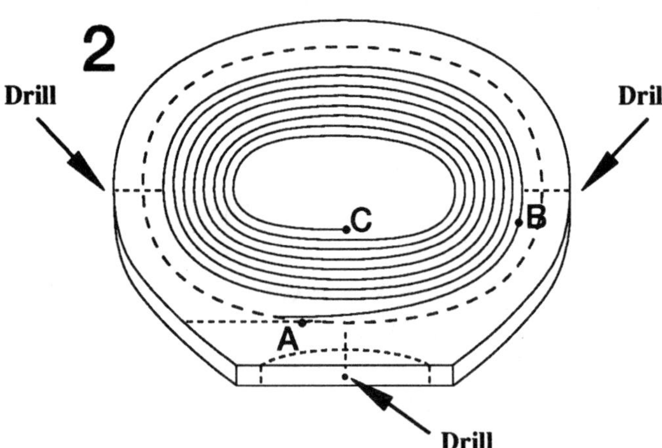

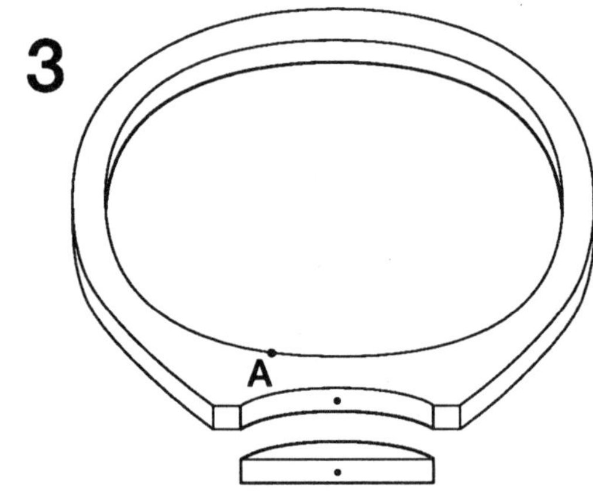

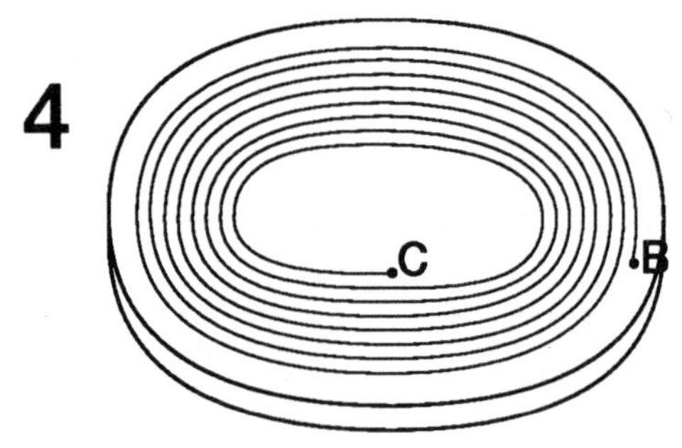

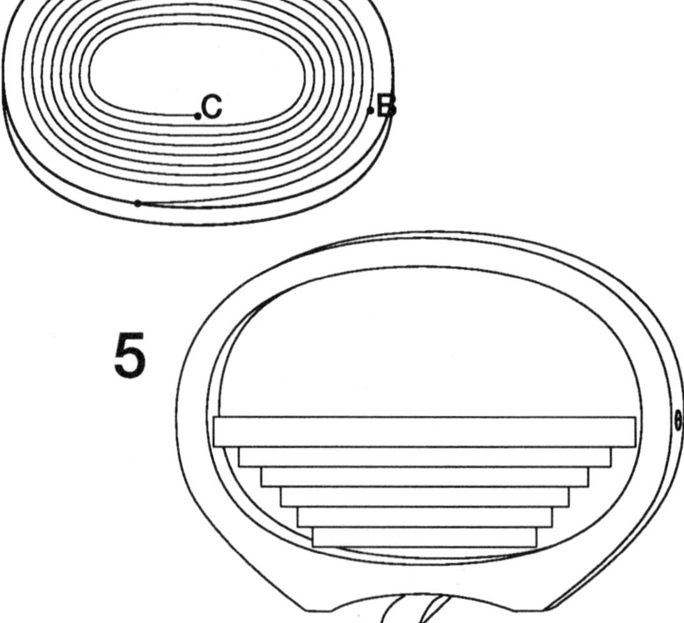

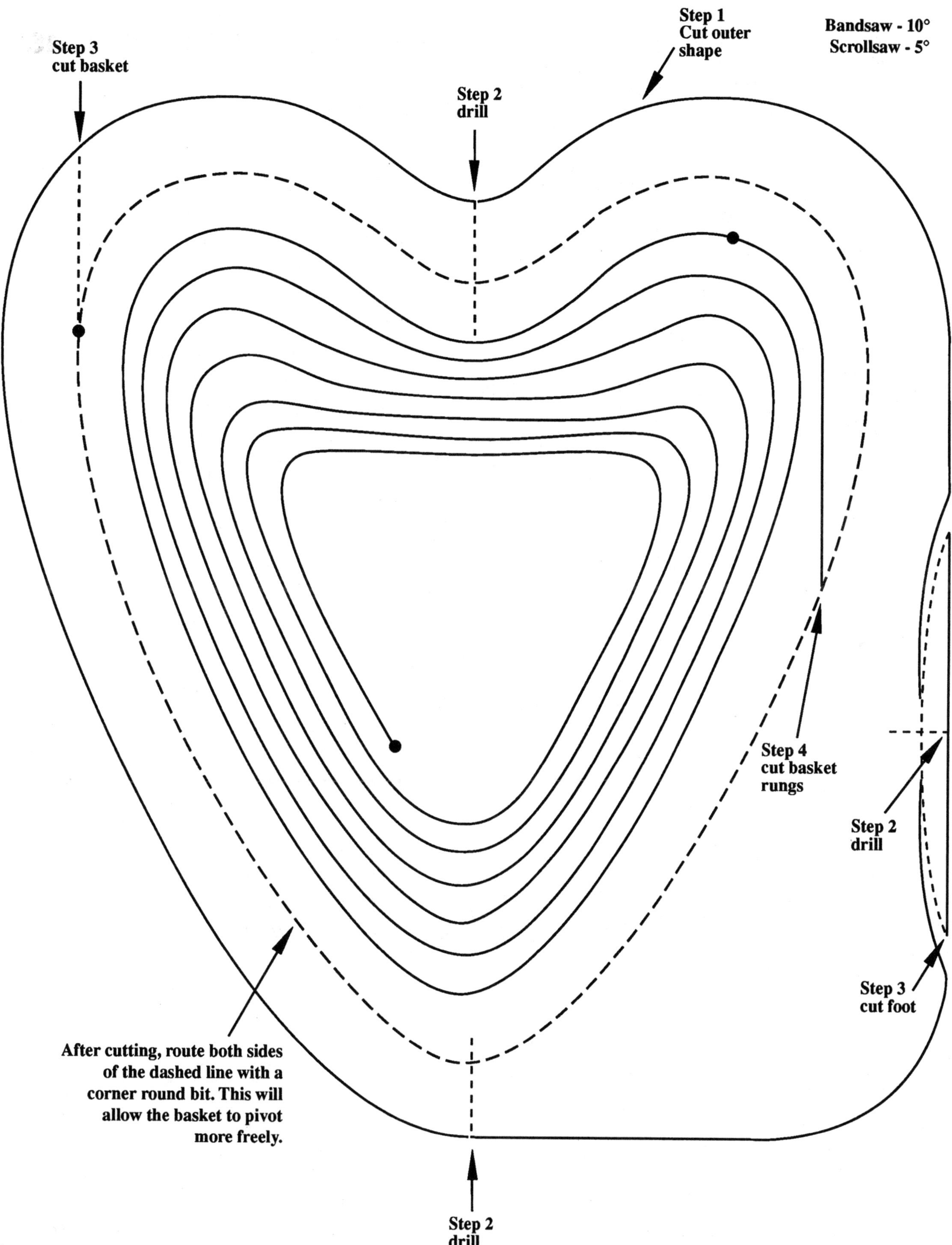
Step 1
Cut outer
shape
Bandsaw - 10°
Scrollsaw - 5°
Step 3
cut basket
Step 2
drill
Step 4
cut basket
rungs
Step 2
drill
Step 3
cut foot
After cutting, route both sides
of the dashed line with a
corner round bit. This will
allow the basket to pivot
more freely.
Step 2
drill

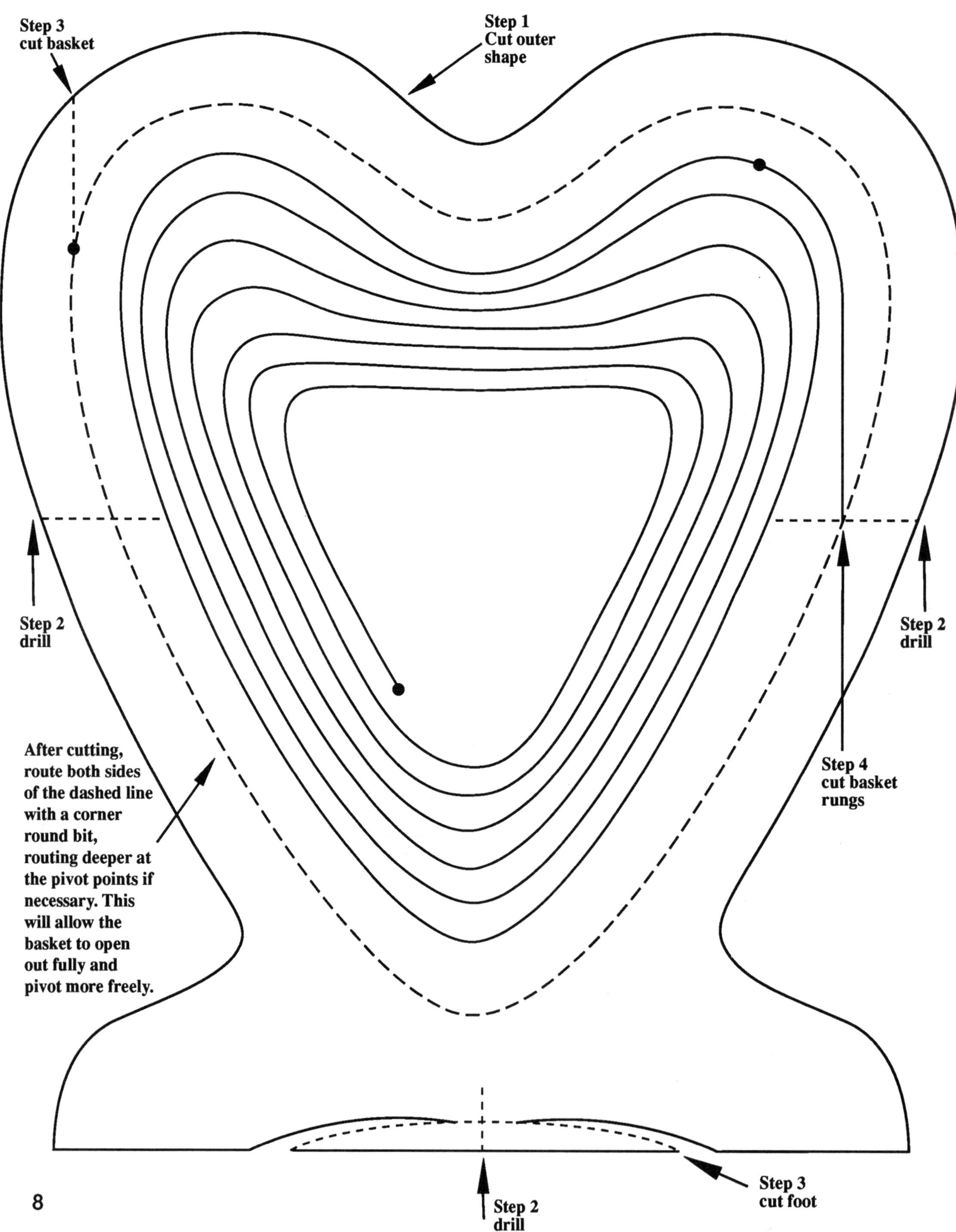
Bandsaw - 10°
Scrollsaw - 5°
Step 3
cut basket
Step 1
Cut outer
shape
Step 2
drill
Step 2
drill
After cutting,
route both sides
of the dashed line
with a corner
round bit,
routing deeper at
the pivot points if
necessary. This
will allow the
basket to open
out fully and
pivot more freely.
Step 4
cut basket
rungs
Step 3
cut foot
Step 2
drill

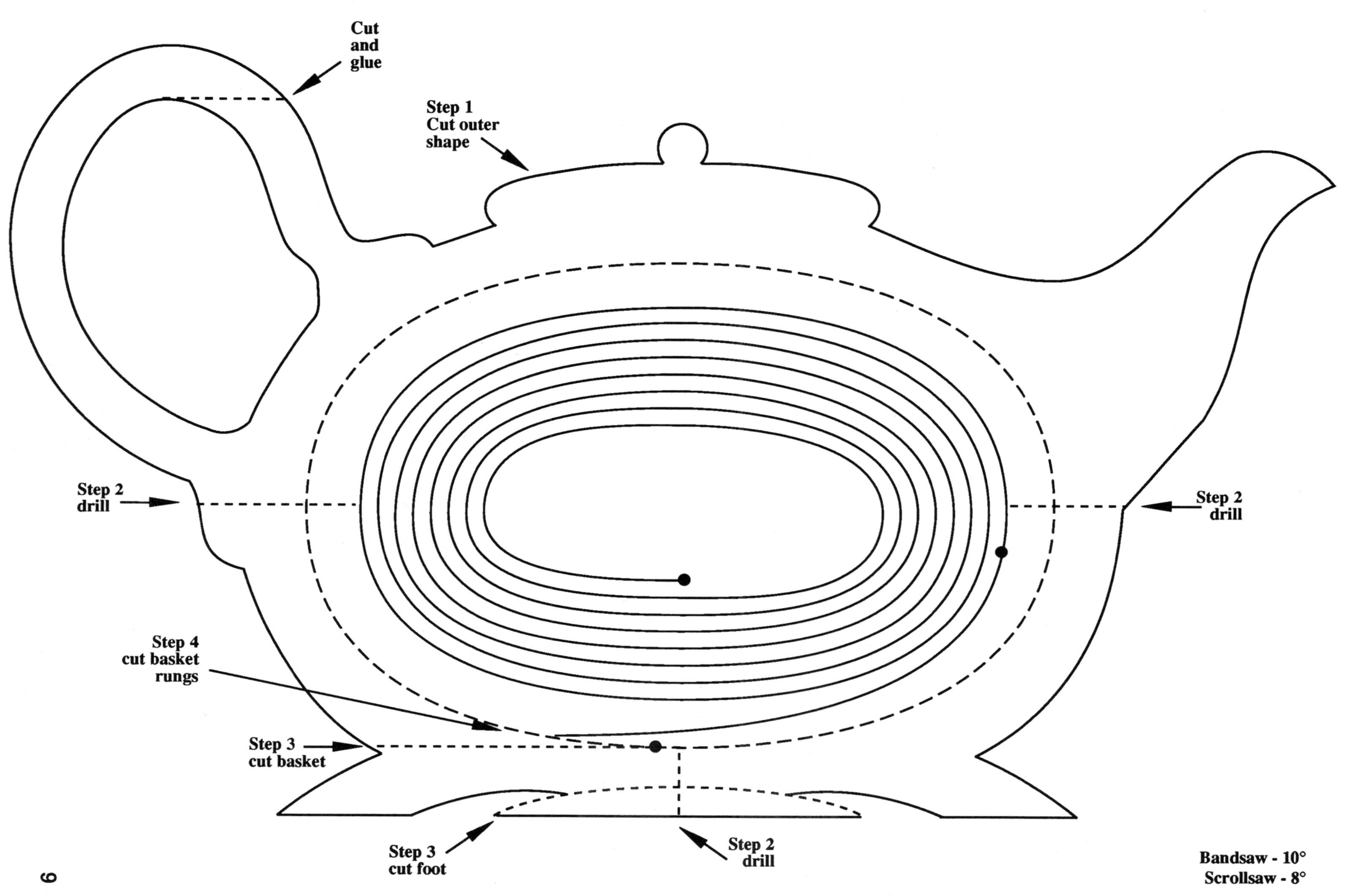
Cut
and
glue
Step 1
Cut outer
shape
Step 2
drill
Step 2
drill
Step 4
cut basket
rungs
Step 3
cut basket
Step 3
cut foot
Step 2
drill
Bandsaw - 10°
Scrollsaw - 8°

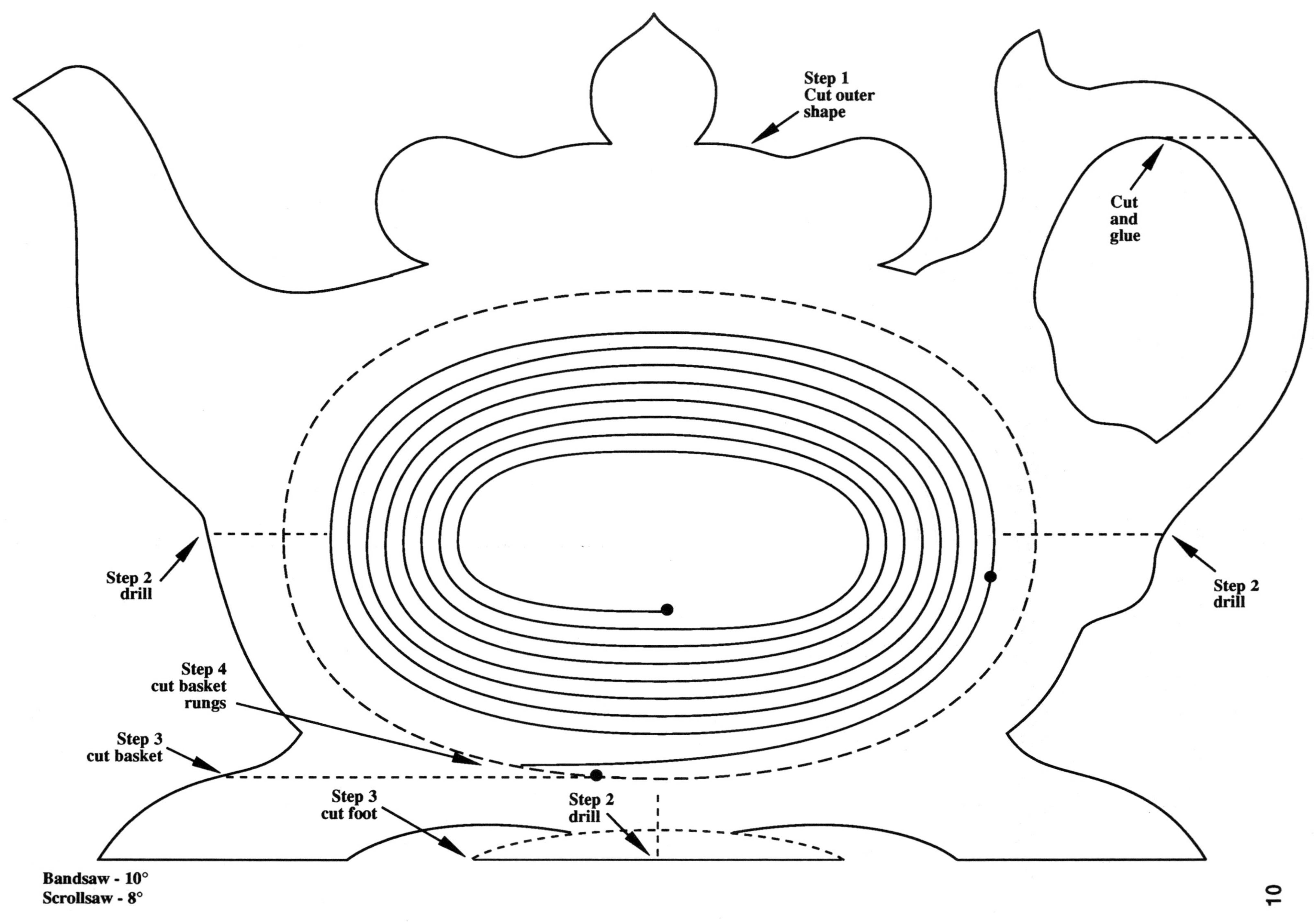
Step 1
Cut outer
shape
Cut
and
glue
Step 2
drill
Step 2
drill
Step 4
cut basket
rungs
Step 3
cut basket
Step 3
cut foot
Step 2
drill
Bandsaw - 10°
Scrollsaw - 8°

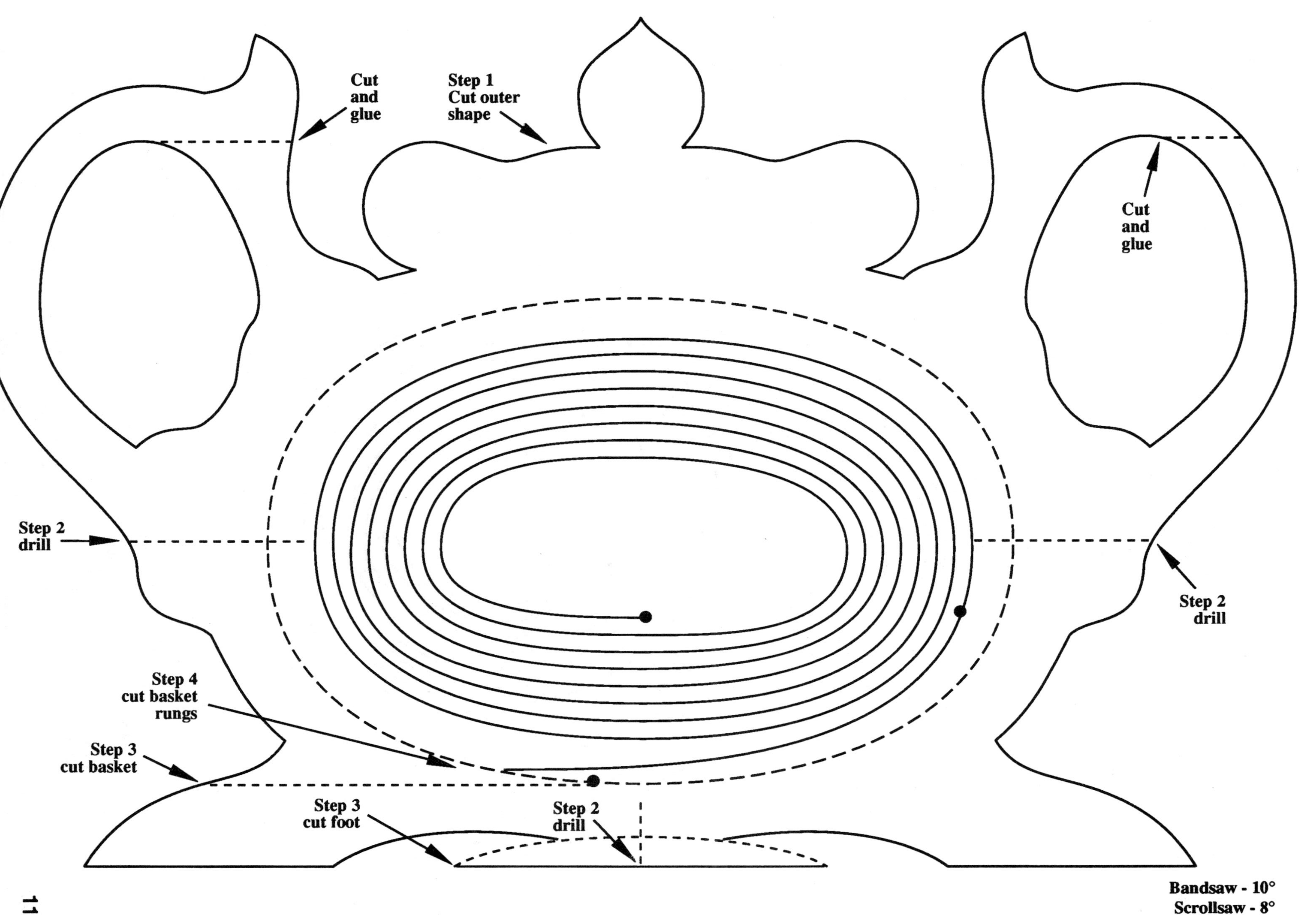

Cut
and
glue
Step 1
Cut outer
shape
Cut
and
glue
Step 2
drill
Step 2
drill
Step 4
cut basket
rungs
Step 3
cut basket
Step 3
cut foot
Step 2
drill
Bandsaw - 10°
Scrollsaw - 8°

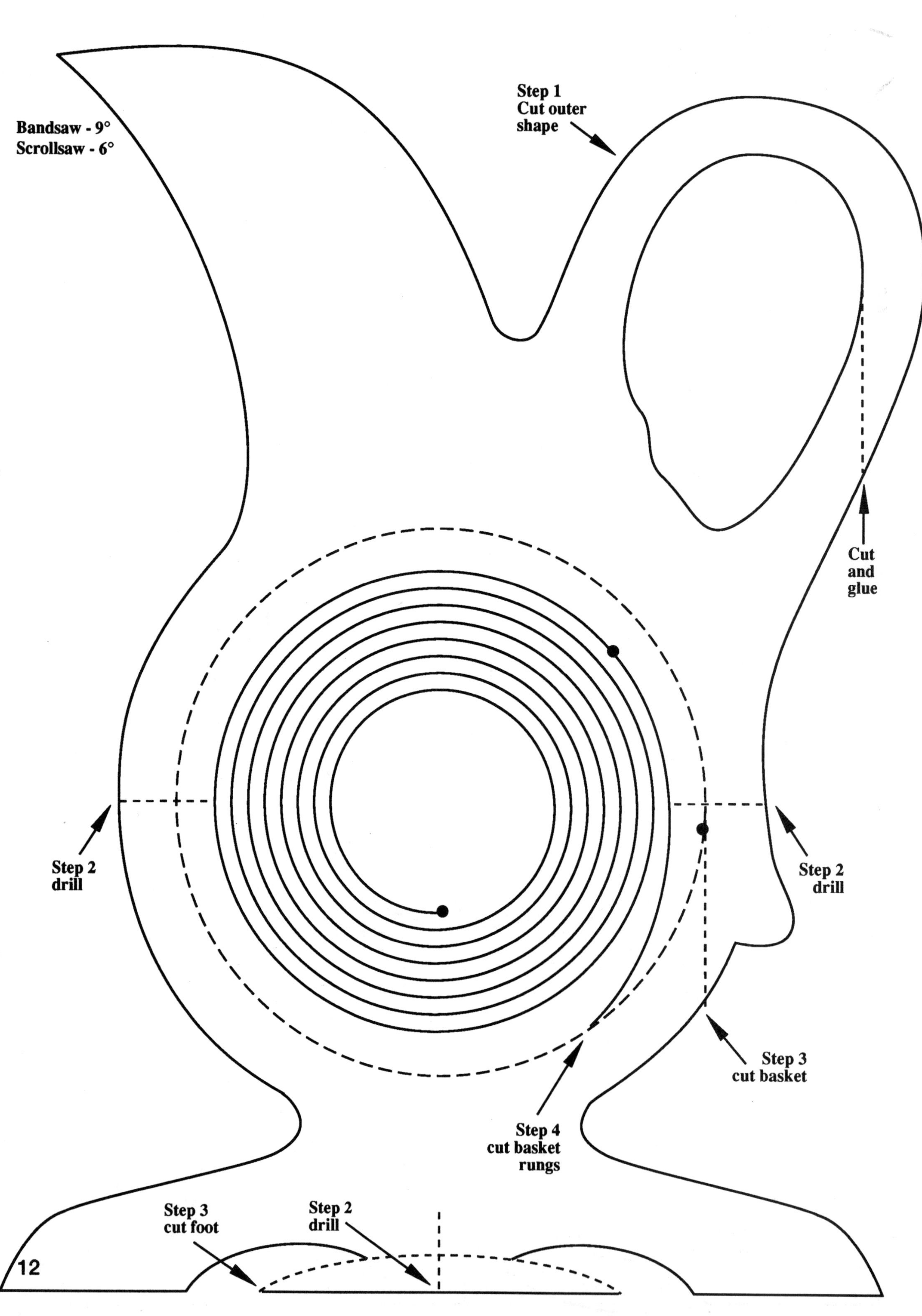
Bandsaw - 9°
Scrollsaw - 6°
Step 1
Cut outer
shape
Cut
and
glue
Step 2
drill
Step 2
drill
Step 3
cut basket
Step 4
cut basket
rungs
Step 3
cut foot
Step 2
drill

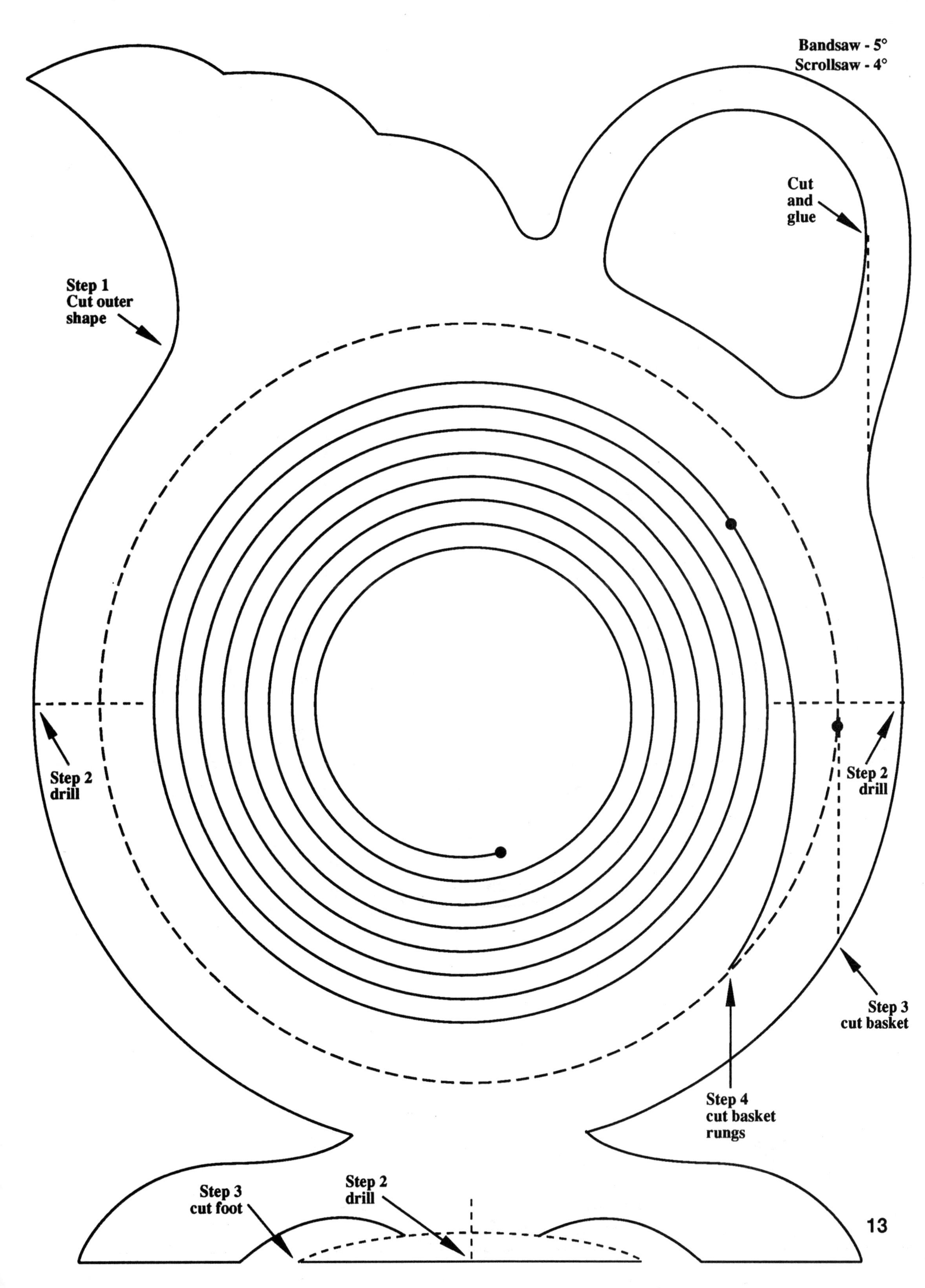
Bandsaw - 5°
Scrollsaw - 4°
Cut and glue
Step 1 Cut outer shape
Step 2 drill
Step 2 drill
Step 3 cut basket
Step 4 cut basket rungs
Step 3 cut foot
Step 2 drill

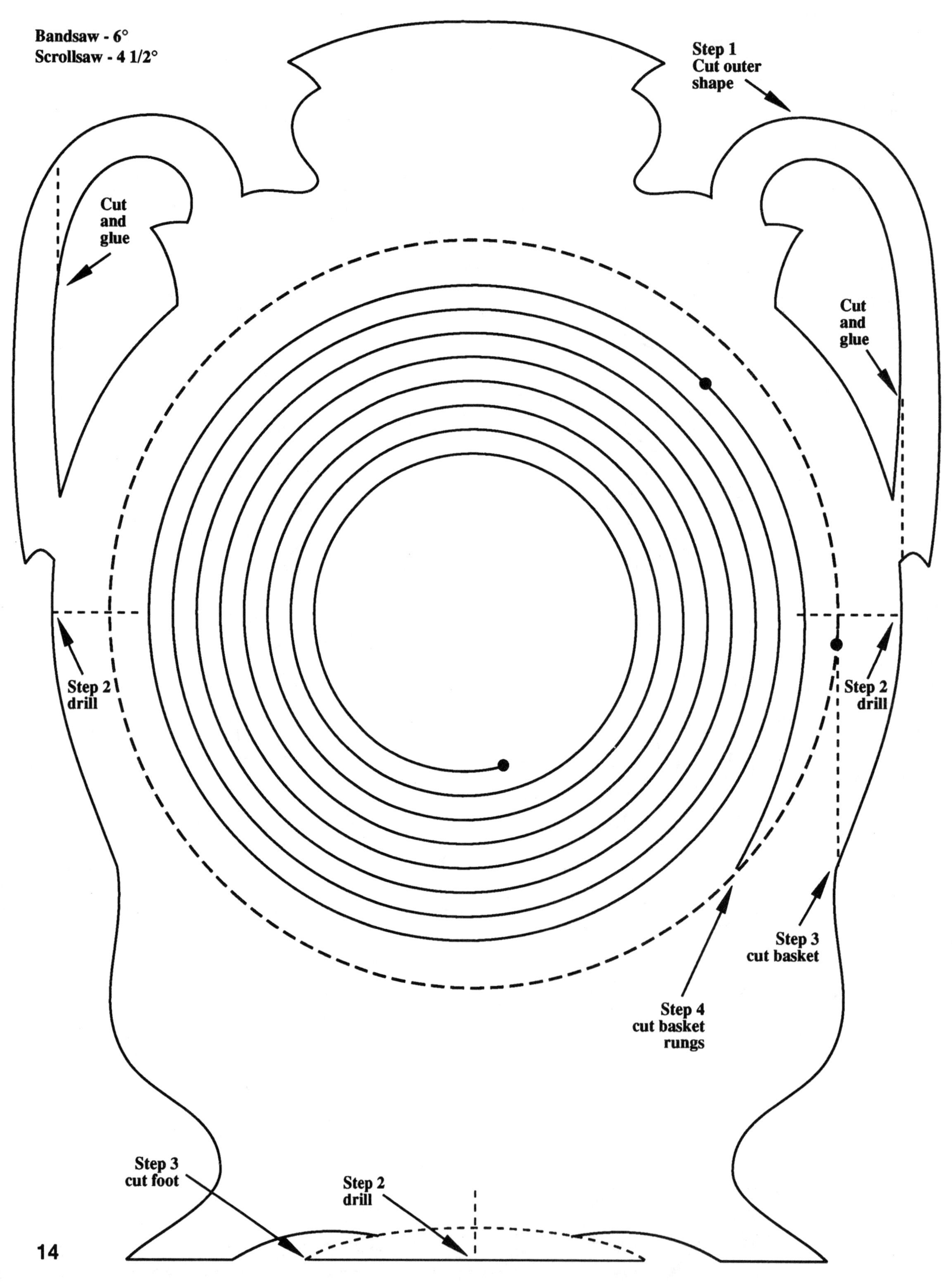
Bandsaw - 6°
Scrollsaw - 4 1/2°
Step 1
Cut outer
shape
Cut
and
glue
Cut
and
glue
Step 2
drill
Step 2
drill
Step 3
cut basket
Step 4
cut basket
rungs
Step 3
cut foot
Step 2
drill

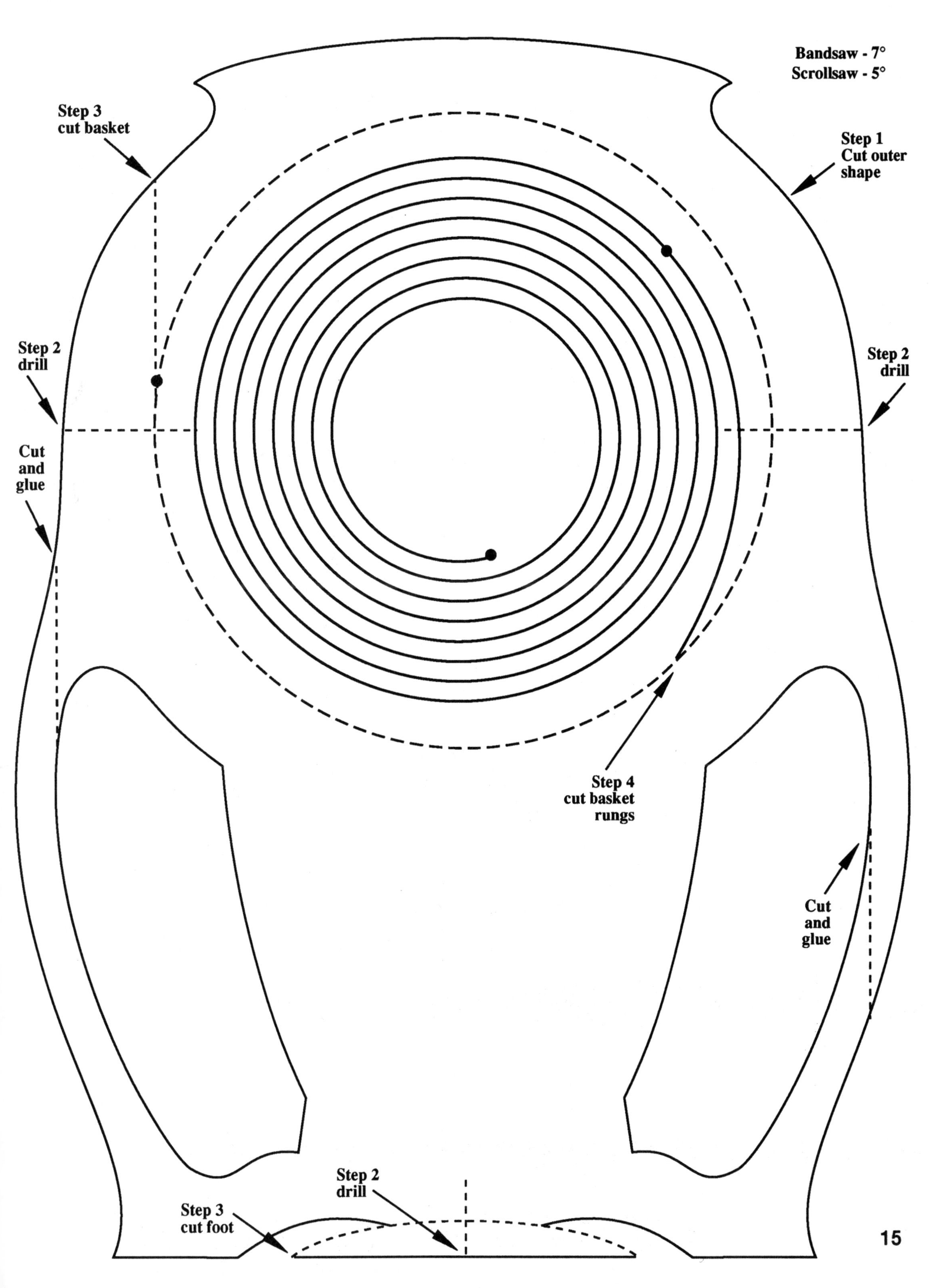
Bandsaw - 7°
Scrollsaw - 5°
Step 3
cut basket
Step 1
Cut outer
shape
Step 2
drill
Step 2
drill
Cut
and
glue
Step 4
cut basket
rungs
Cut
and
glue
Step 2
drill
Step 3
cut foot

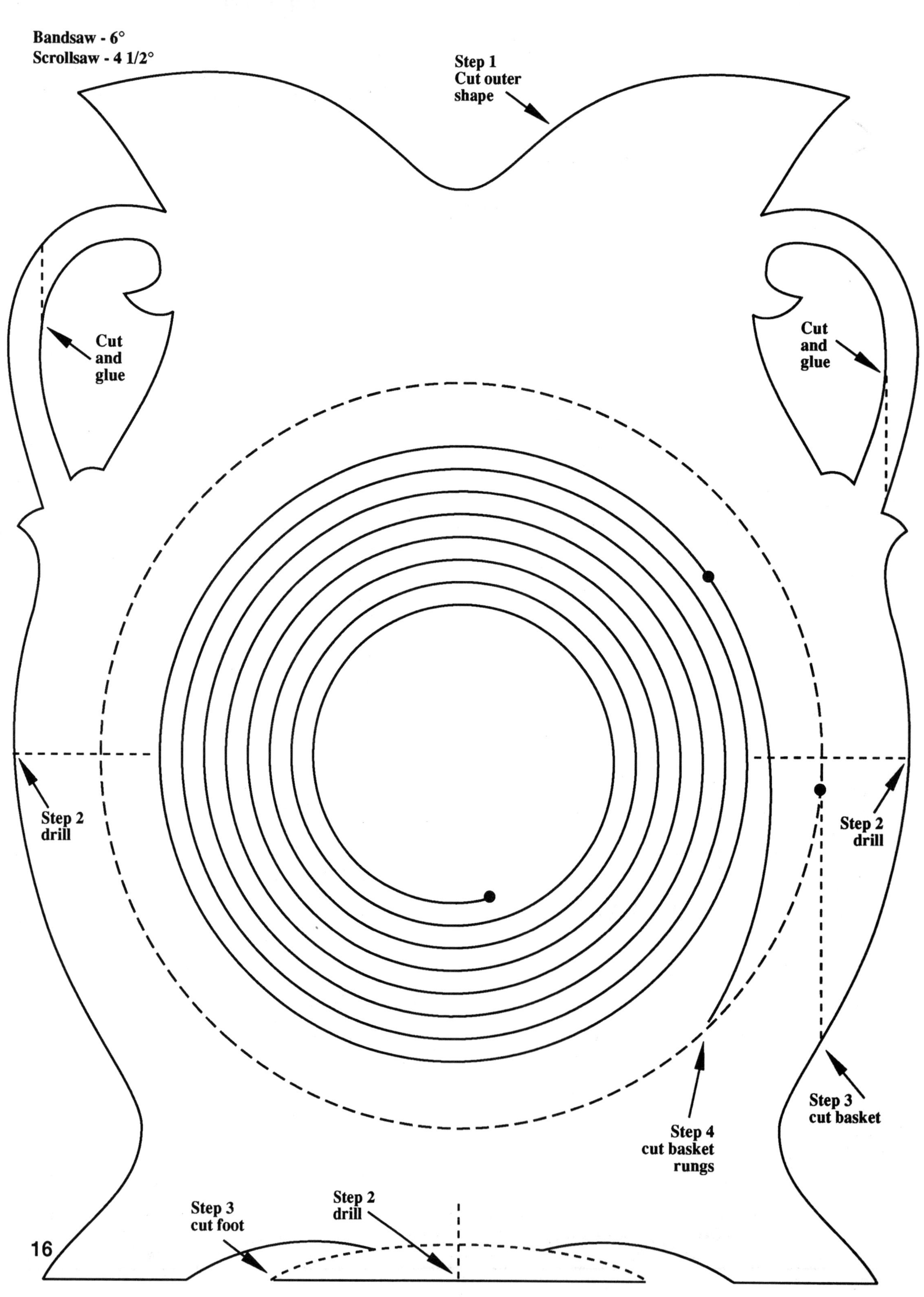
Bandsaw - 6°
Scrollsaw - 4 1/2°
Step 1
Cut outer
shape
Cut
and
glue
Cut
and
glue
Step 2
drill
Step 2
drill
Step 3
cut basket
Step 4
cut basket
rungs
Step 3
cut foot
Step 2
drill

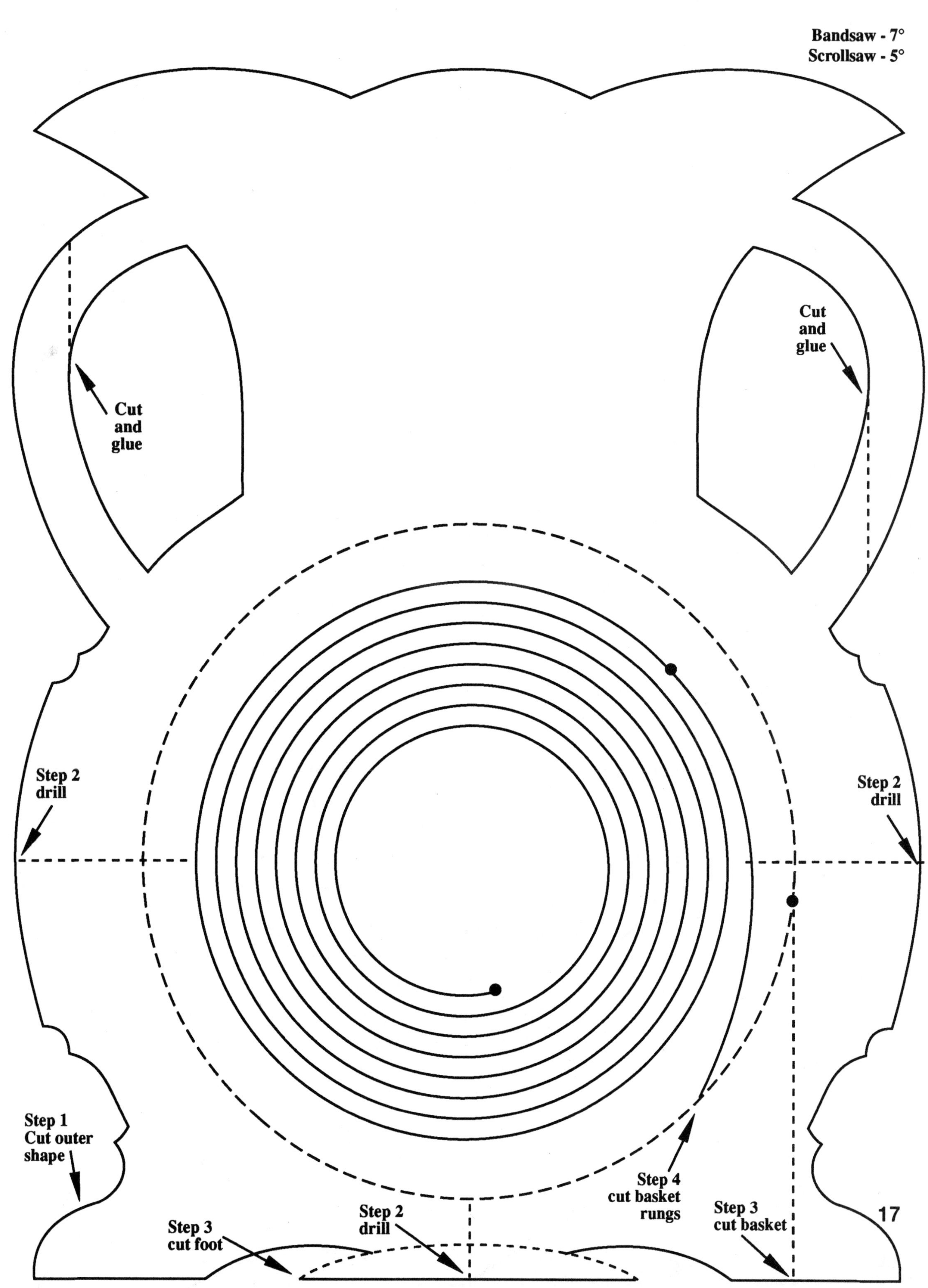
Bandsaw - 7°
Scrollsaw - 5°
Cut
and
glue
Cut
and
glue
Step 2
drill
Step 2
drill
Step 1
Cut outer
shape
Step 3
cut foot
Step 2
drill
Step 4
cut basket
rungs
Step 3
cut basket

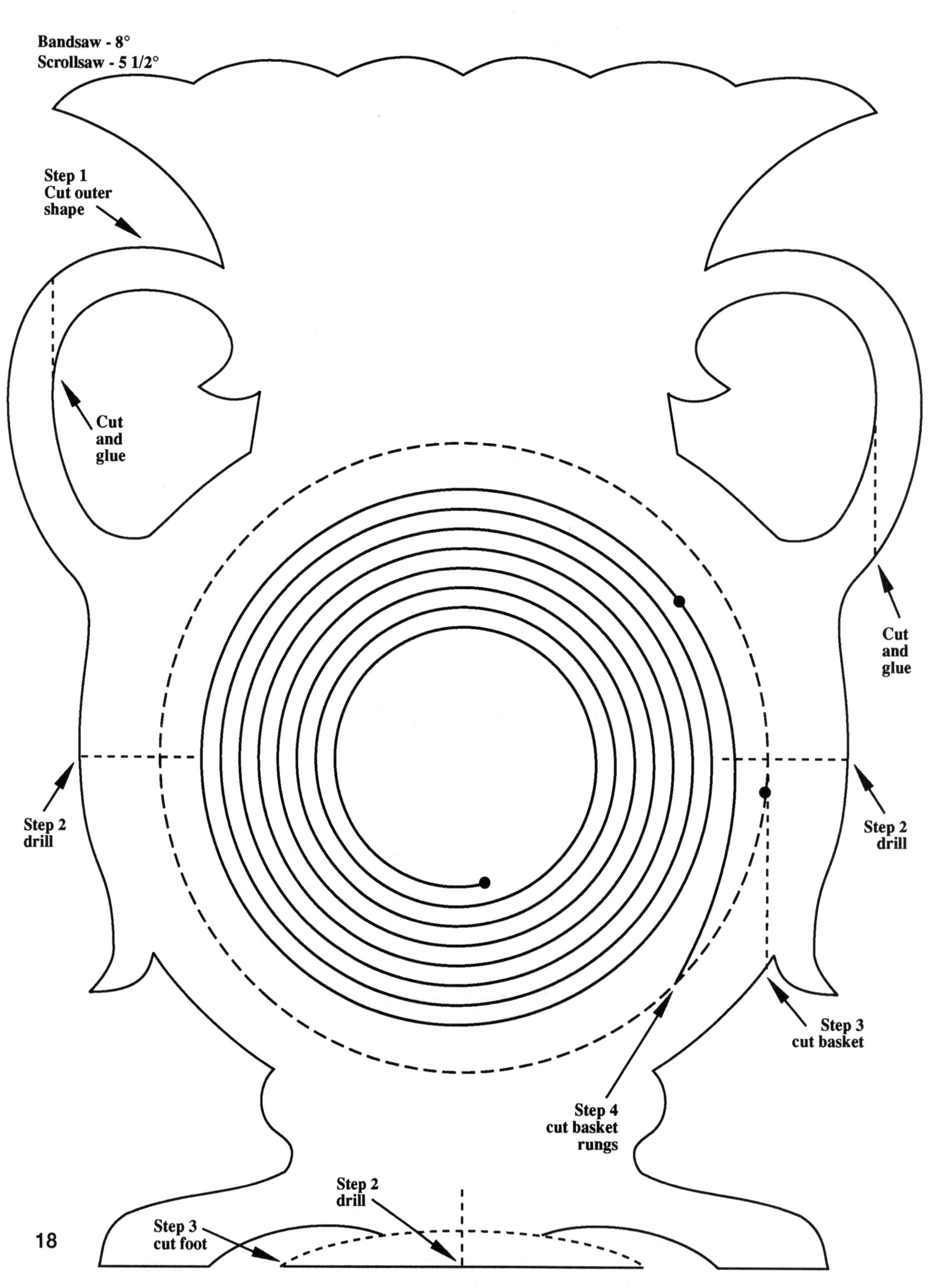
Bandsaw - 8°
Scrollsaw - 5 1/2°
Step 1
Cut outer
shape
Cut
and
glue
Cut
and
glue
Step 2
drill
Step 2
drill
Step 3
cut basket
Step 4
cut basket
rungs
Step 2
drill
Step 3
cut foot

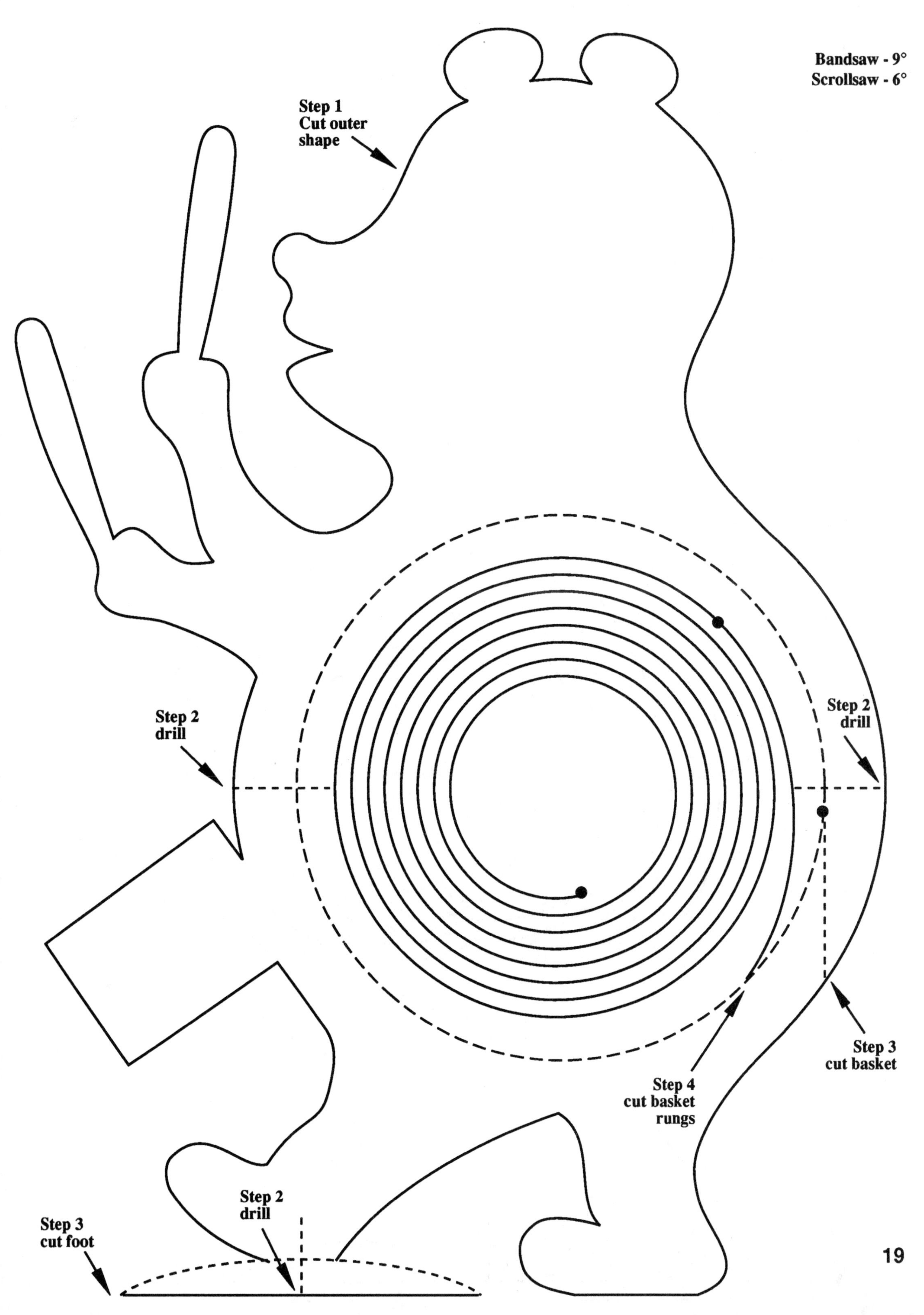
Bandsaw - 9°
Scrollsaw - 6°
Step 1
Cut outer
shape
Step 2
drill
Step 2
drill
Step 3
cut basket
Step 4
cut basket
rungs
Step 2
drill
Step 3
cut foot

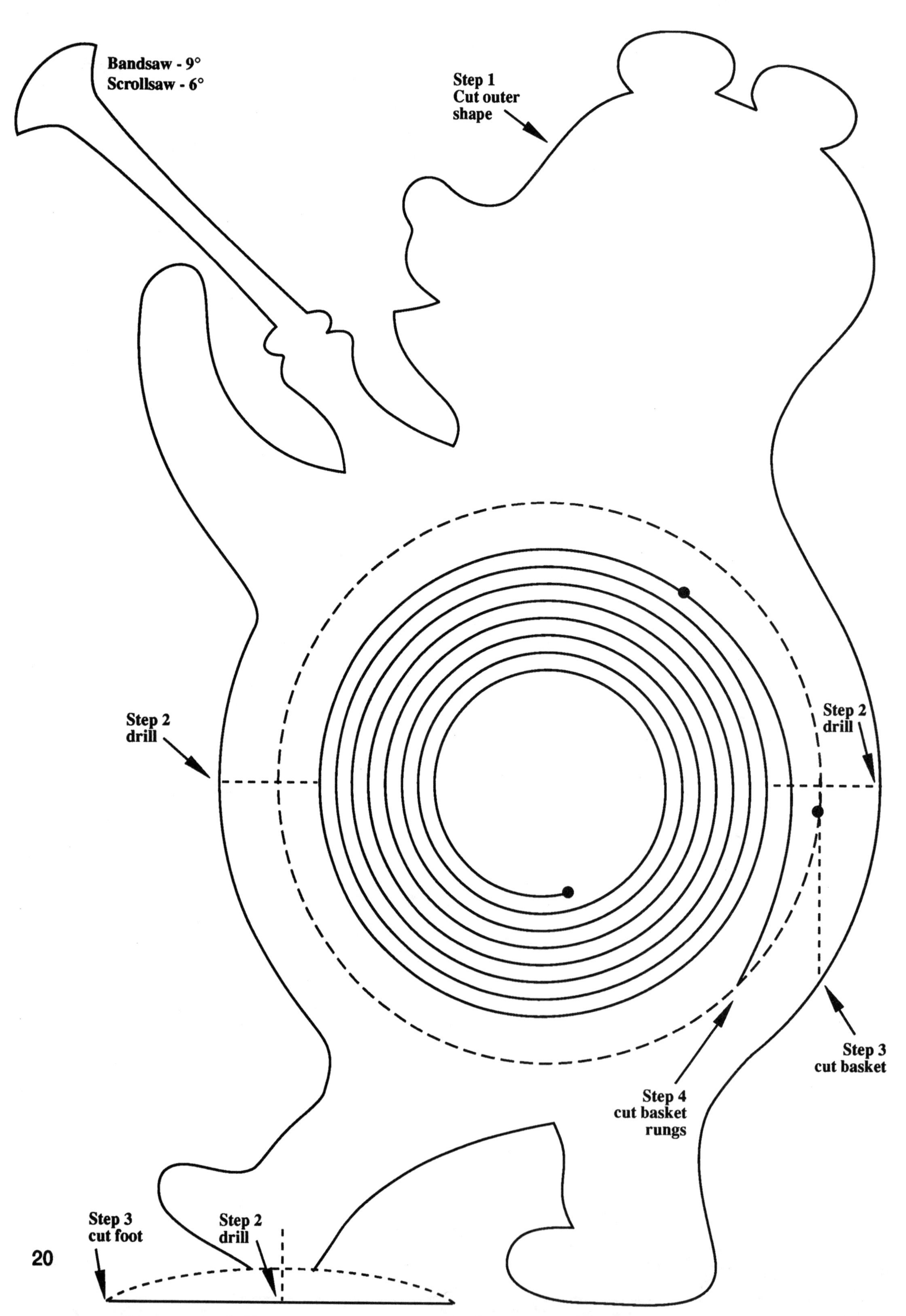
Bandsaw - 9°
Scrollsaw - 6°
Step 1
Cut outer
shape
Step 2
drill
Step 2
drill
Step 3
cut basket
Step 4
cut basket
rungs
Step 3
cut foot
Step 2
drill

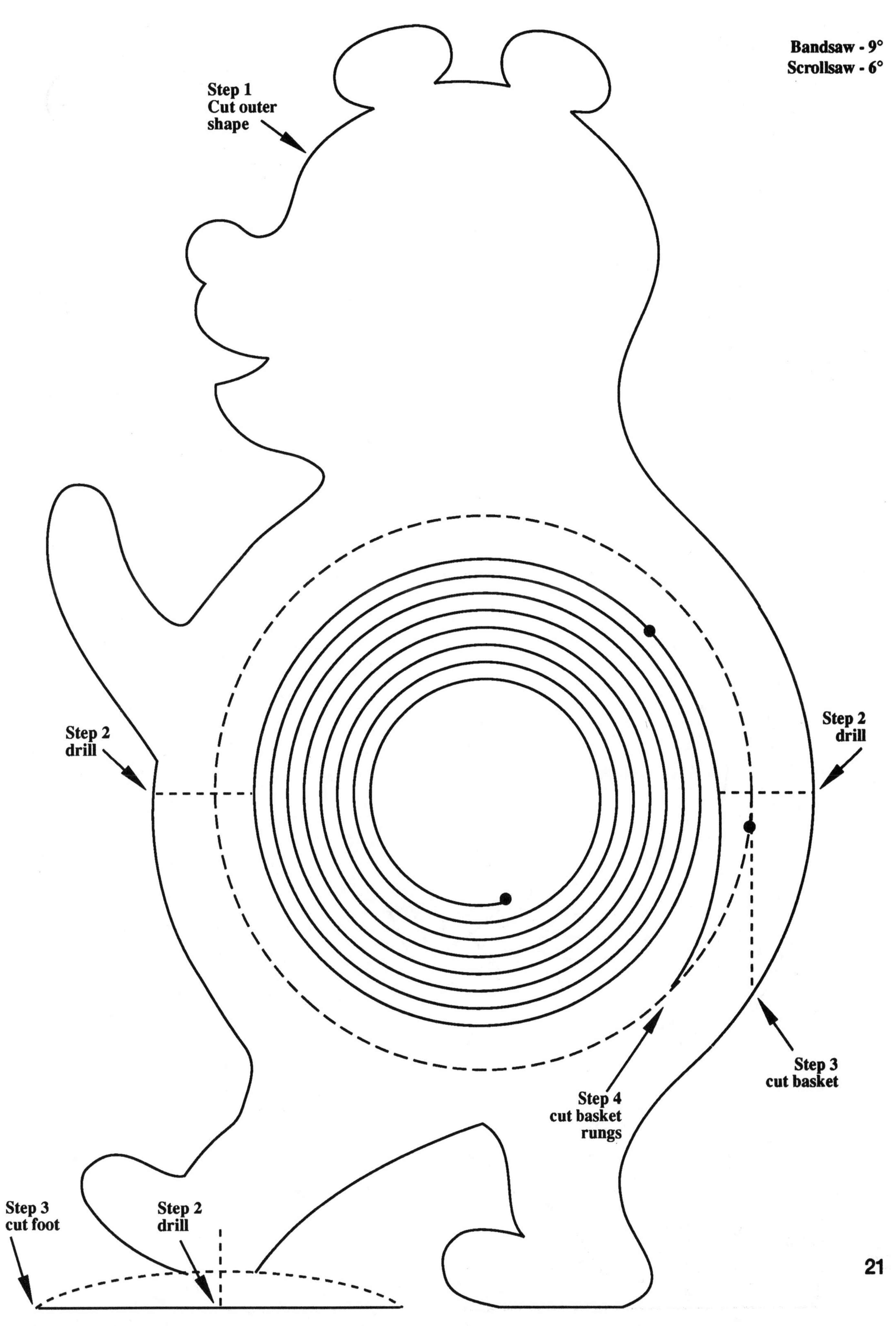
Bandsaw - 9°
Scrollsaw - 6°
Step 1
Cut outer
shape
Step 2
drill
Step 2
drill
Step 3
cut basket
Step 4
cut basket
rungs
Step 3
cut foot
Step 2
drill

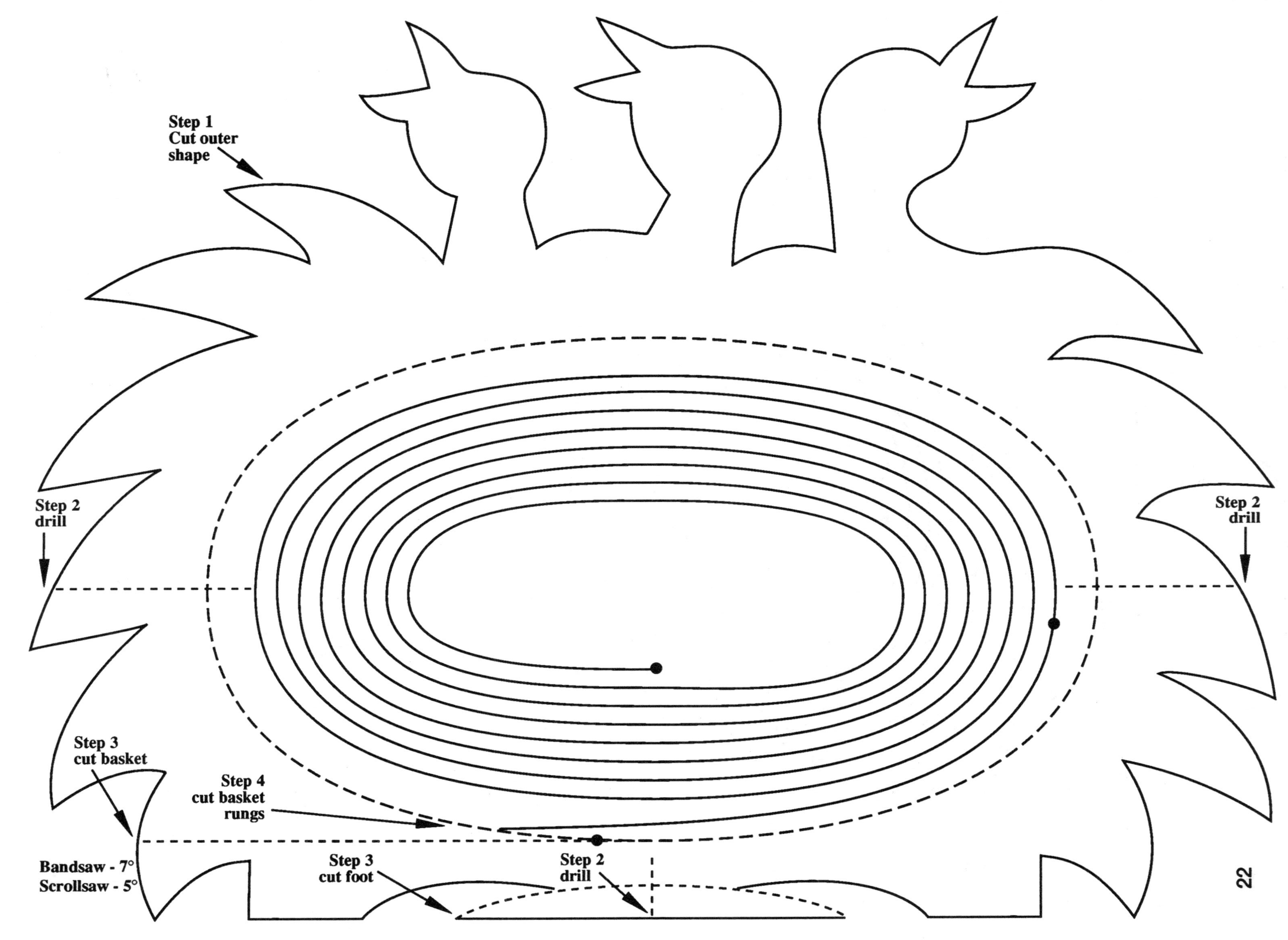
Step 1
Cut outer
shape
Step 2
drill
Step 2
drill
Step 3
cut basket
Step 4
cut basket
rungs
Bandsaw - 7°
Scrollsaw - 5°
Step 3
cut foot
Step 2
drill

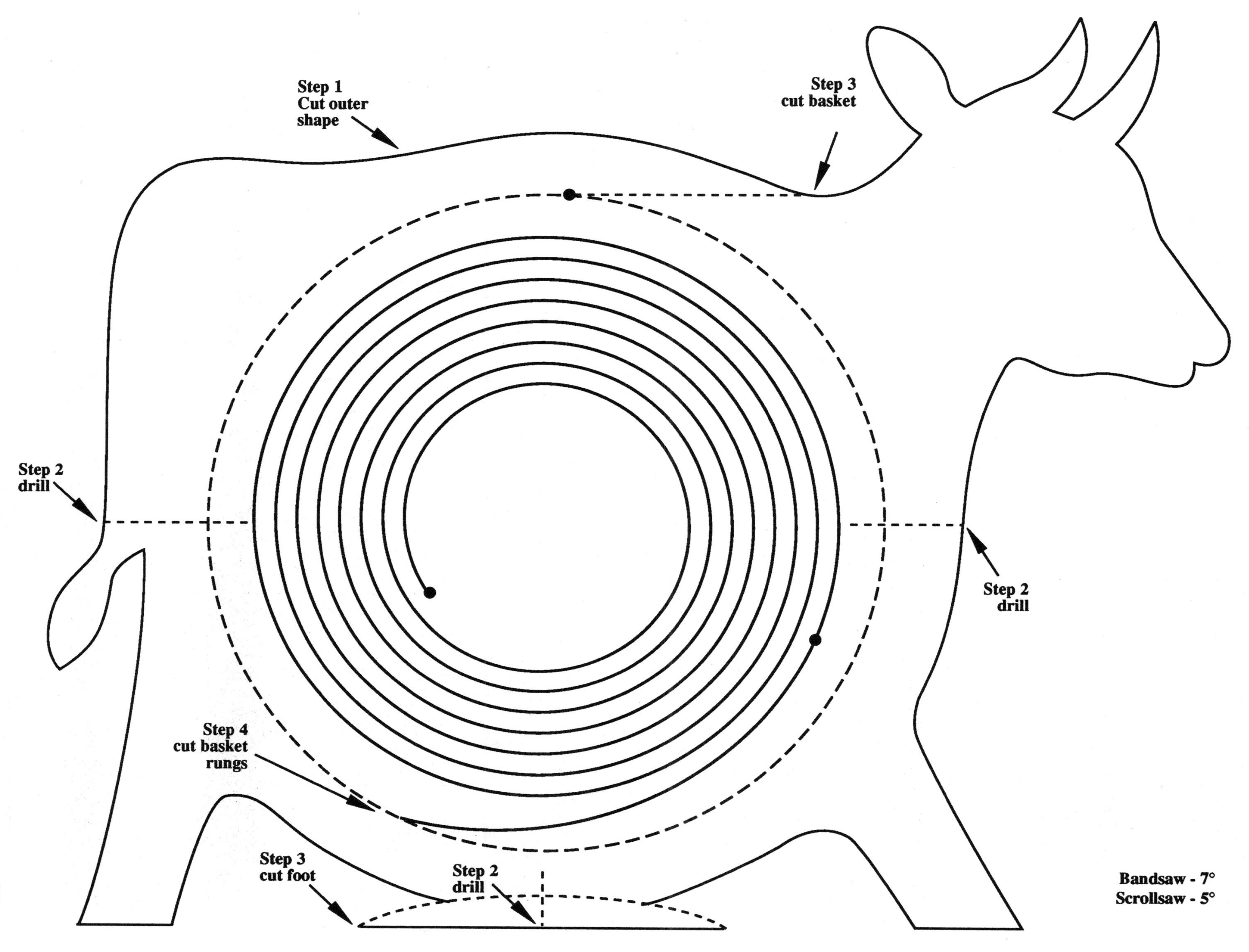
Step 1
Cut outer
shape
Step 3
cut basket
Step 2
drill
Step 2
drill
Step 4
cut basket
rungs
Step 3
cut foot
Step 2
drill
Bandsaw - 7°
Scrollsaw - 5°

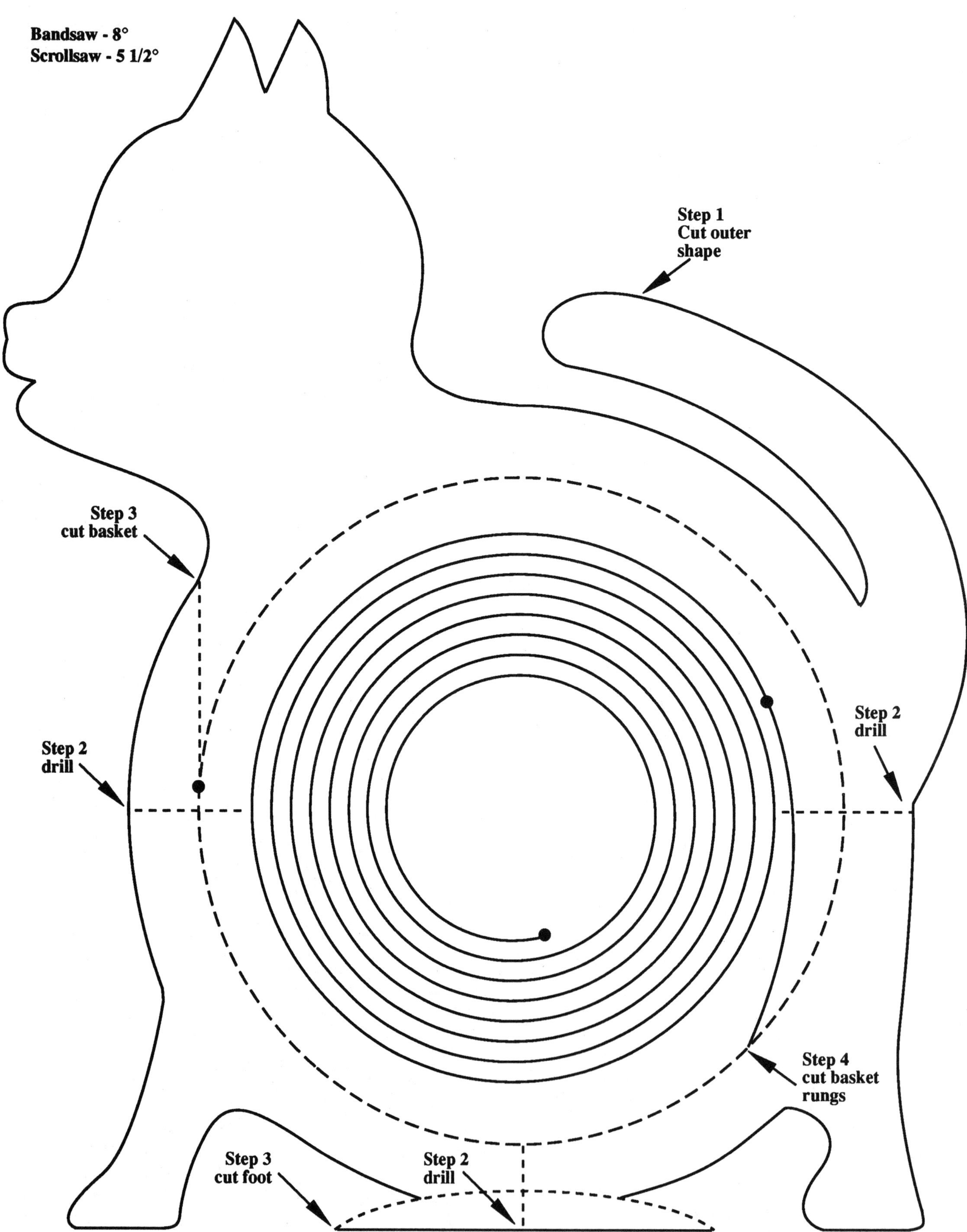
Bandsaw - 8°
Scrollsaw - 5 1/2°
Step 1
Cut outer
shape
Step 3
cut basket
Step 2
drill
Step 2
drill
Step 4
cut basket
rungs
Step 3
cut foot
Step 2
drill

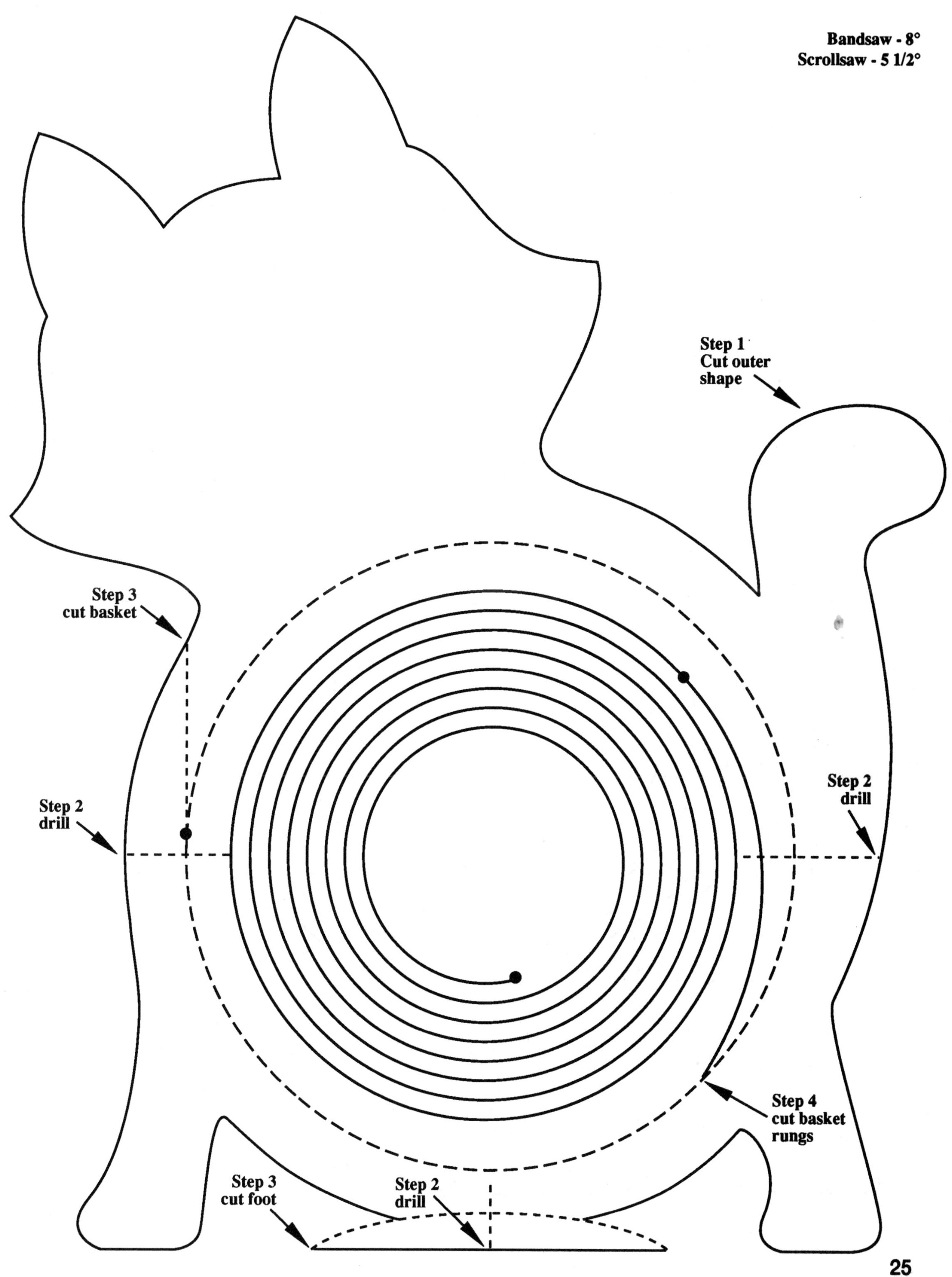
Bandsaw - 8°
Scrollsaw - 5 1/2°
Step 1
Cut outer shape
Step 3
cut basket
Step 2
drill
Step 2
drill
Step 4
cut basket rungs
Step 3
cut foot
Step 2
drill

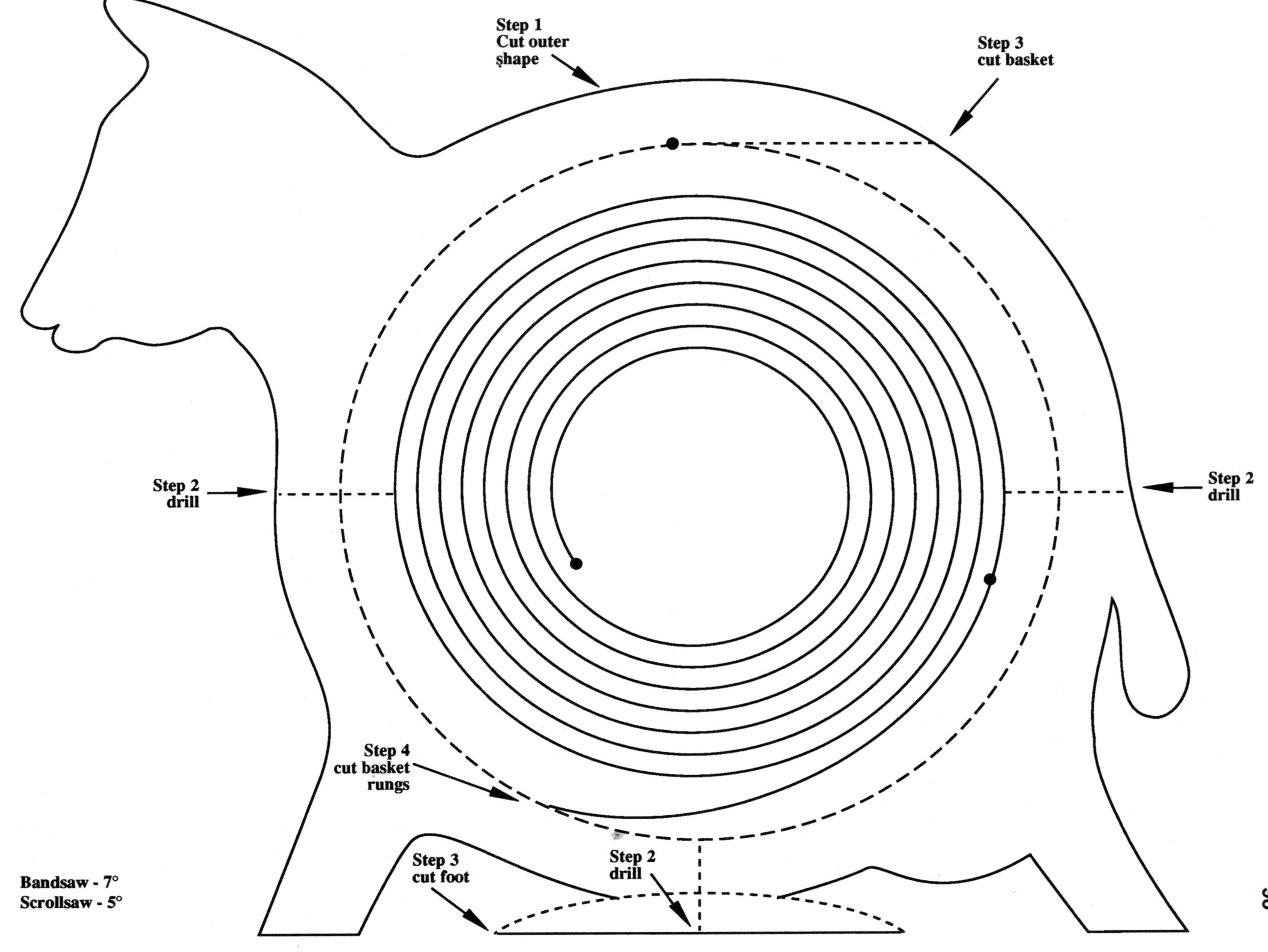
Step 1
Cut outer
shape
Step 3
cut basket
Step 2
drill
Step 2
drill
Step 4
cut basket
rungs
Step 3
cut foot
Step 2
drill
Bandsaw - 7°
Scrollsaw - 5°

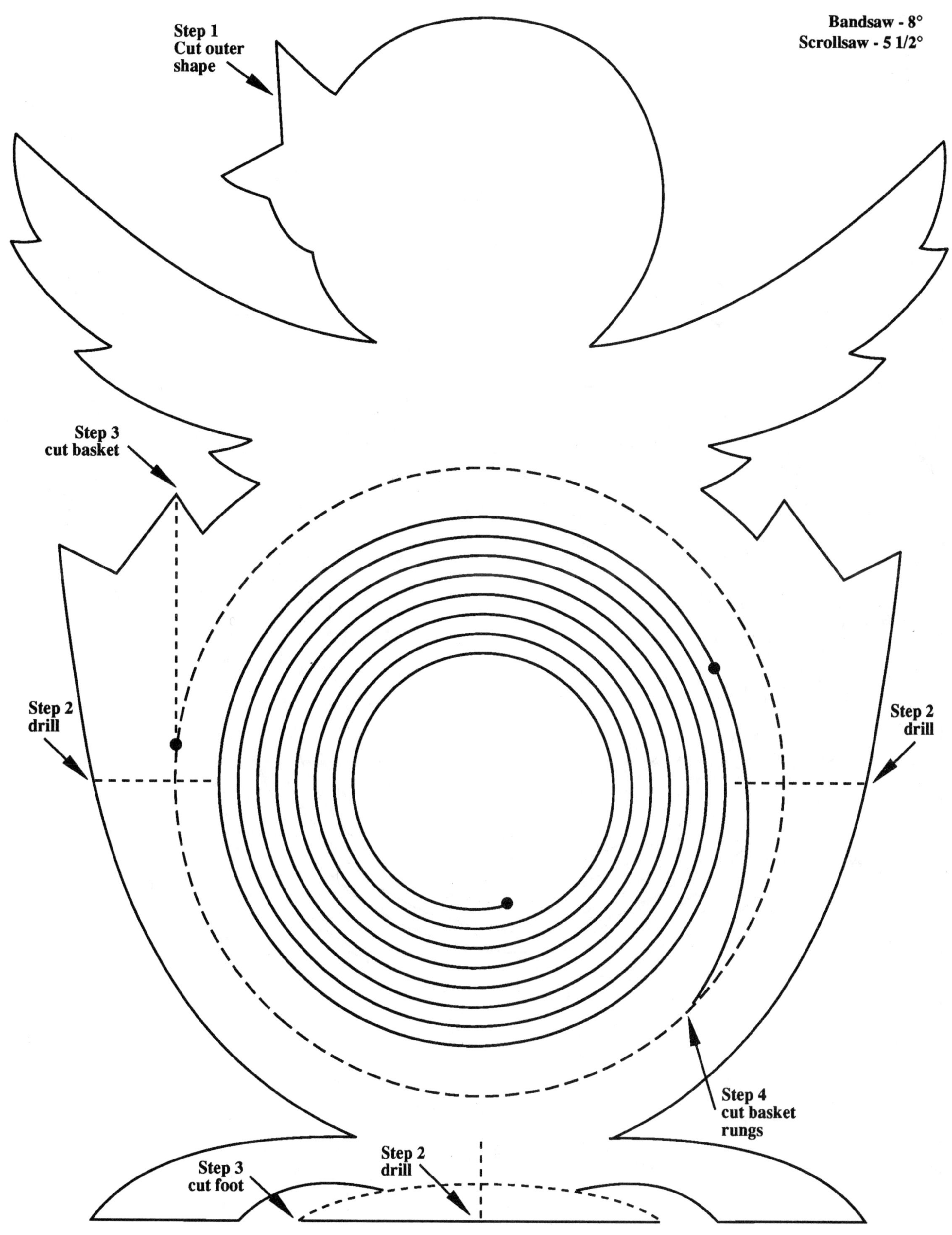
Step 1
Cut outer
shape
Bandsaw - 8°
Scrollsaw - 5 1/2°
Step 3
cut basket
Step 2
drill
Step 2
drill
Step 4
cut basket
rungs
Step 3
cut foot
Step 2
drill

Step 1
Cut outer
shape

Step 3
cut basket

Step 2
drill

Step 2
drill

Step 4
cut basket
rungs

Step 3
cut foot

Step 2
drill

Bandsaw - 7°
Scrollsaw - 5°

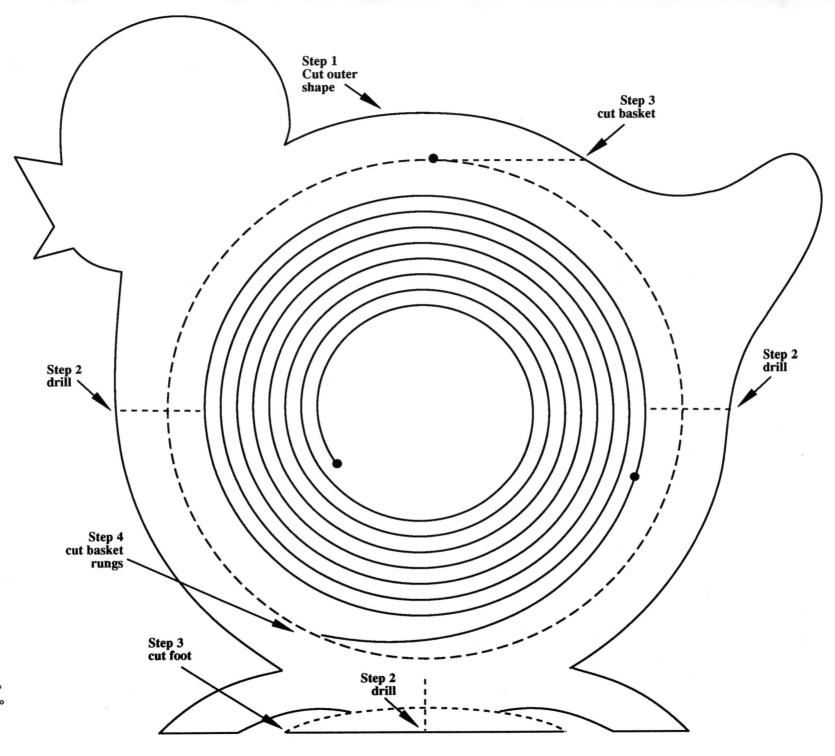

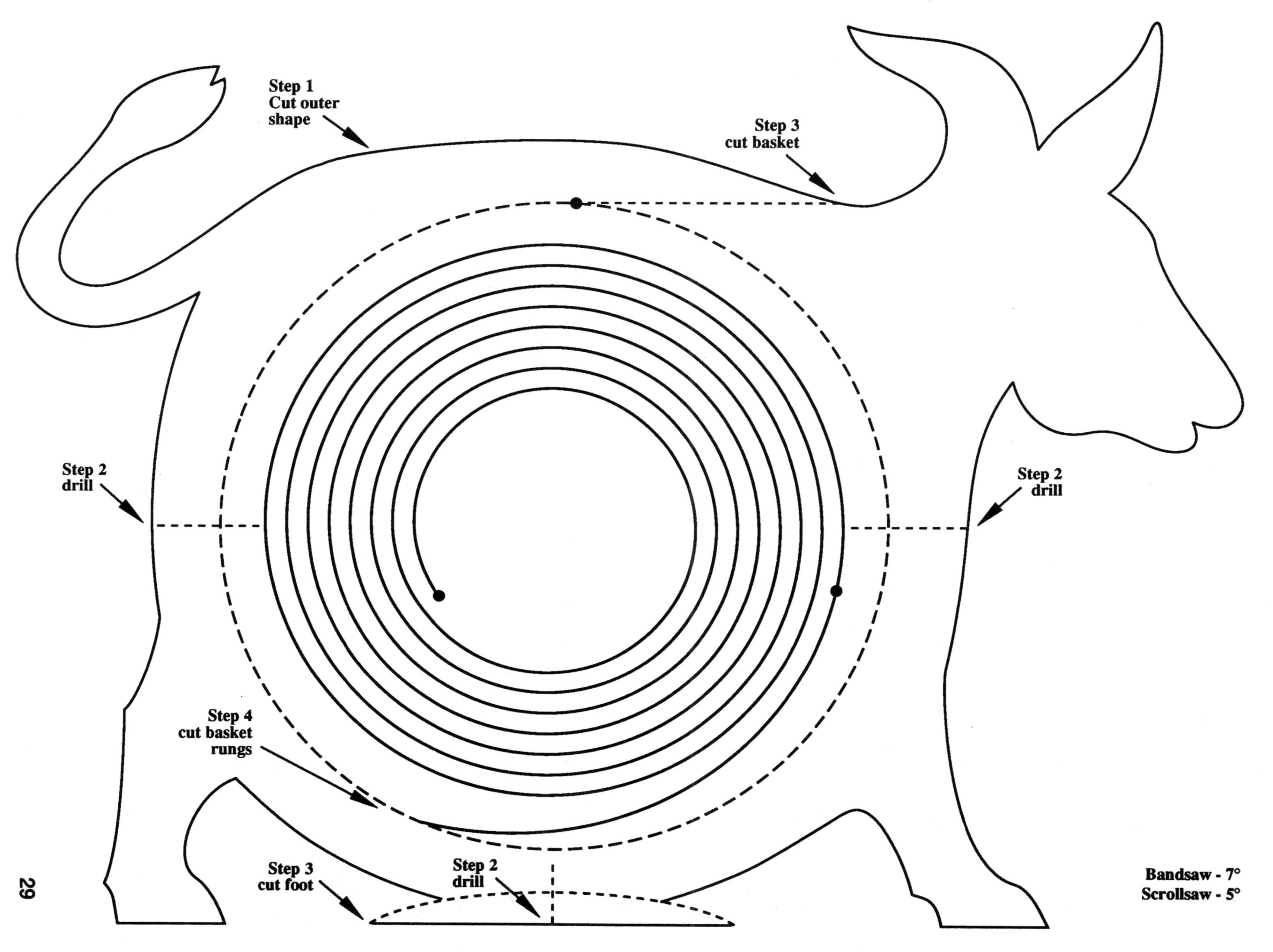
Step 1
Cut outer
shape
Step 3
cut basket
Step 2
drill
Step 2
drill
Step 4
cut basket
rungs
Step 3
cut foot
Step 2
drill
Bandsaw - 7°
Scrollsaw - 5°

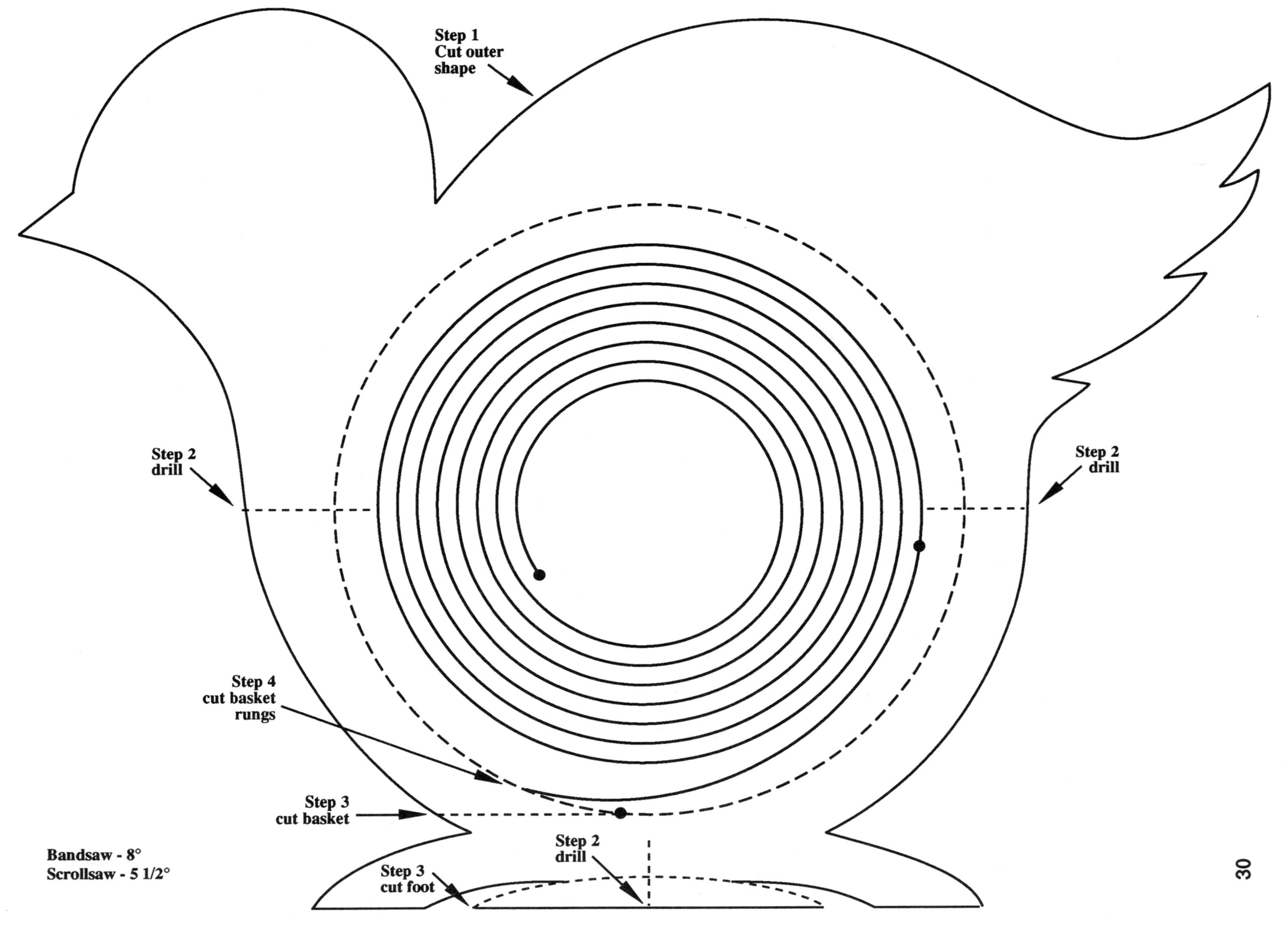

Step 1
Cut outer
shape
Step 2
drill
Step 2
drill
Step 4
cut basket
rungs
Step 3
cut basket
Step 2
drill
Step 3
cut foot
Bandsaw - 8°
Scrollsaw - 5 1/2°

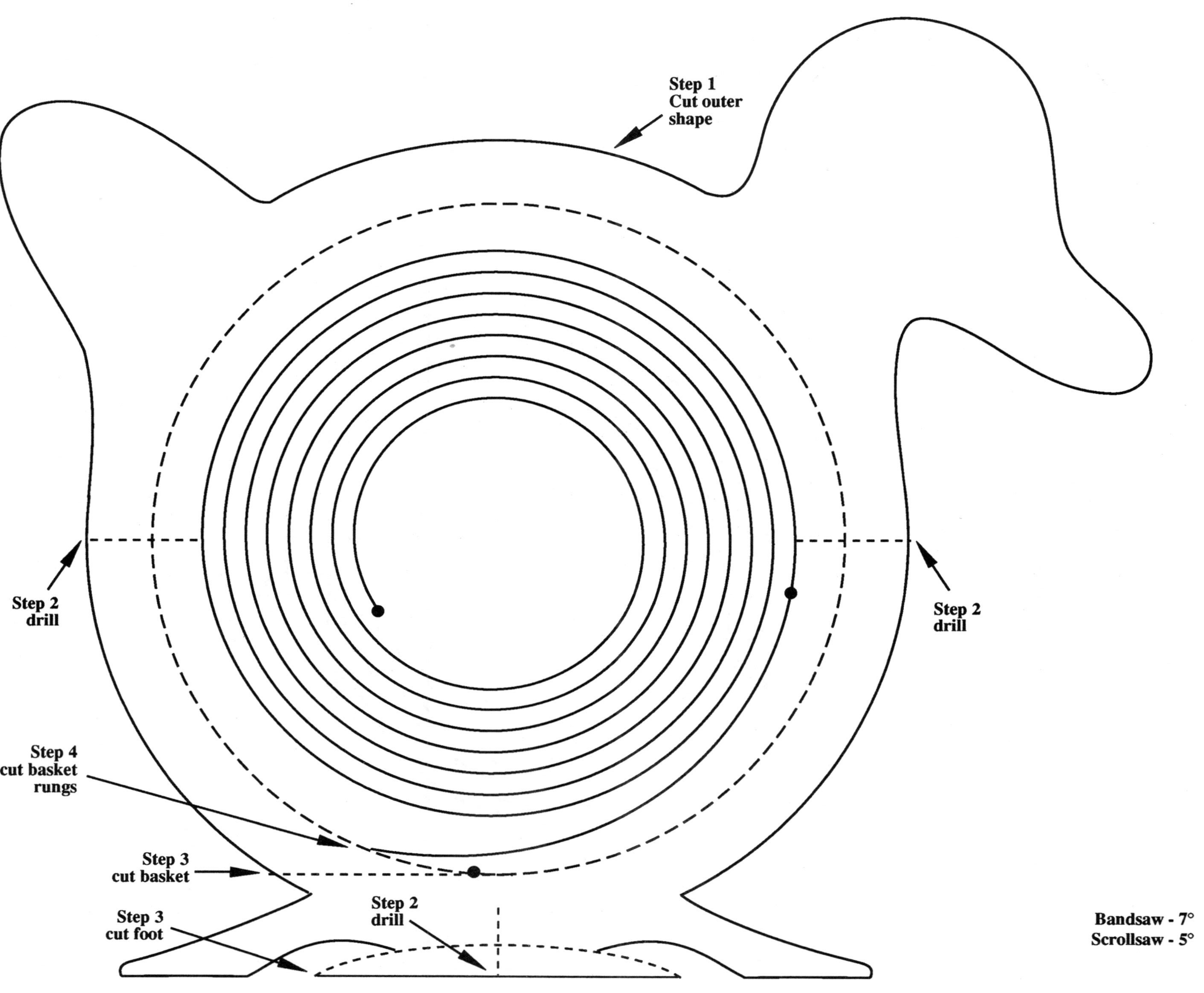
Step 1
Cut outer
shape
Step 2
drill
Step 2
drill
Step 4
cut basket
rungs
Step 3
cut basket
Step 3
cut foot
Step 2
drill
Bandsaw - 7°
Scrollsaw - 5°

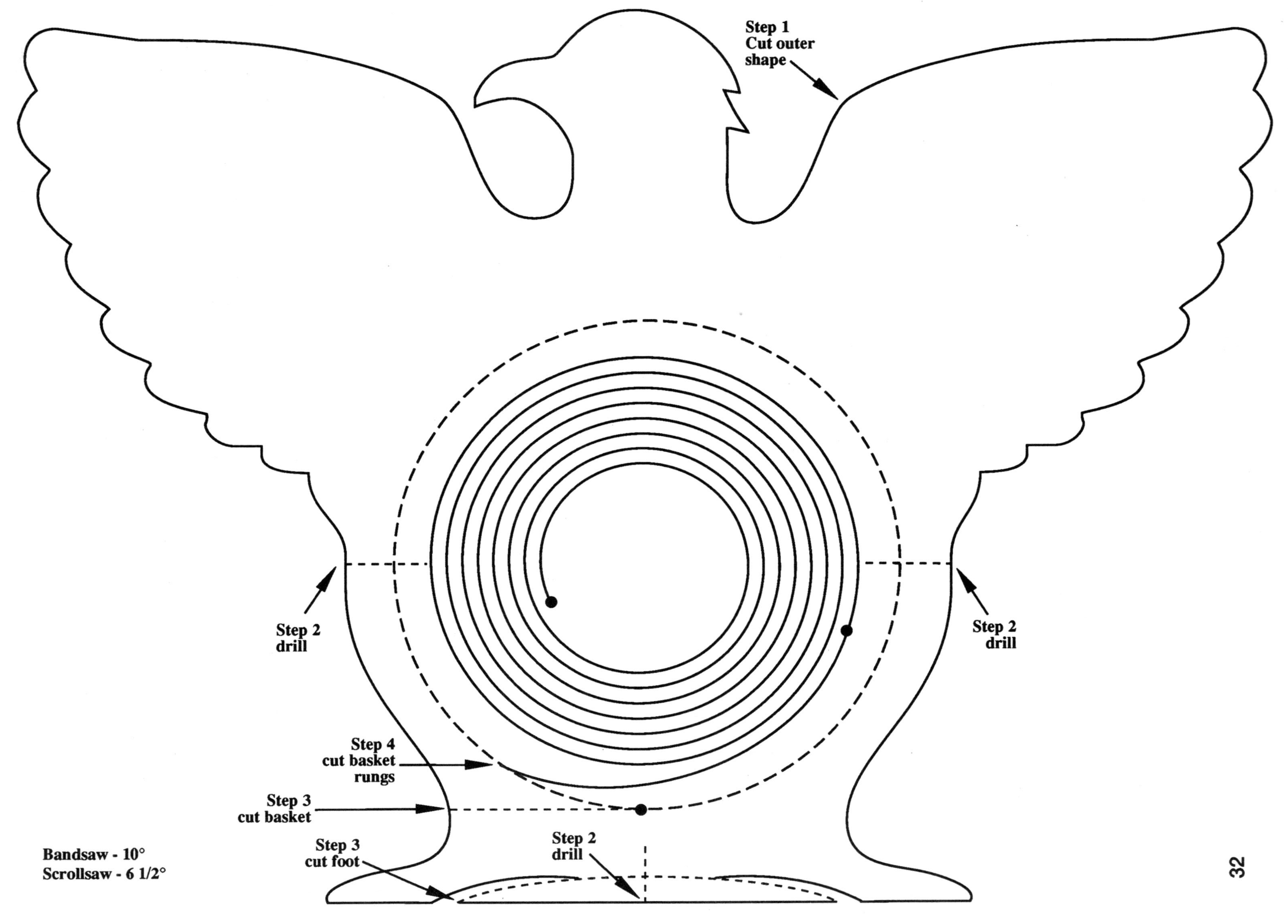
Step 1
Cut outer
shape
Step 2
drill
Step 2
drill
Step 4
cut basket
rungs
Step 3
cut basket
Step 3
cut foot
Step 2
drill
Bandsaw - 10°
Scrollsaw - 6 1/2°

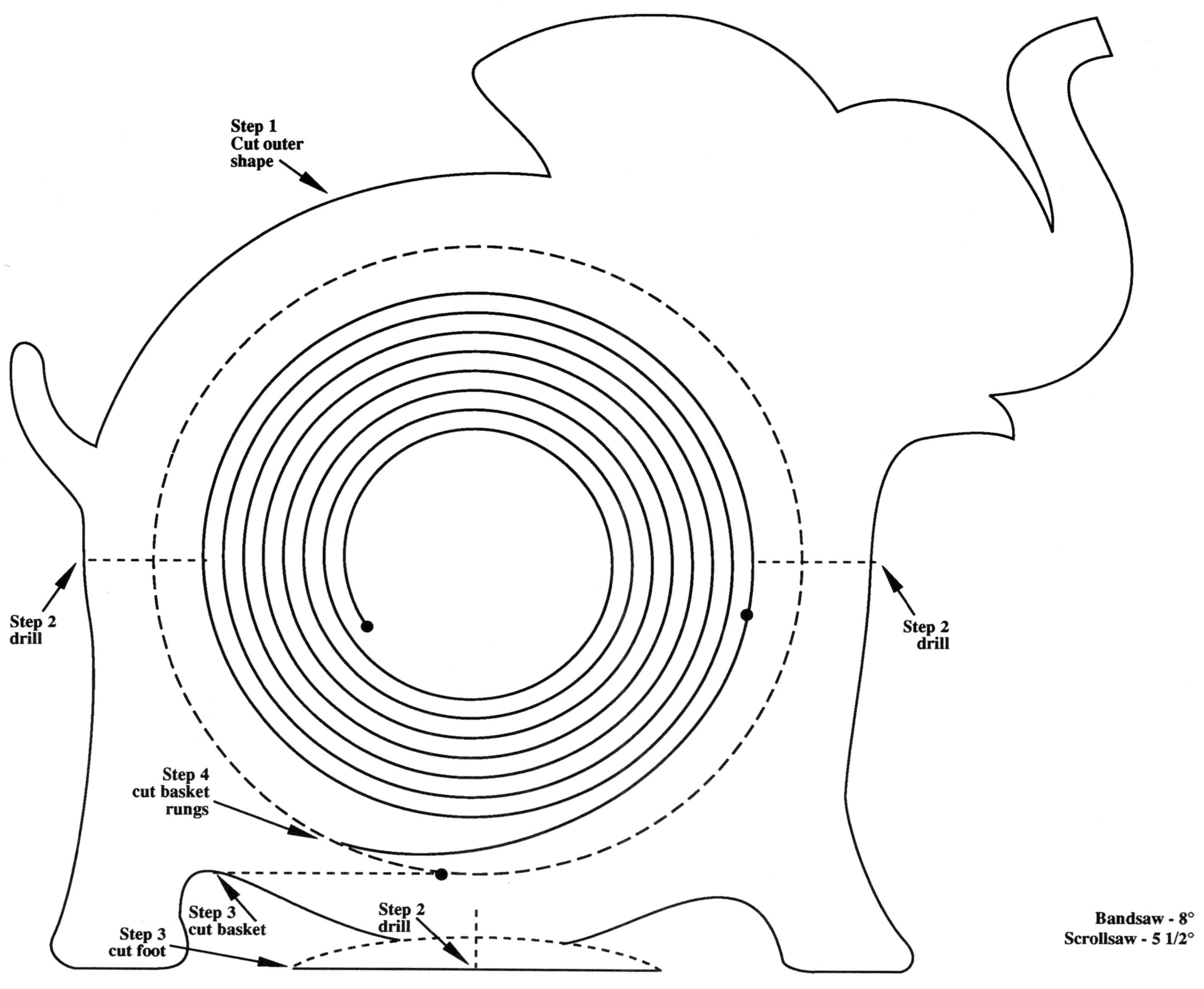
Step 1
Cut outer
shape
Step 2
drill
Step 2
drill
Step 4
cut basket
rungs
Step 3
cut basket
Step 2
drill
Step 3
cut foot
Bandsaw - 8°
Scrollsaw - 5 1/2°

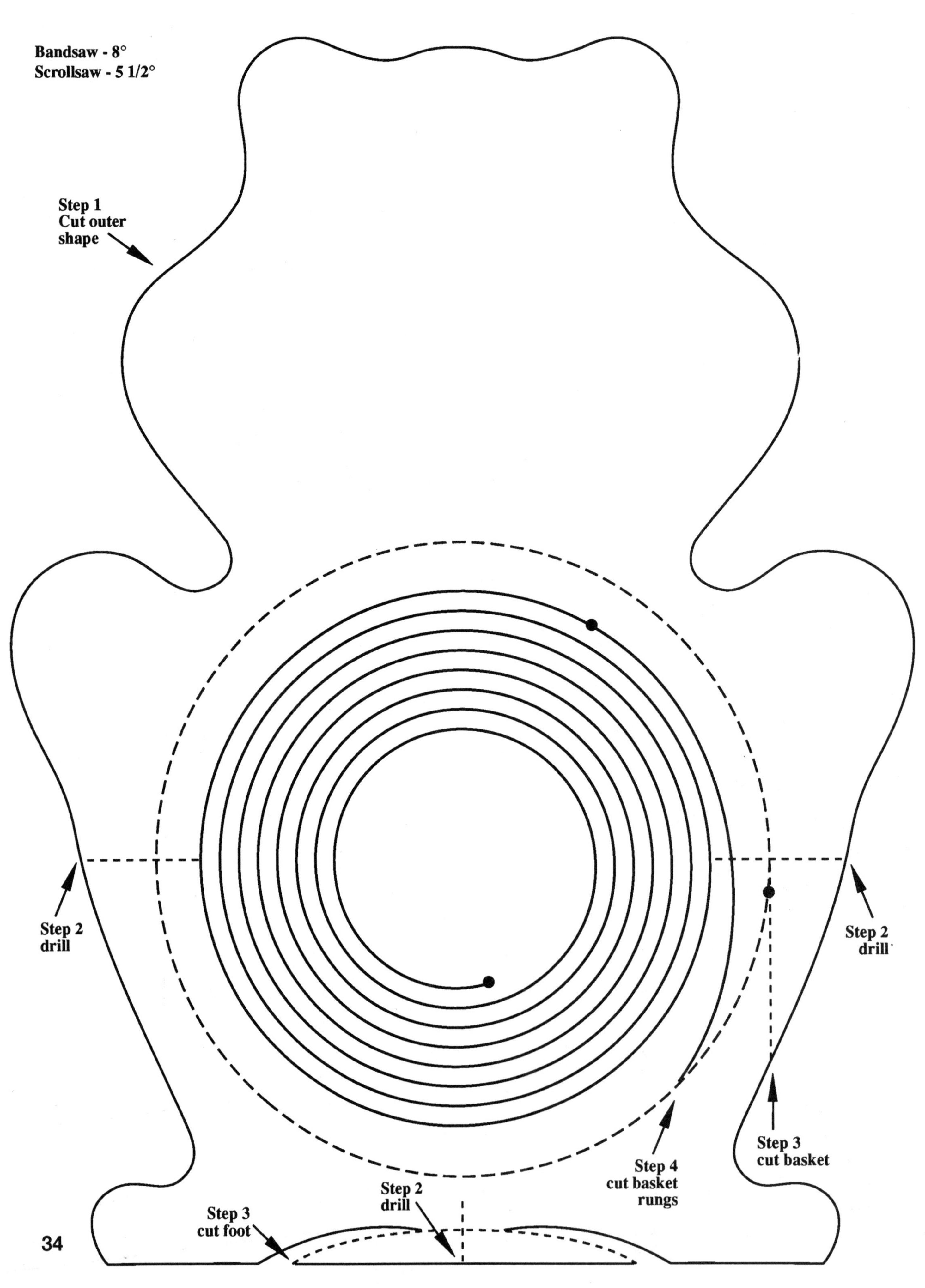
Bandsaw - 8°
Scrollsaw - 5 1/2°
Step 1
Cut outer
shape
Step 2
drill
Step 2
drill
Step 3
cut basket
Step 4
cut basket
rungs
Step 2
drill
Step 3
cut foot

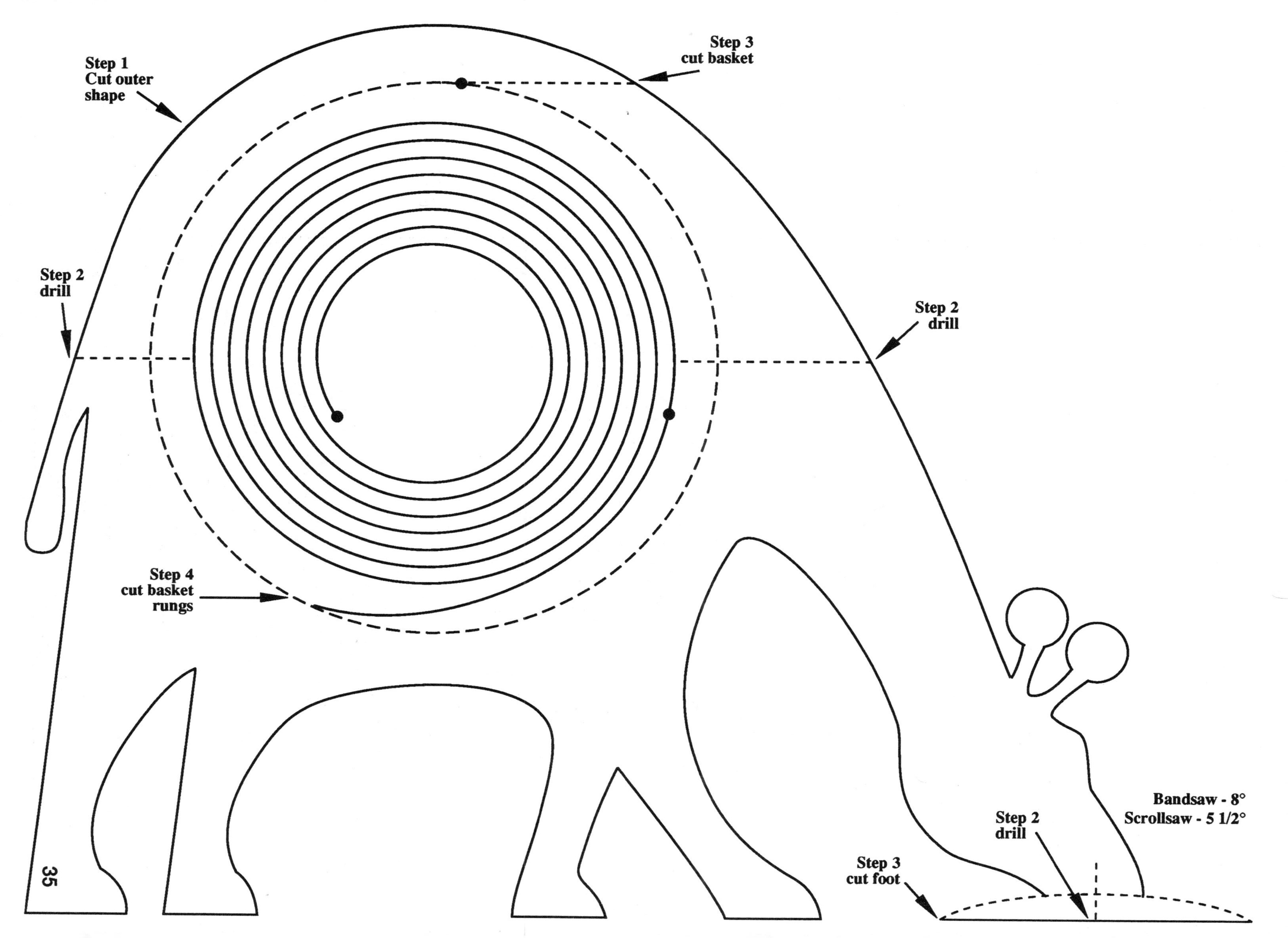

Step 1
Cut outer
shape
Step 3
cut basket
Step 2
drill
Step 2
drill
Step 4
cut basket
rungs
Bandsaw - 8°
Scrollsaw - 5 1/2°
Step 2
drill
Step 3
cut foot
35

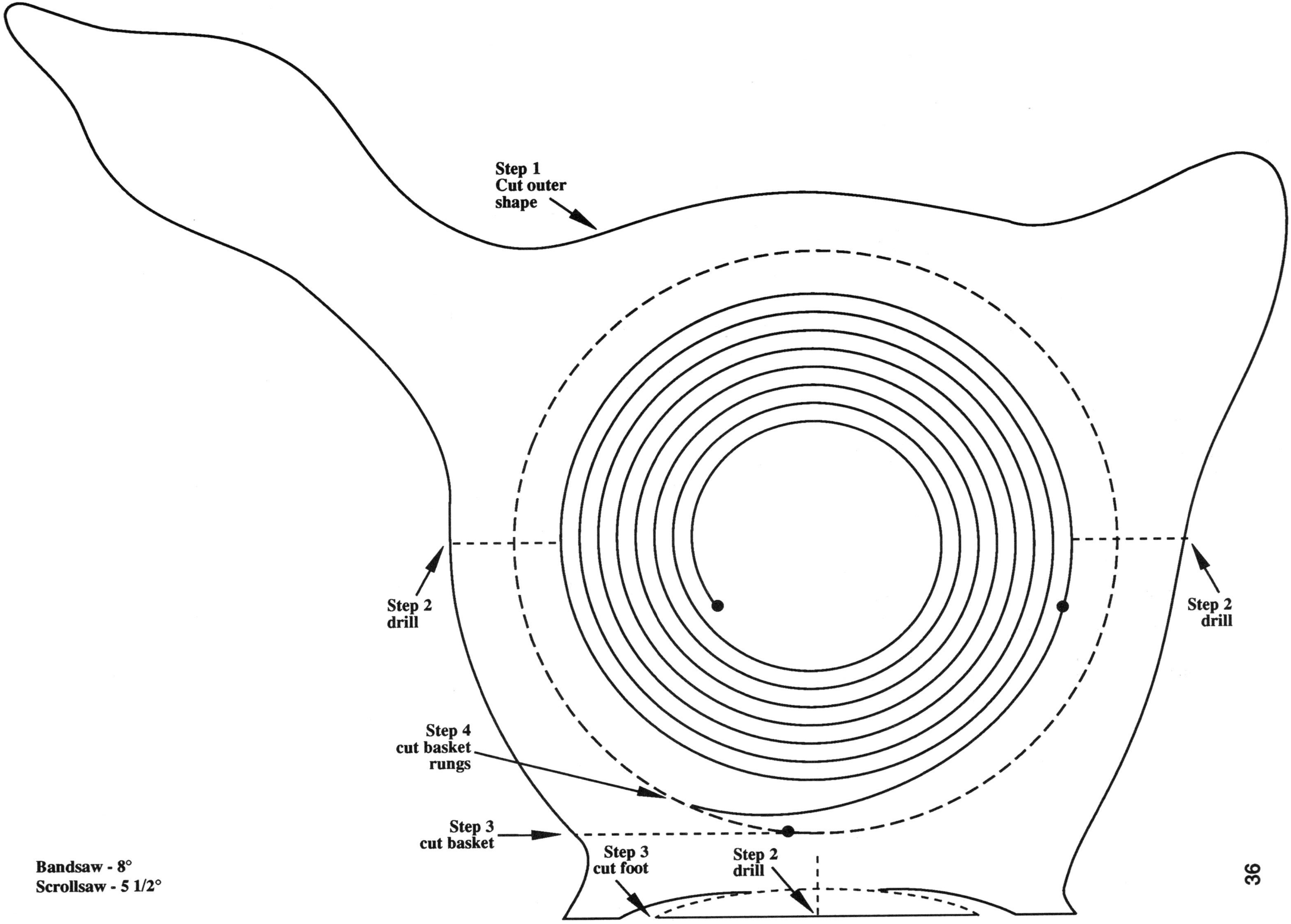

Step 1
Cut outer
shape

Step 2
drill

Step 2
drill

Step 4
cut basket
rungs

Step 3
cut basket

Step 3
cut foot

Step 2
drill

Bandsaw - 8°
Scrollsaw - 5 1/2°

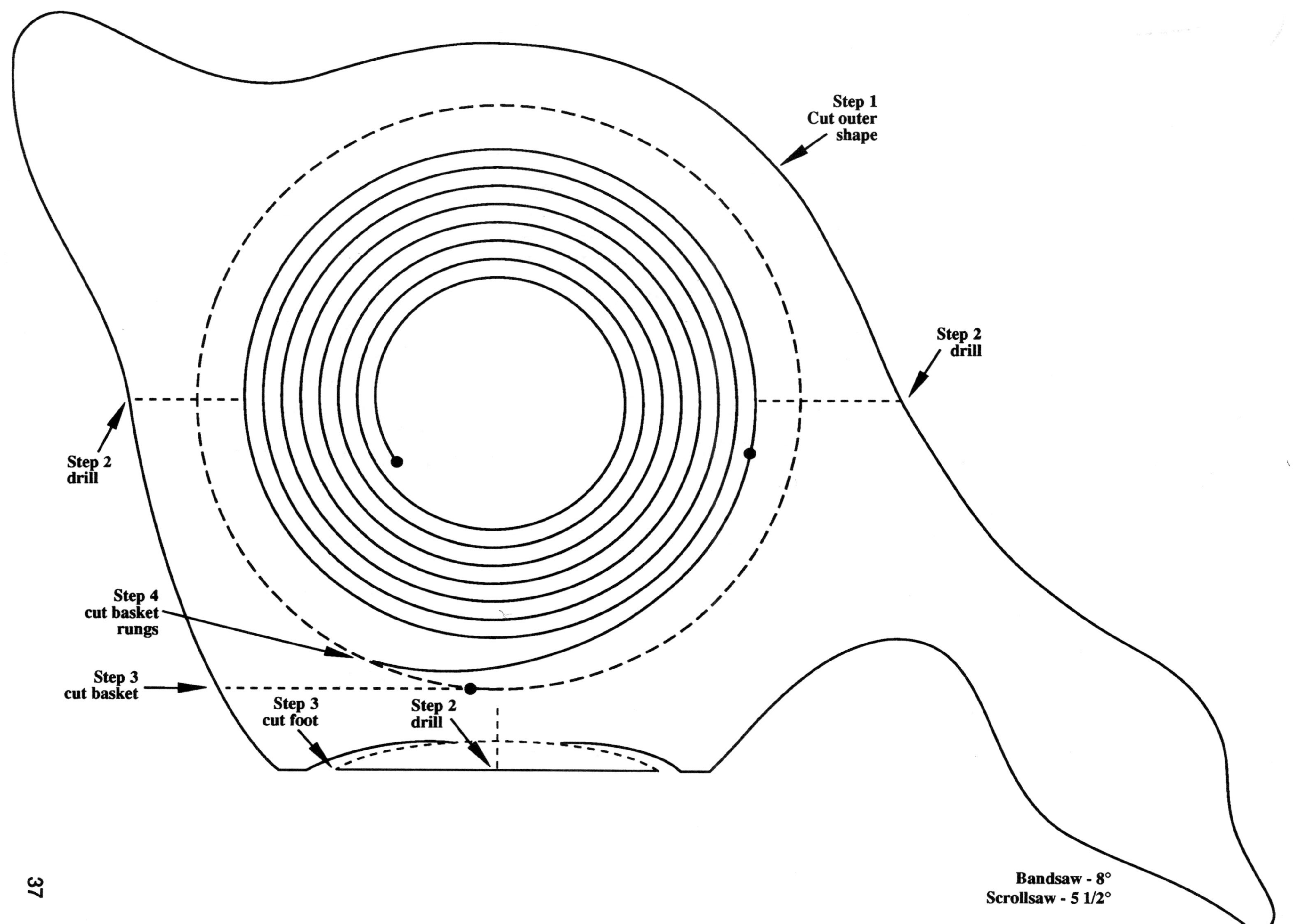

Step 1
Cut outer
shape
Step 2
drill
Step 2
drill
Step 4
cut basket
rungs
Step 3
cut basket
Step 3
cut foot
Step 2
drill
Bandsaw - 8°
Scrollsaw - 5 1/2°

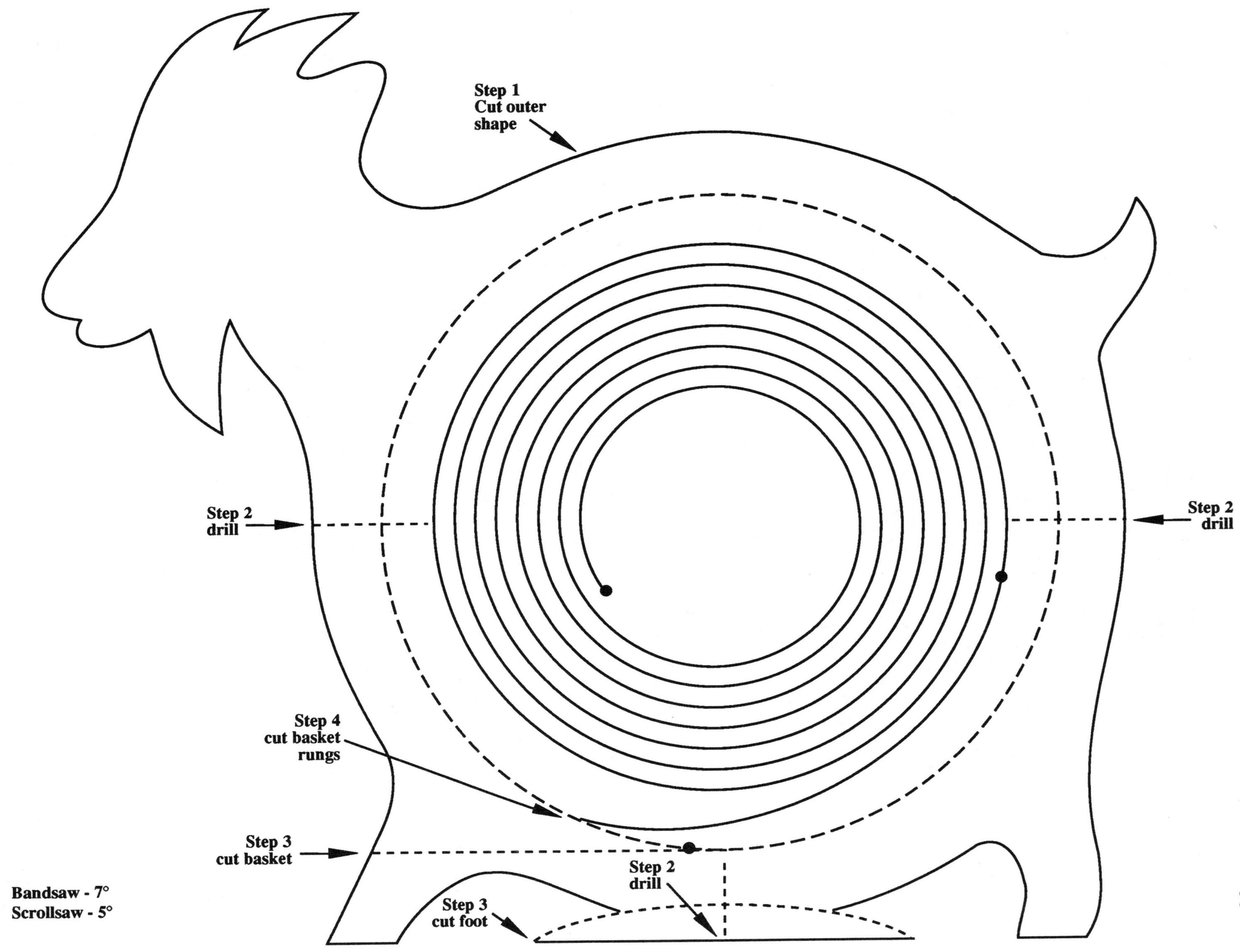

Bandsaw - 7°
Scrollsaw - 5°

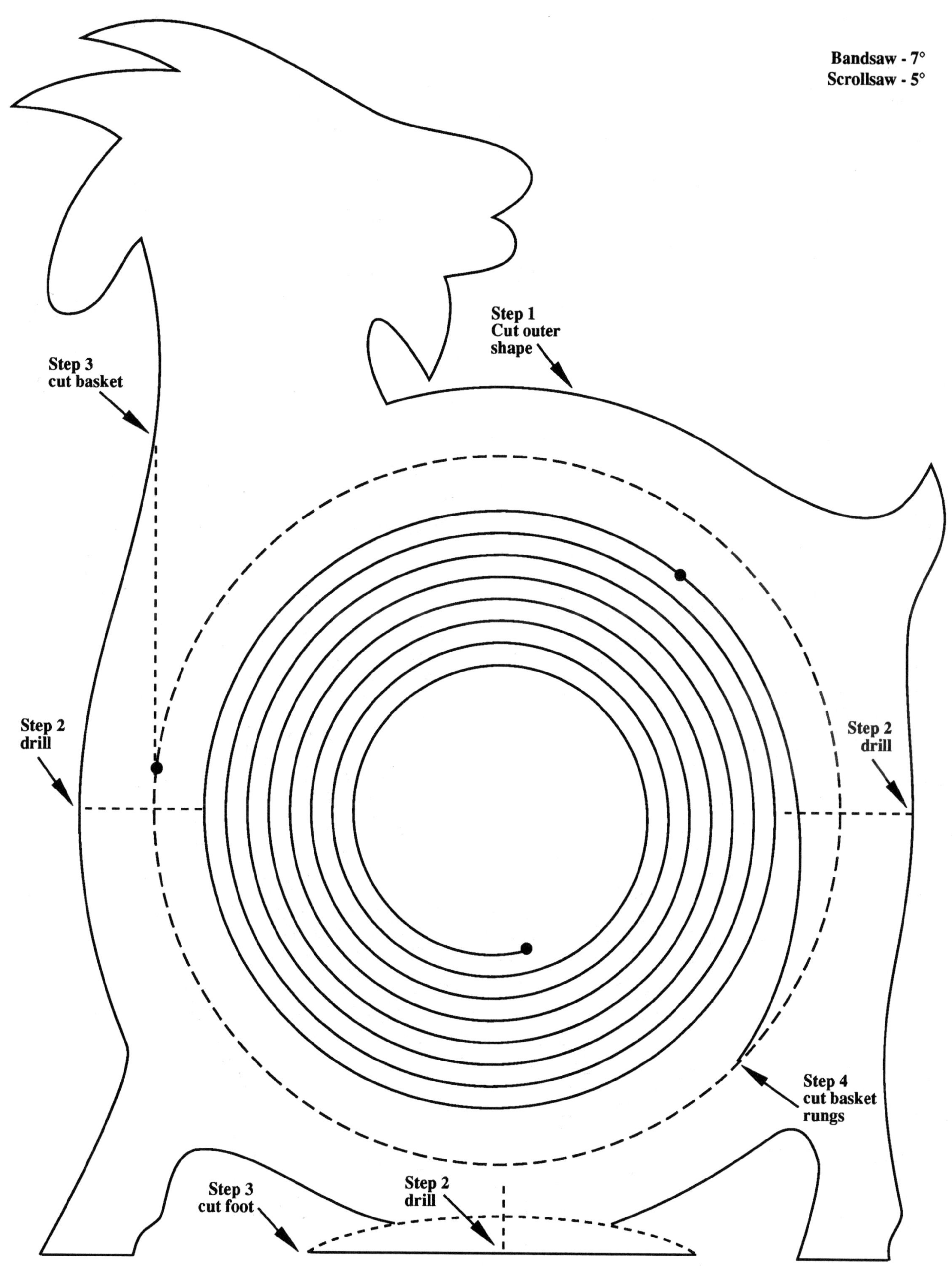
Bandsaw - 7°
Scrollsaw - 5°
Step 1
Cut outer
shape
Step 3
cut basket
Step 2
drill
Step 2
drill
Step 4
cut basket
rungs
Step 3
cut foot
Step 2
drill

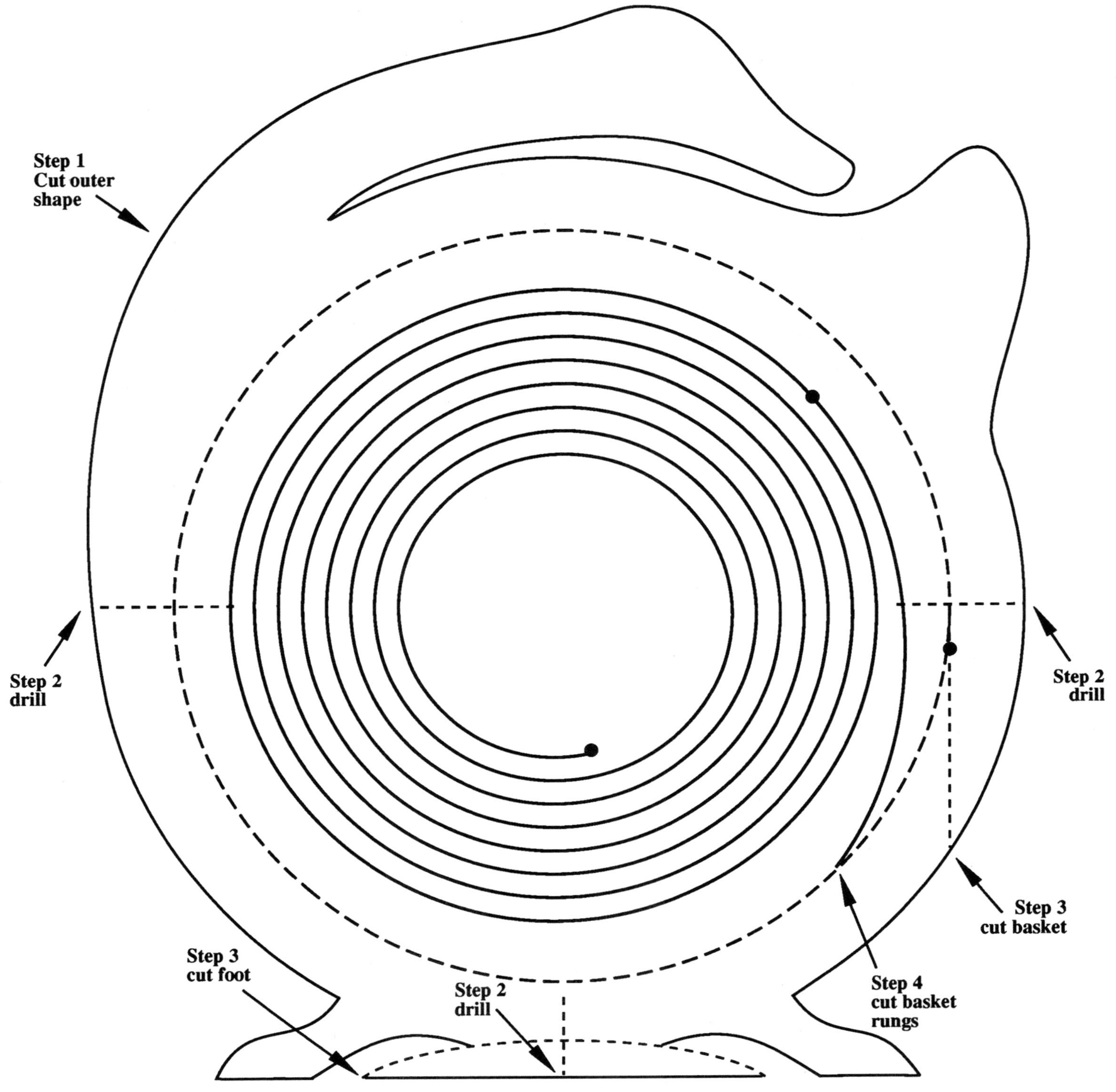

Bandsaw - 7°
Scrollsaw - 5°

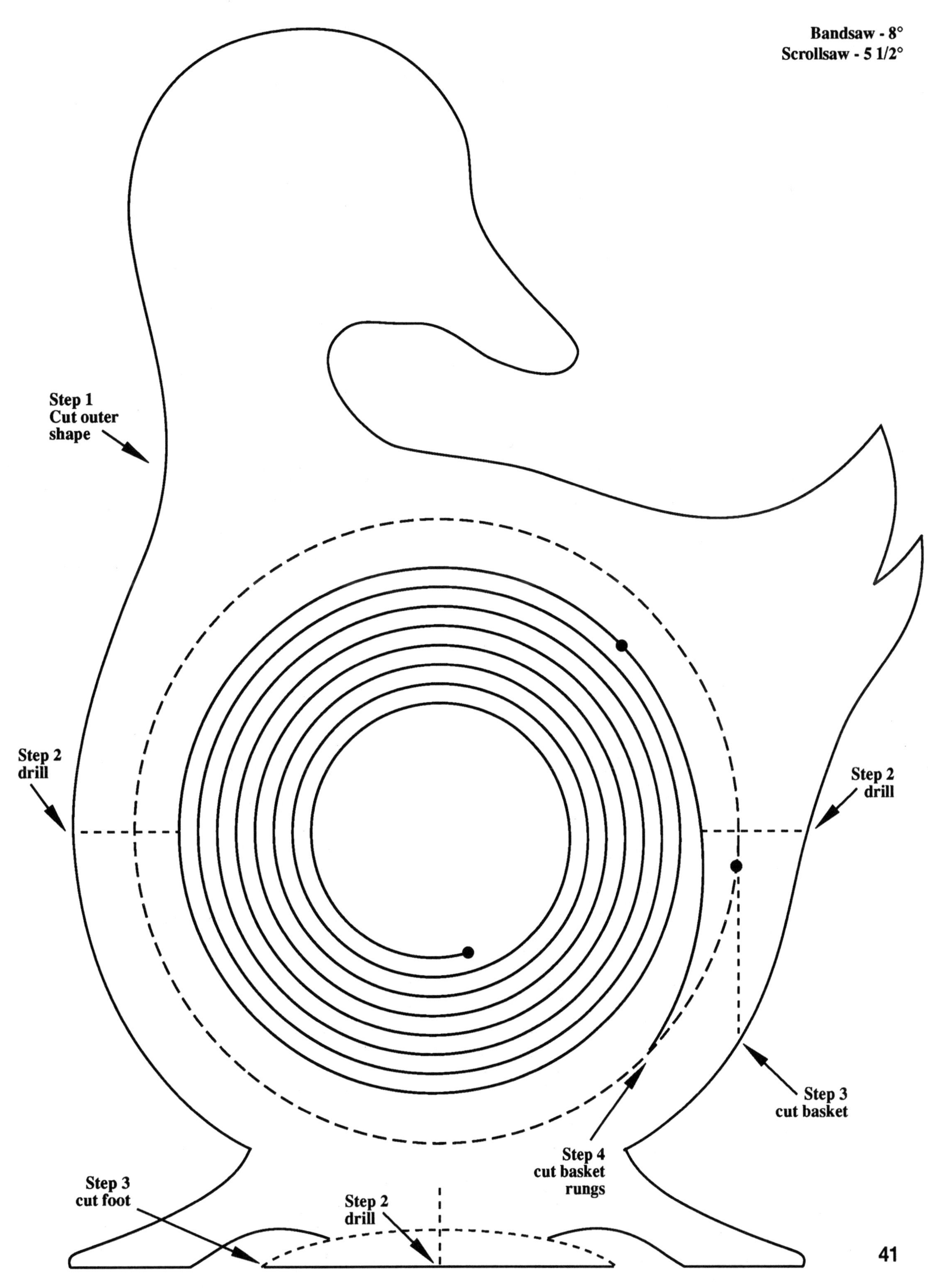
Bandsaw - 8°
Scrollsaw - 5 1/2°
Step 1
Cut outer
shape
Step 2
drill
Step 2
drill
Step 3
cut basket
Step 4
cut basket
rungs
Step 3
cut foot
Step 2
drill

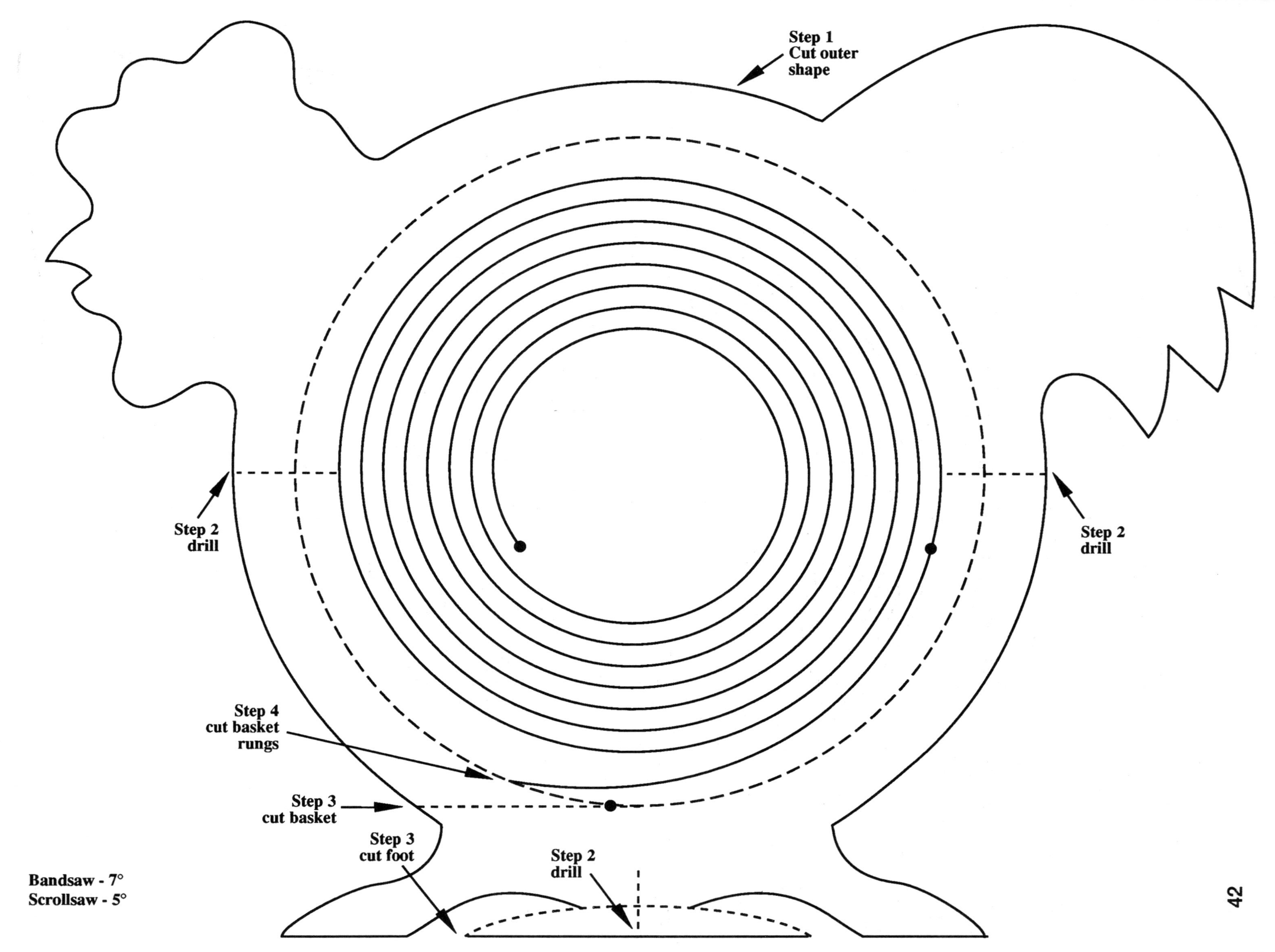
Step 1
Cut outer
shape
Step 2
drill
Step 2
drill
Step 4
cut basket
rungs
Step 3
cut basket
Step 3
cut foot
Step 2
drill
Bandsaw - 7°
Scrollsaw - 5°

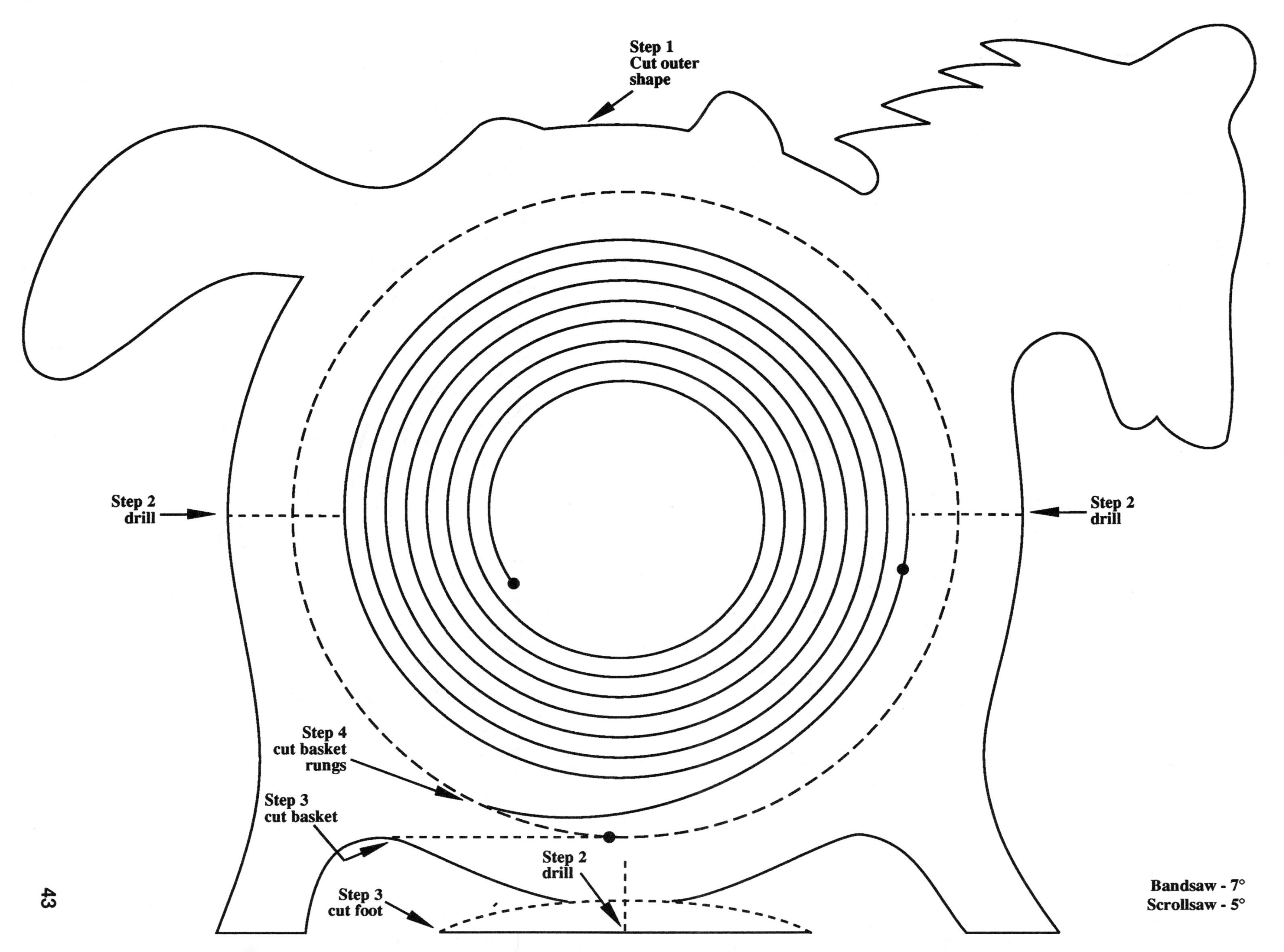

Step 1
Cut outer
shape
Step 2
drill
Step 2
drill
Step 4
cut basket
rungs
Step 3
cut basket
Step 2
drill
Step 3
cut foot
Bandsaw - 7°
Scrollsaw - 5°

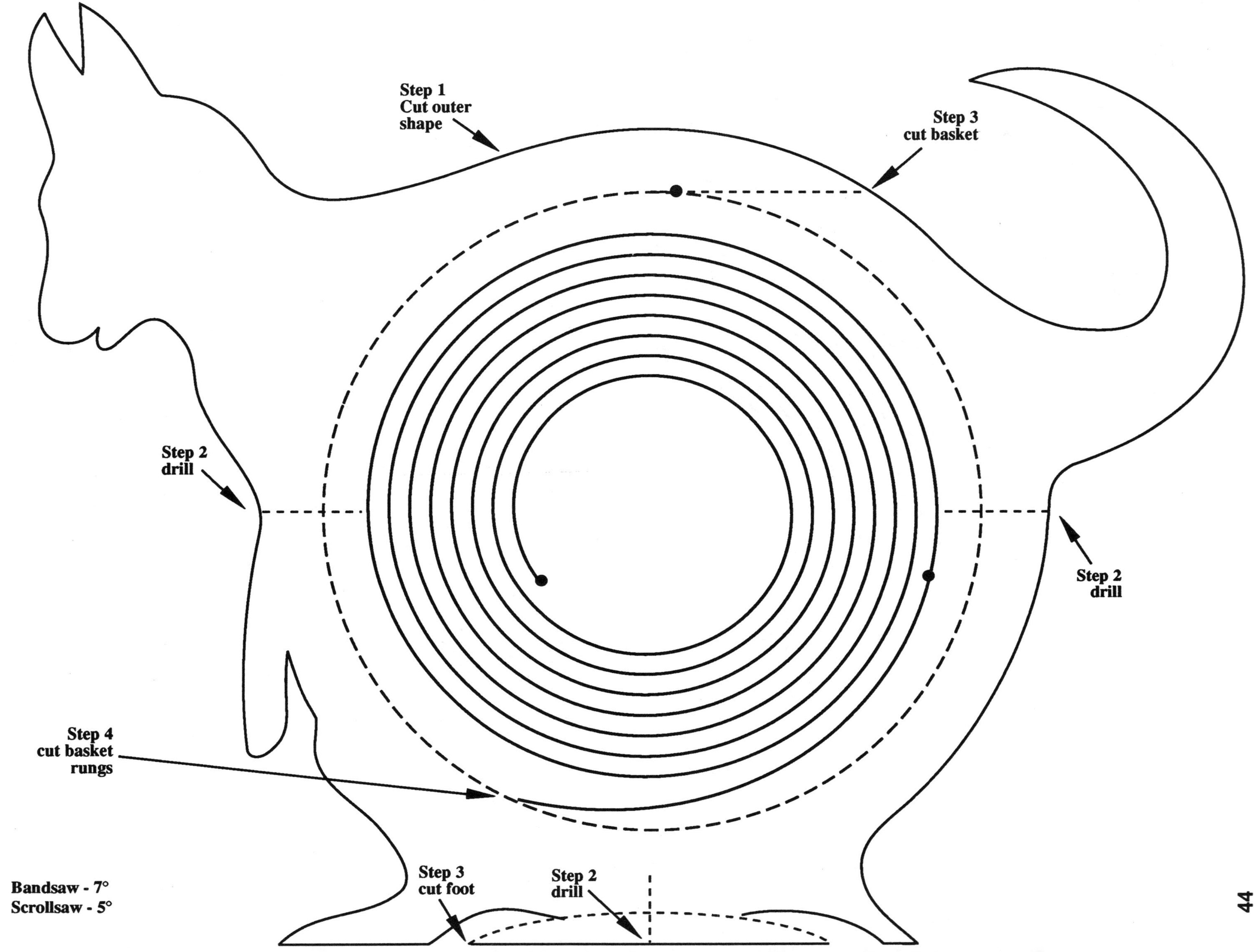
Step 1
Cut outer
shape
Step 3
cut basket
Step 2
drill
Step 2
drill
Step 4
cut basket
rungs
Step 3
cut foot
Step 2
drill
Bandsaw - 7°
Scrollsaw - 5°

Bandsaw - 9°
Scrollsaw - 6°

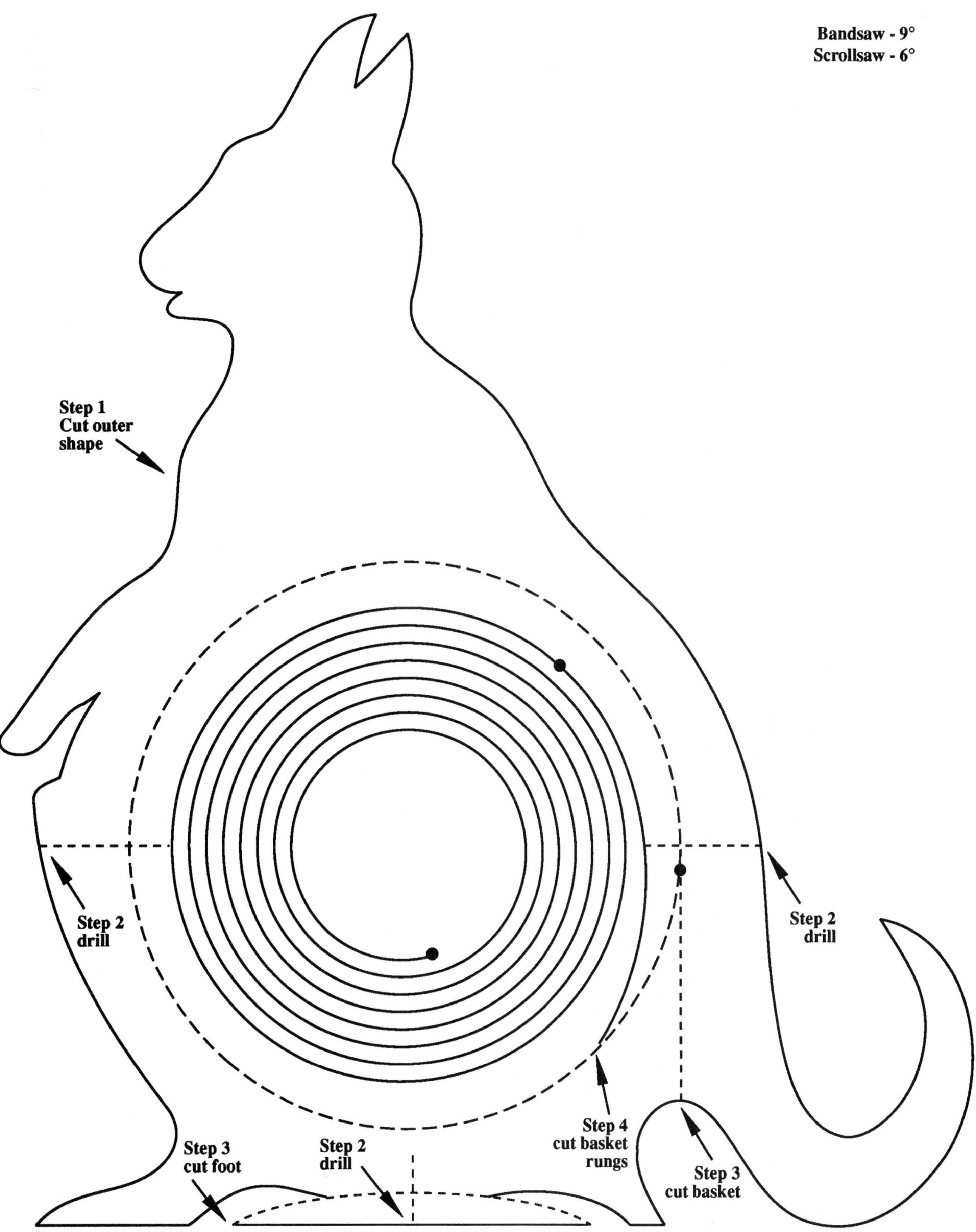

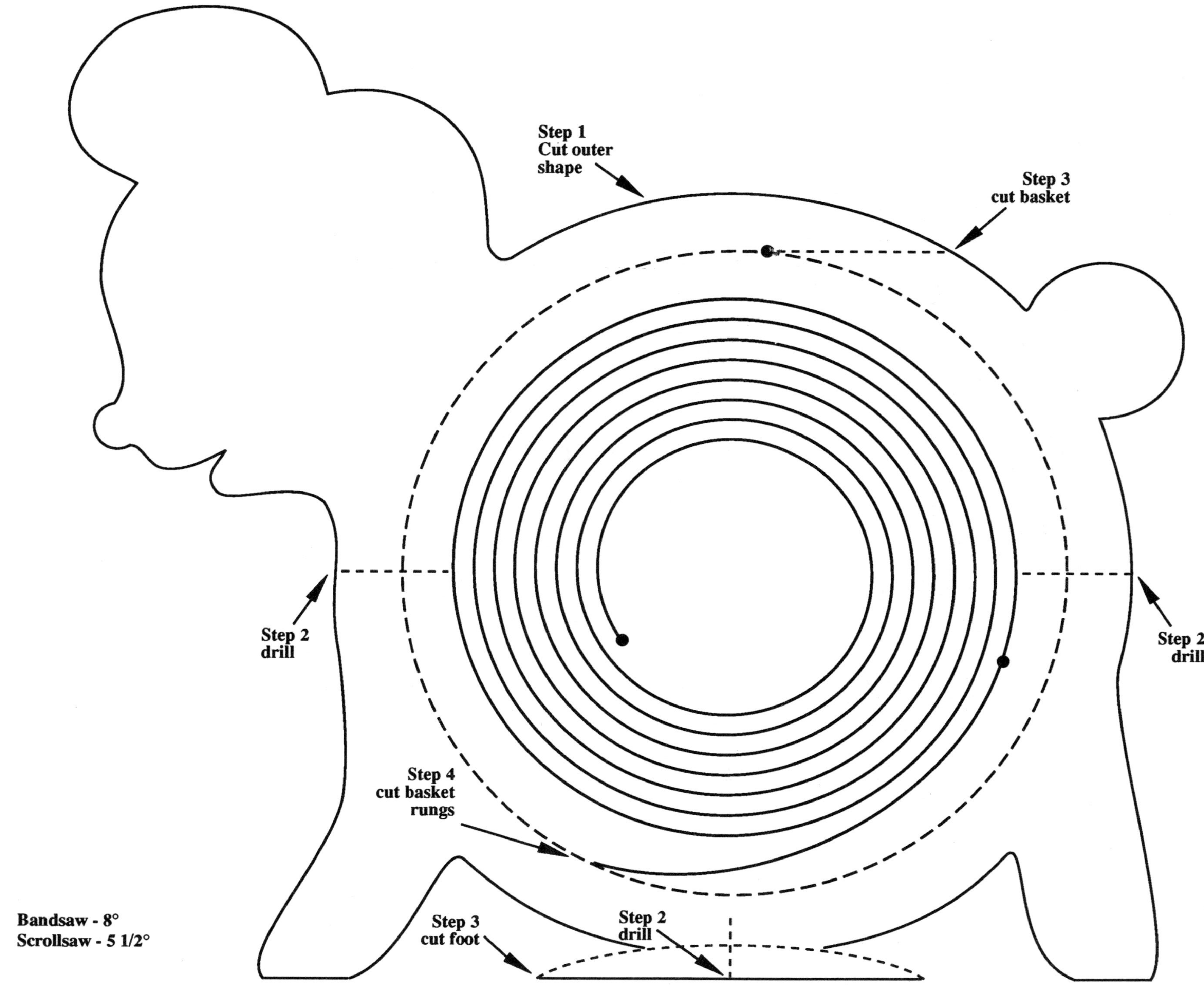

Bandsaw - 8°
Scrollsaw - 5 1/2°

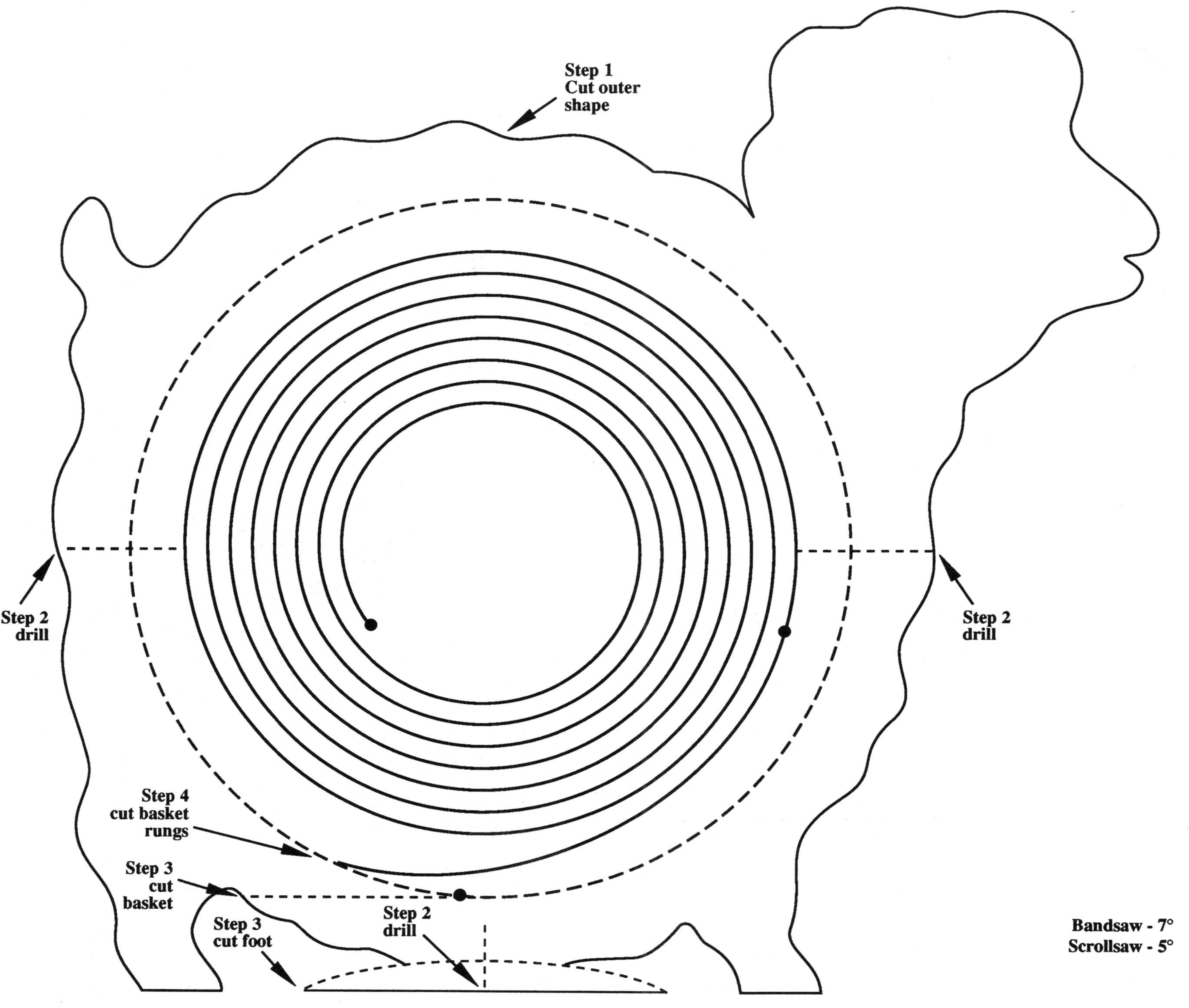
Step 1
Cut outer
shape
Step 2
drill
Step 2
drill
Step 4
cut basket
rungs
Step 3
cut
basket
Step 3
cut foot
Step 2
drill
Bandsaw - 7°
Scrollsaw - 5°

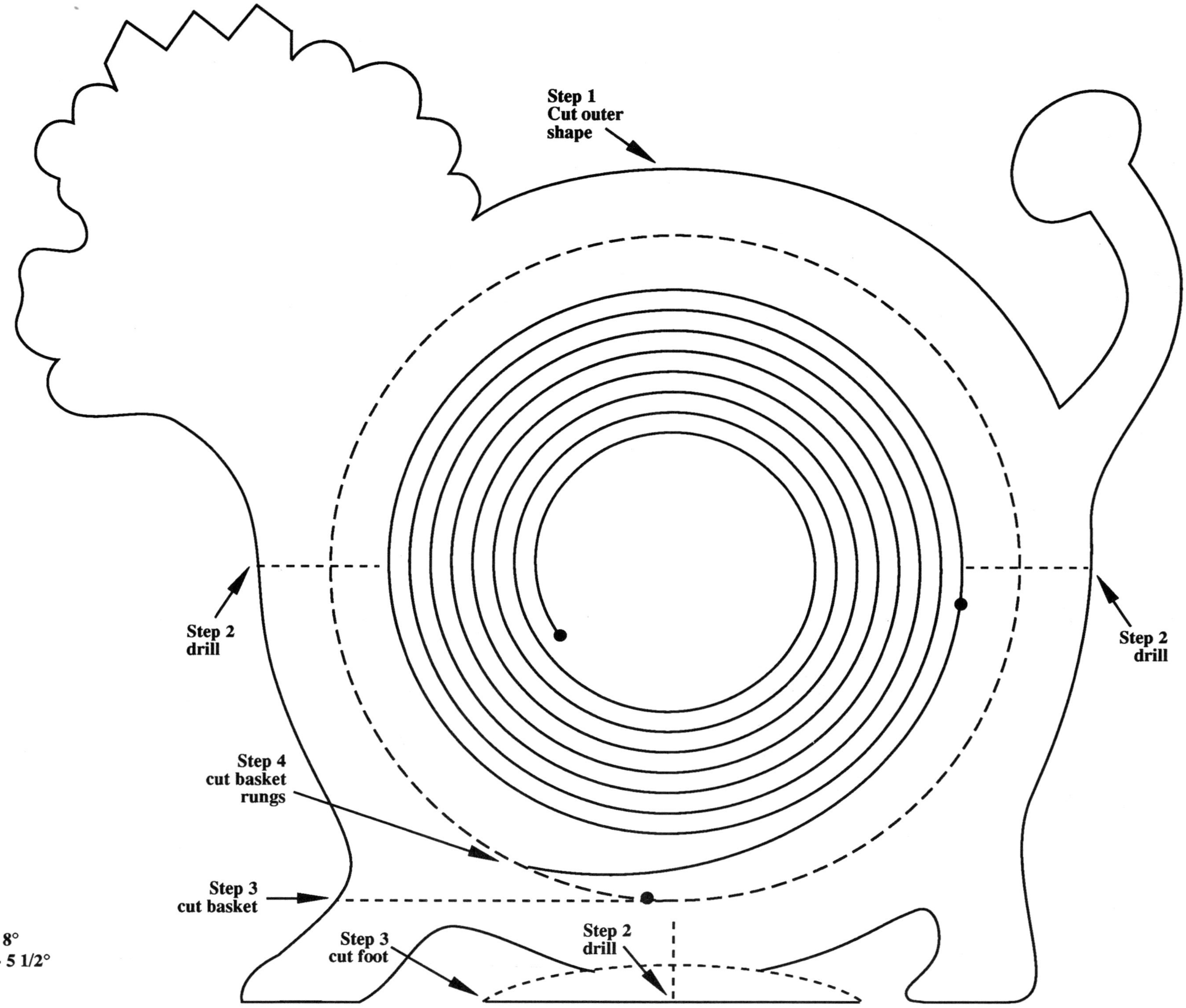

Step 1
Cut outer
shape

Step 2
drill

Step 2
drill

Step 4
cut basket
rungs

Step 3
cut basket

Step 3
cut foot

Step 2
drill

Bandsaw - 8°
Scrollsaw - 5 1/2°

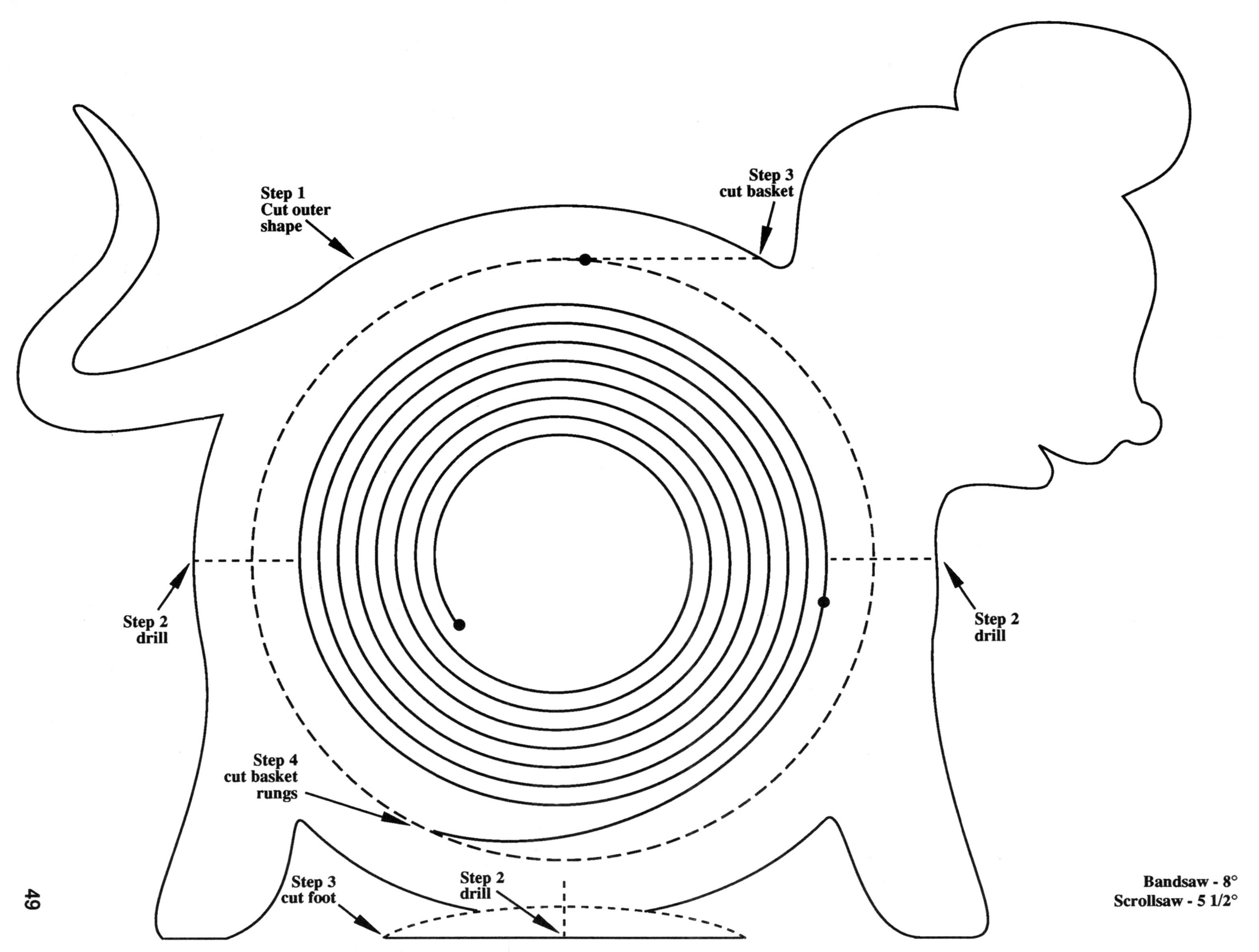
Step 1
Cut outer
shape
Step 3
cut basket
Step 2
drill
Step 2
drill
Step 4
cut basket
rungs
Step 3
cut foot
Step 2
drill
Bandsaw - 8°
Scrollsaw - 5 1/2°

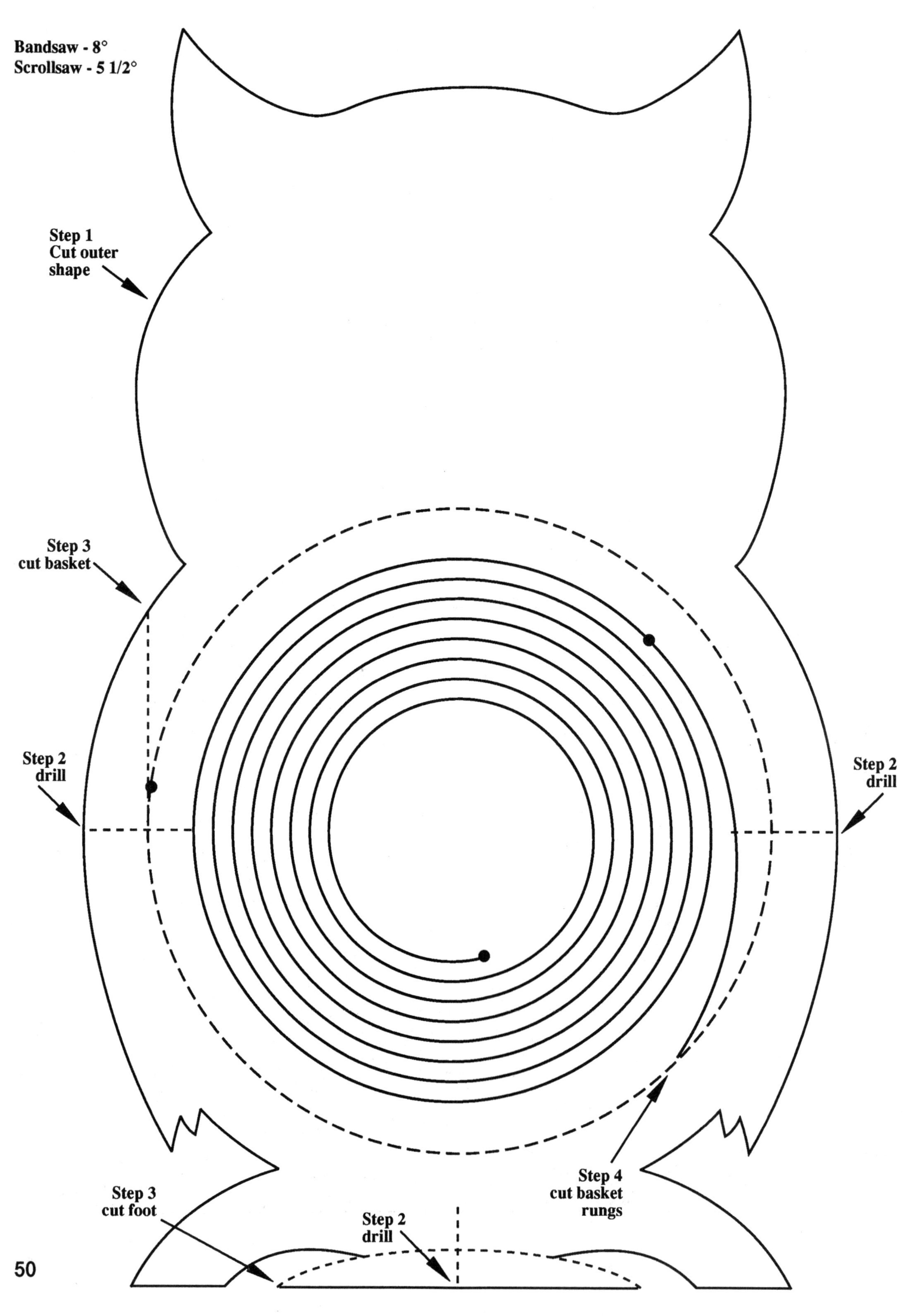
Bandsaw - 8°
Scrollsaw - 5 1/2°
Step 1
Cut outer
shape
Step 3
cut basket
Step 2
drill
Step 2
drill
Step 4
cut basket
rungs
Step 3
cut foot
Step 2
drill

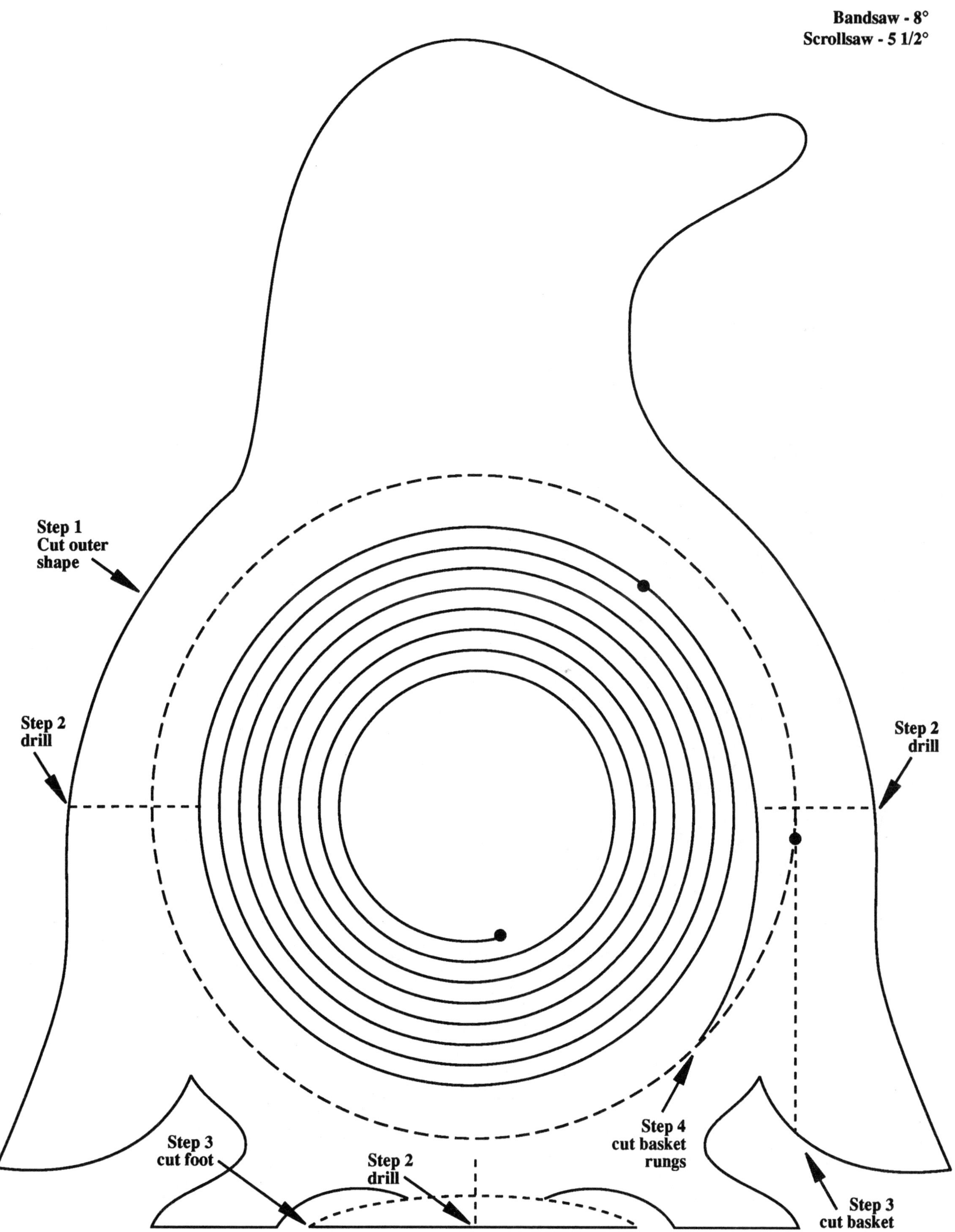
Bandsaw - 8°
Scrollsaw - 5 1/2°
Step 1
Cut outer
shape
Step 2
drill
Step 2
drill
Step 3
cut foot
Step 2
drill
Step 4
cut basket
rungs
Step 3
cut basket

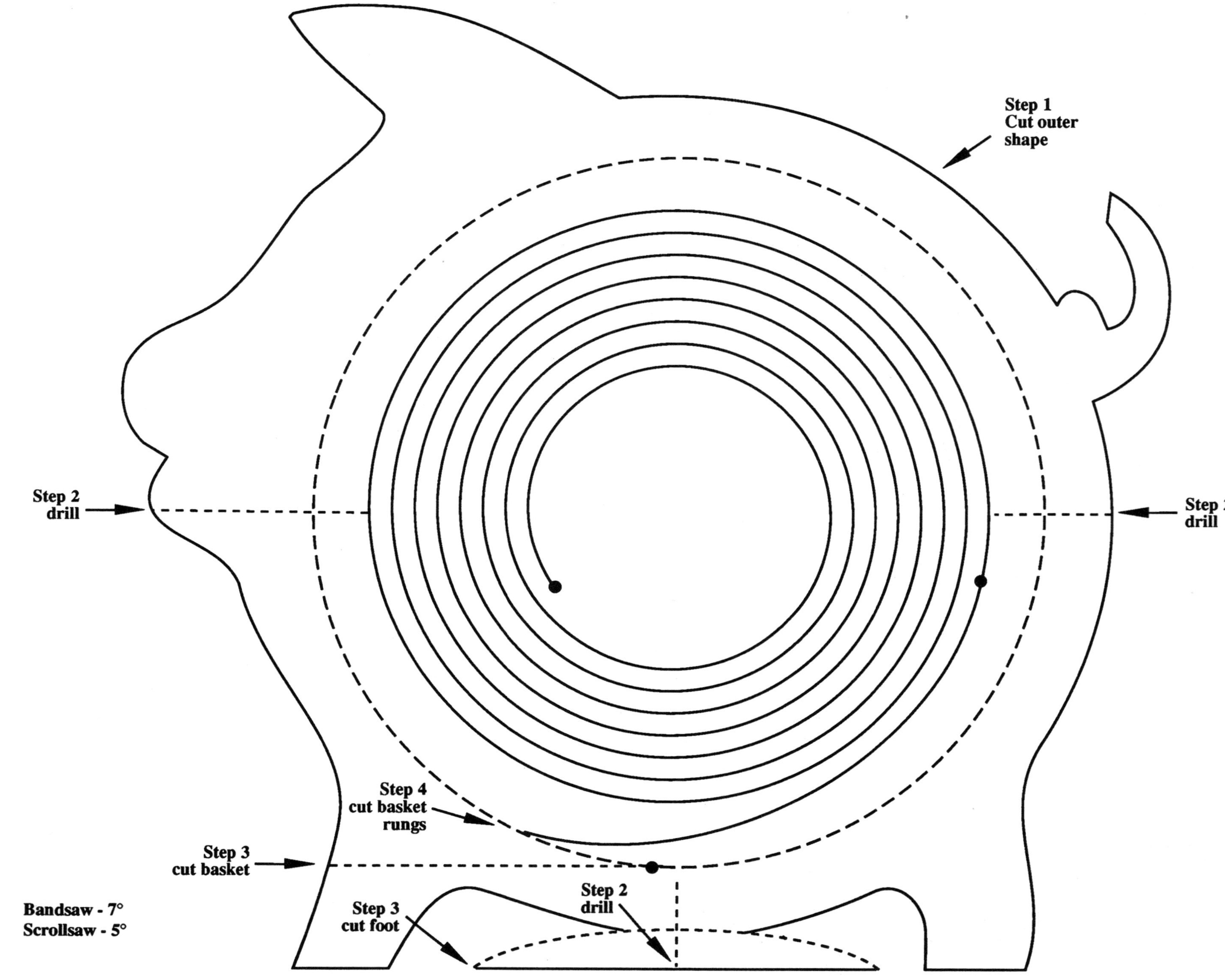
Step 1
Cut outer
shape
Step 2
drill
Step 2
drill
Step 4
cut basket
rungs
Step 3
cut basket
Step 2
drill
Step 3
cut foot
Bandsaw - 7°
Scrollsaw - 5°

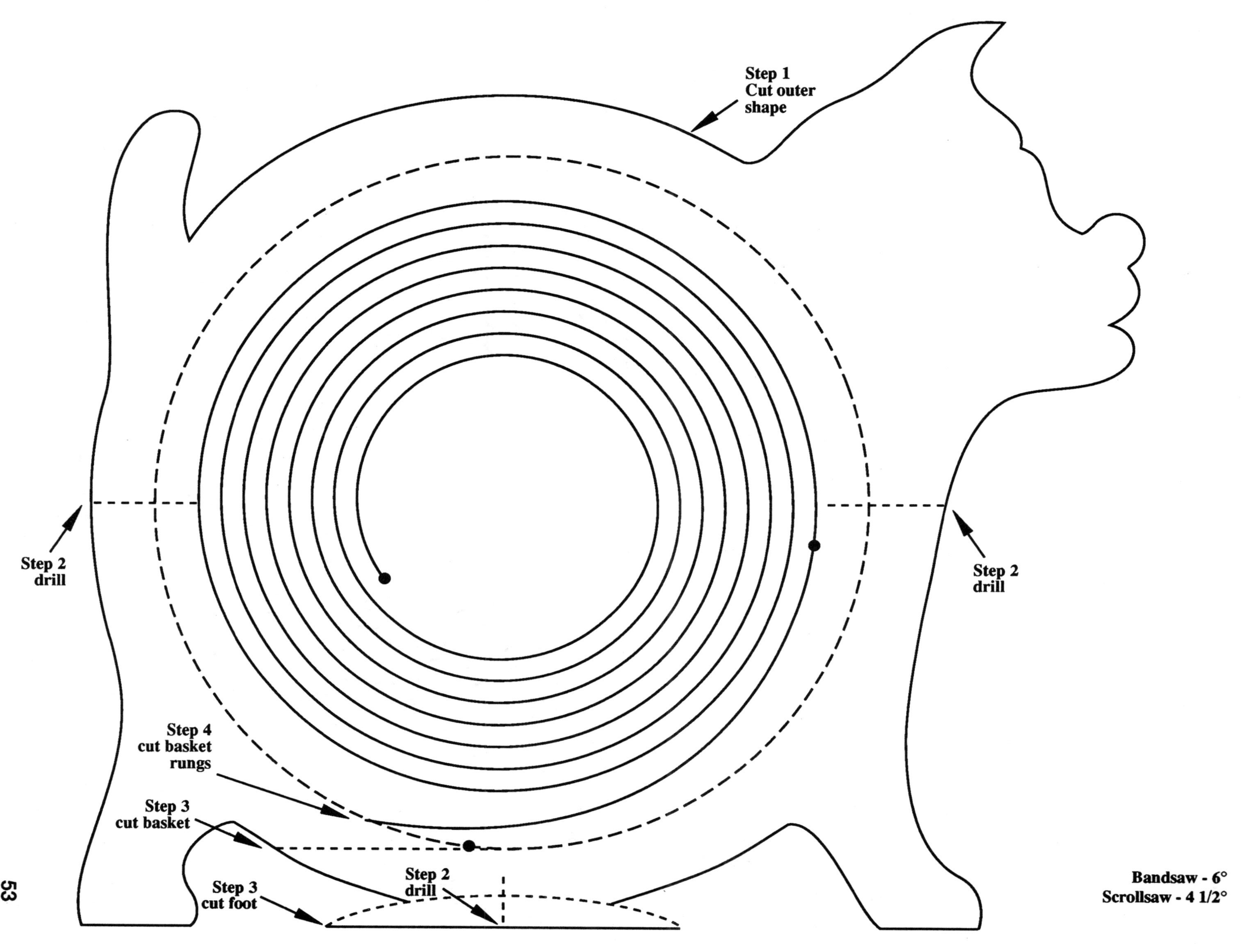
Step 1
Cut outer
shape
Step 2
drill
Step 2
drill
Step 4
cut basket
rungs
Step 3
cut basket
Step 3
cut foot
Step 2
drill
Bandsaw - 6°
Scrollsaw - 4 1/2°

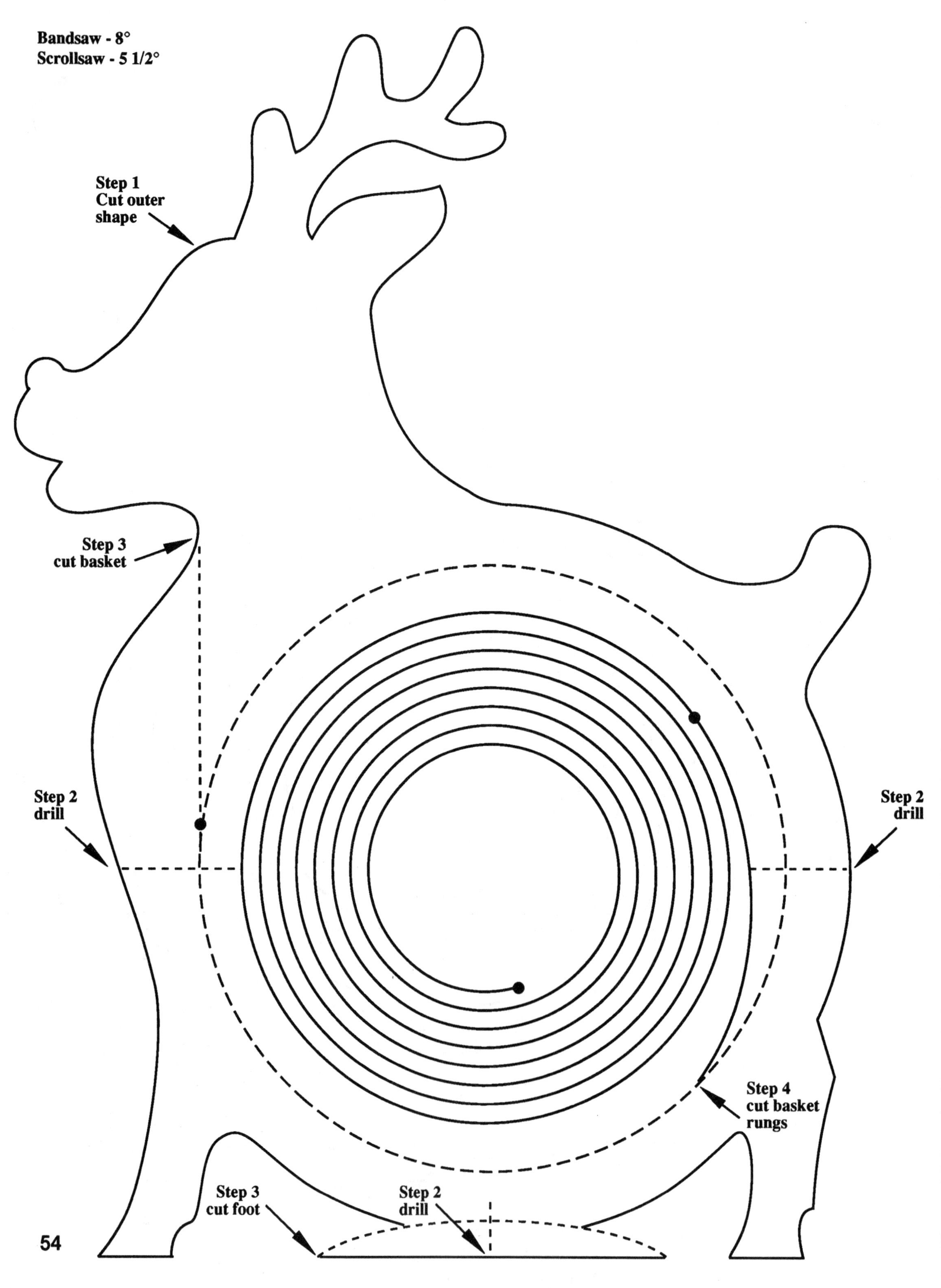
Bandsaw - 8°
Scrollsaw - 5 1/2°
Step 1
Cut outer
shape
Step 3
cut basket
Step 2
drill
Step 2
drill
Step 4
cut basket
rungs
Step 3
cut foot
Step 2
drill

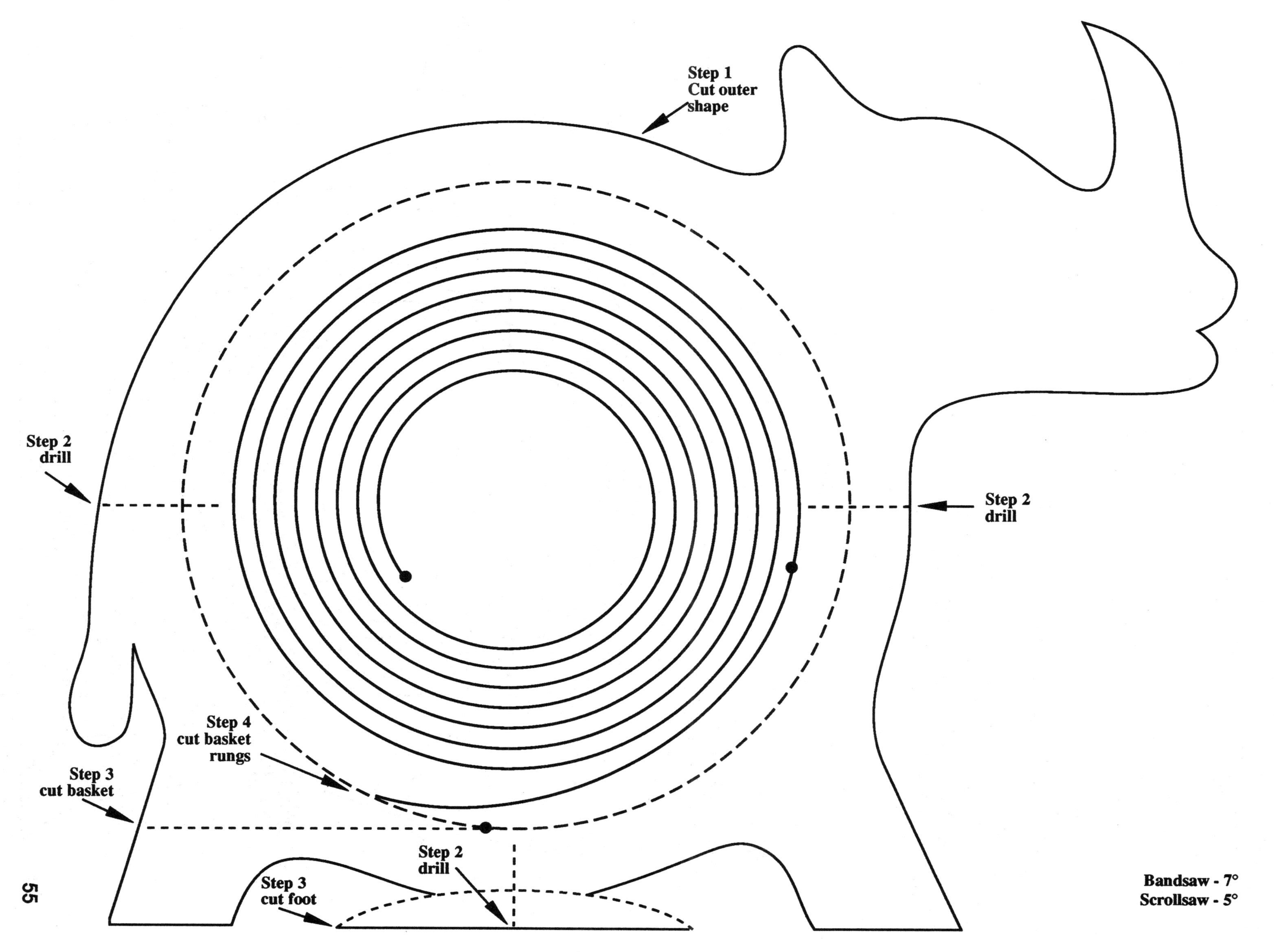

Step 1
Cut outer
shape
Step 2
drill
Step 2
drill
Step 4
cut basket
rungs
Step 3
cut basket
Step 2
drill
Step 3
cut foot
Bandsaw - 7°
Scrollsaw - 5°

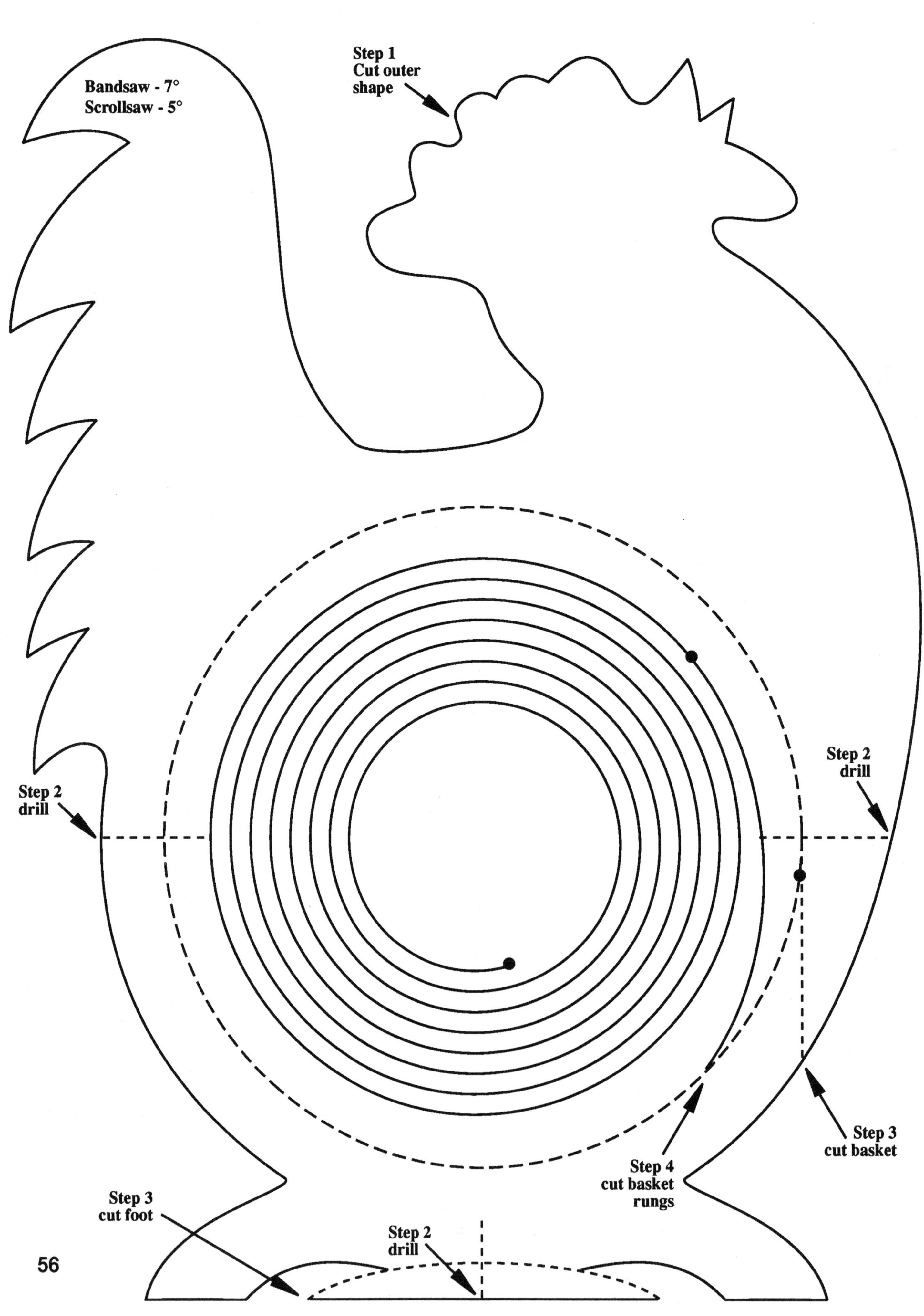
Bandsaw - 7°
Scrollsaw - 5°
Step 1
Cut outer
shape
Step 2
drill
Step 2
drill
Step 3
cut basket
Step 4
cut basket
rungs
Step 3
cut foot
Step 2
drill

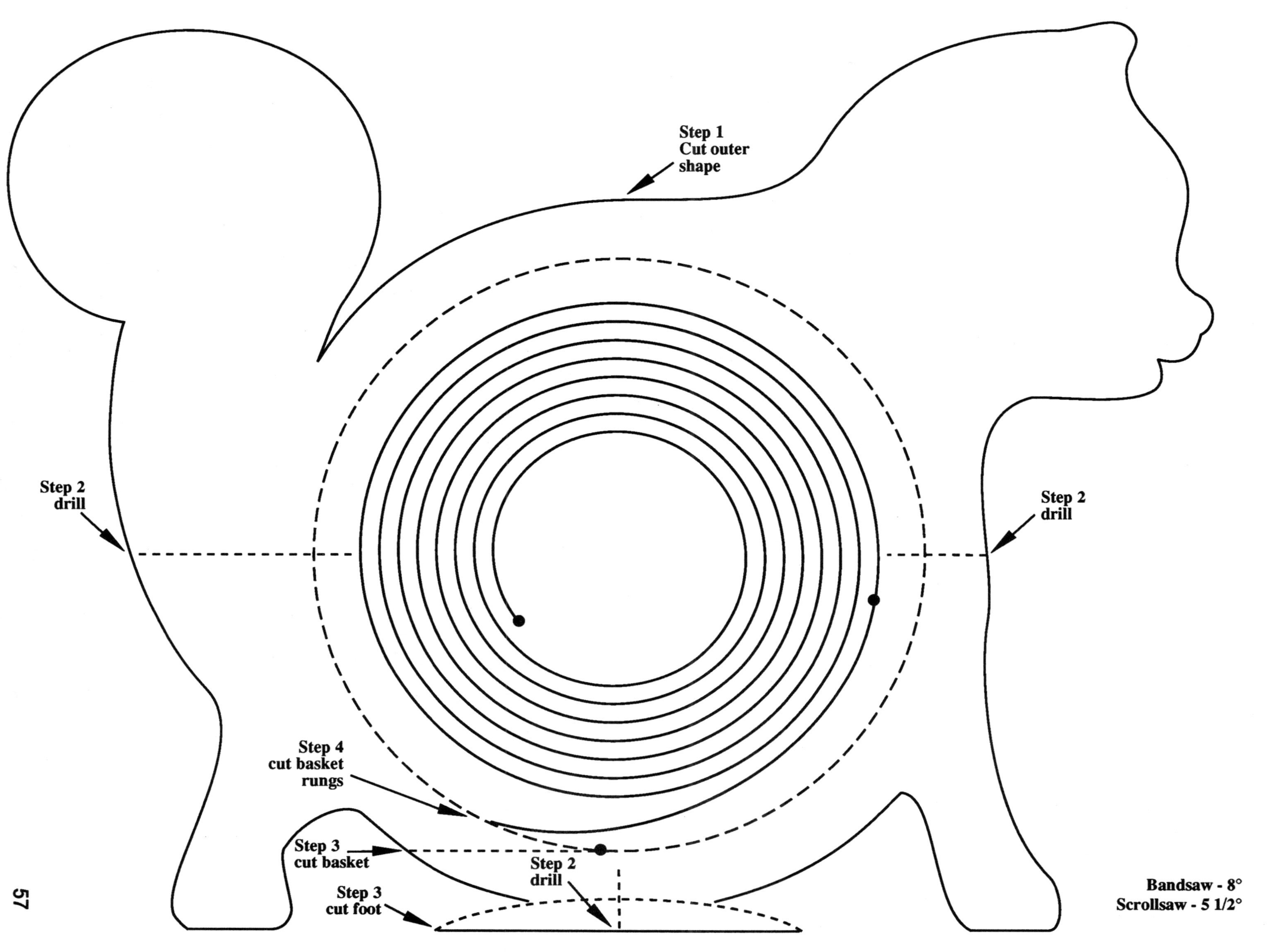
Step 1
Cut outer
shape
Step 2
drill
Step 2
drill
Step 4
cut basket
rungs
Step 3
cut basket
Step 2
drill
Step 3
cut foot
Bandsaw - 8°
Scrollsaw - 5 1/2°

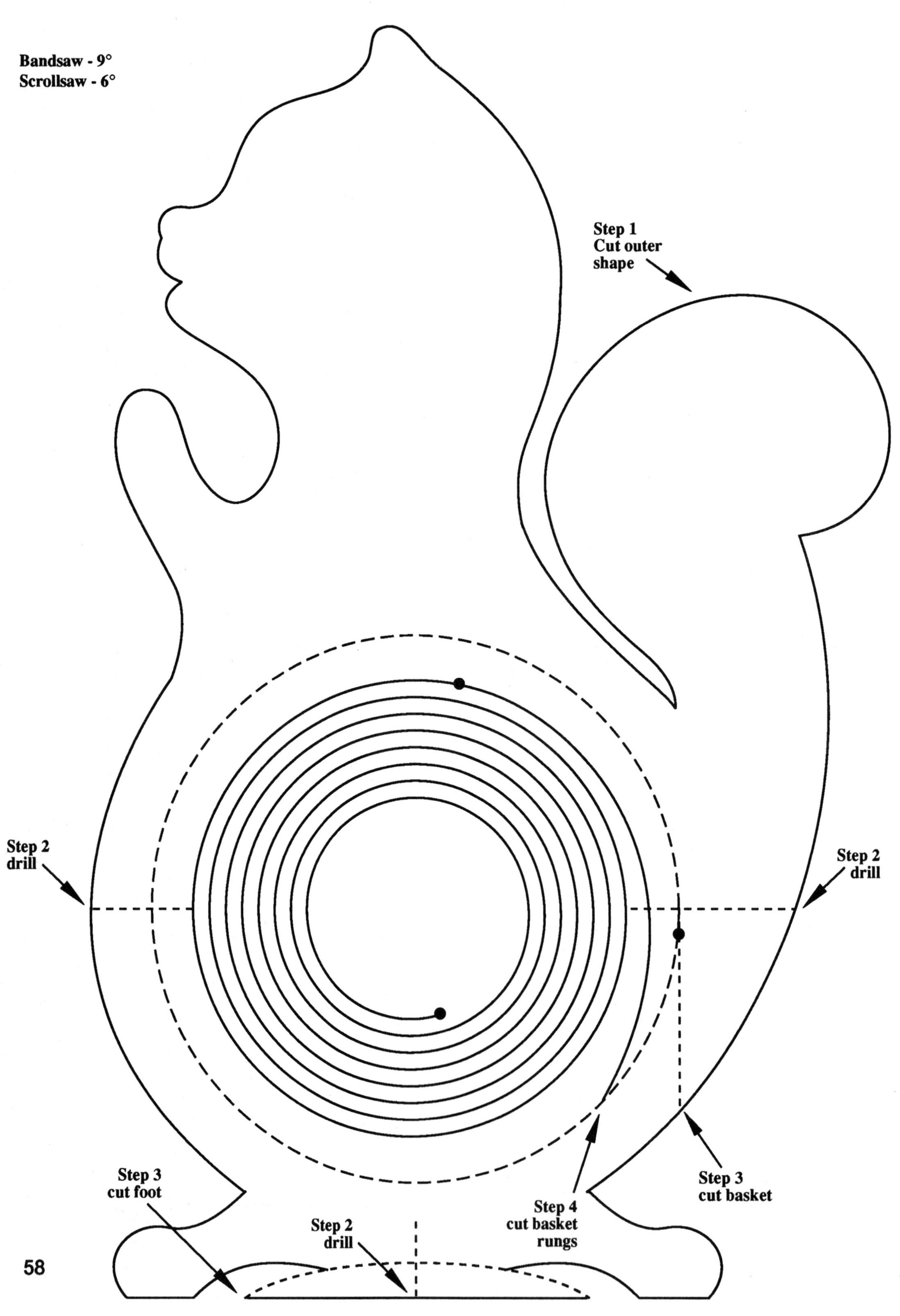

Bandsaw - 9°
Scrollsaw - 6°
Step 1
Cut outer
shape
Step 2
drill
Step 2
drill
Step 3
cut foot
Step 2
drill
Step 4
cut basket
rungs
Step 3
cut basket

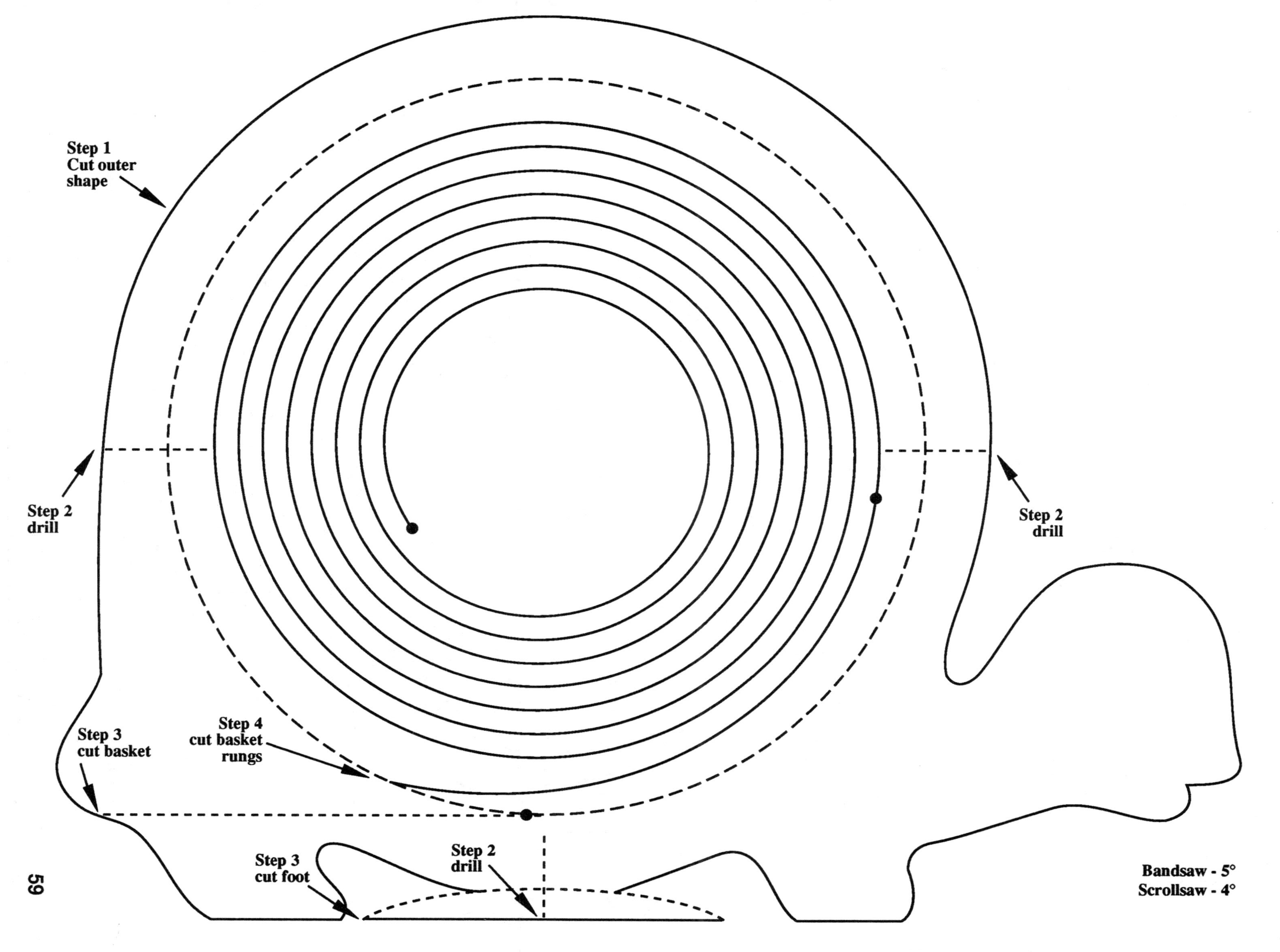

Step 1
Cut outer
shape
Step 2
drill
Step 2
drill
Step 3
cut basket
Step 4
cut basket
rungs
Step 3
cut foot
Step 2
drill
Bandsaw - 5°
Scrollsaw - 4°

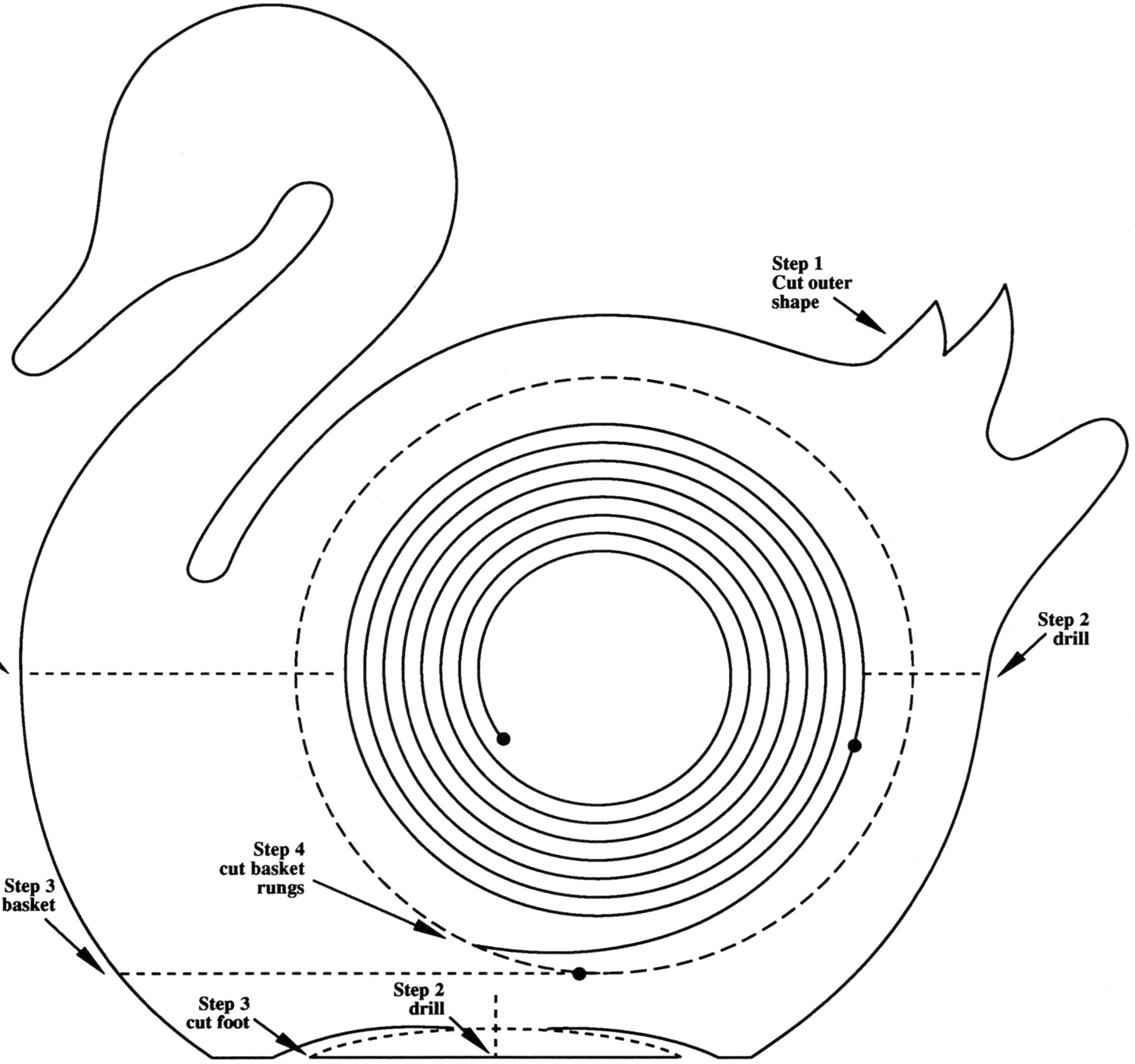

Step 1
Cut outer
shape

Step 2
drill

Step 2
drill

Step 4
cut basket
rungs

Step 3
cut basket

Step 2
drill

Step 3
cut foot

Bandsaw - 9°
Scrollsaw - 6°

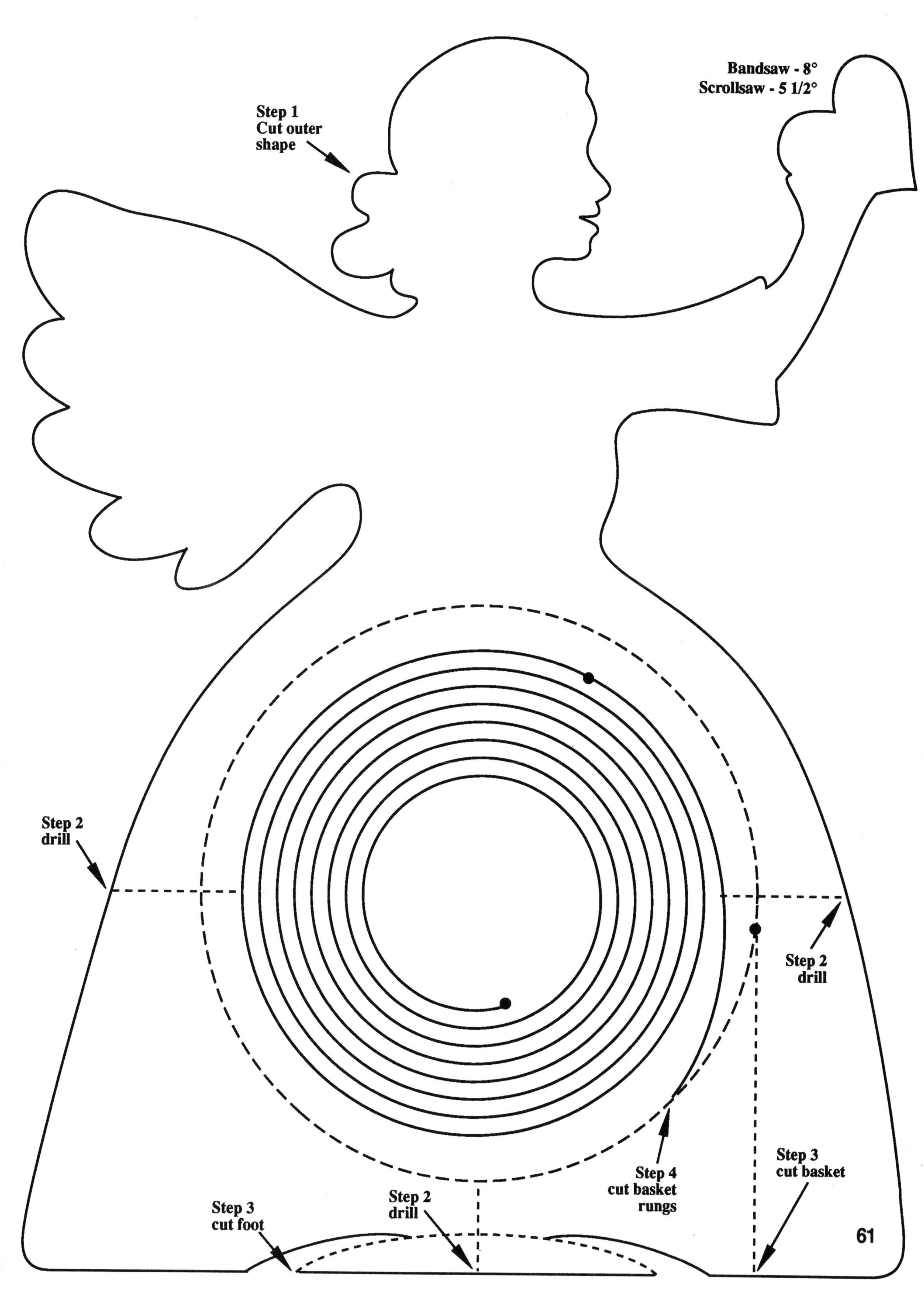
Bandsaw - 8°
Scrollsaw - 5 1/2°
Step 1
Cut outer
shape
Step 2
drill
Step 2
drill
Step 4
cut basket
rungs
Step 3
cut basket
Step 3
cut foot
Step 2
drill

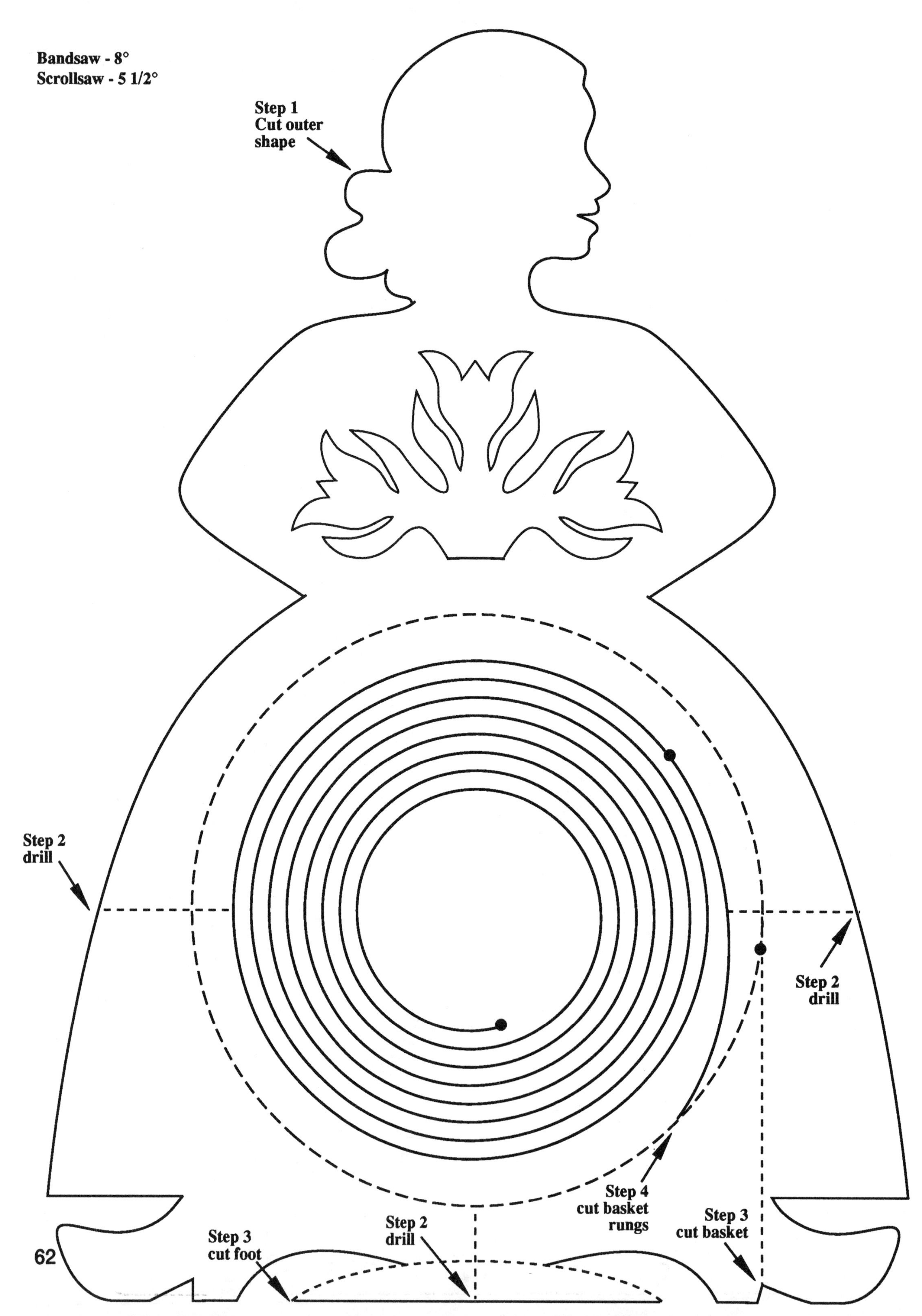

Bandsaw - 8°
Scrollsaw - 5 1/2°
Step 1
Cut outer
shape
Step 2
drill
Step 2
drill
Step 4
cut basket
rungs
Step 3
cut basket
Step 2
drill
Step 3
cut foot

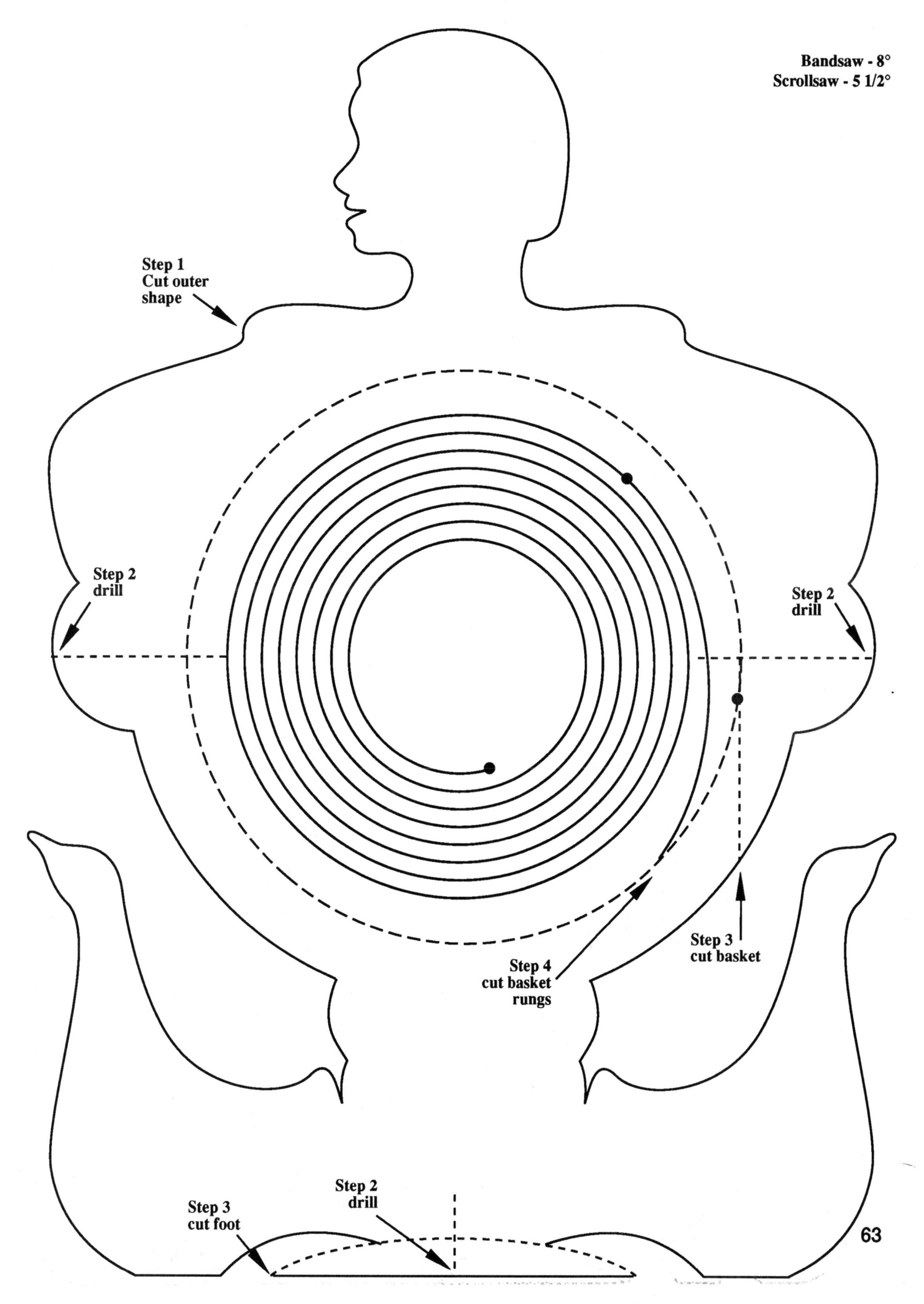
Bandsaw - 8°
Scrollsaw - 5 1/2°
Step 1
Cut outer
shape
Step 2
drill
Step 2
drill
Step 3
cut basket
Step 4
cut basket
rungs
Step 2
drill
Step 3
cut foot

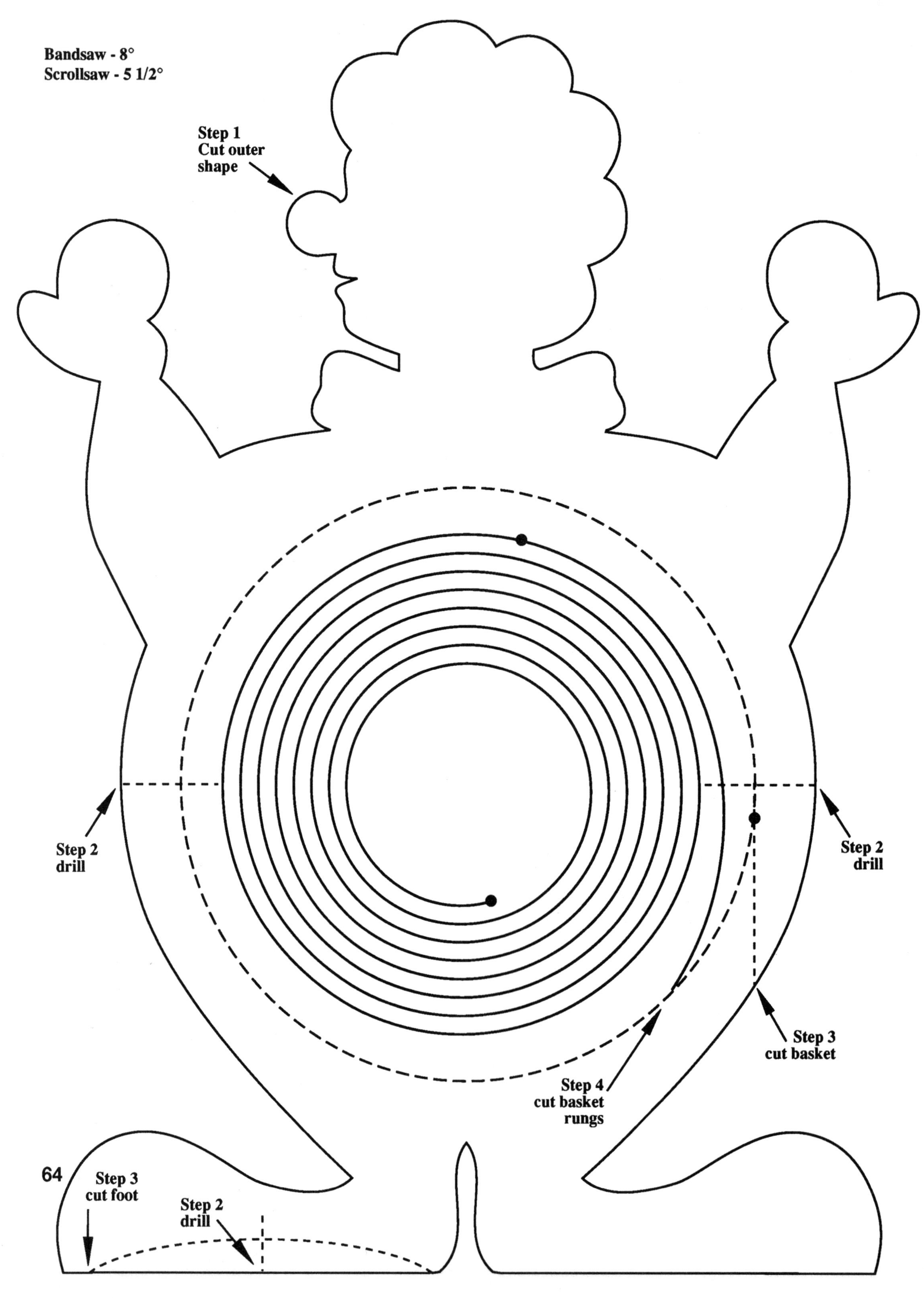
Bandsaw - 8°
Scrollsaw - 5 1/2°
Step 1
Cut outer
shape
Step 2
drill
Step 2
drill
Step 3
cut basket
Step 4
cut basket
rungs
Step 3
cut foot
Step 2
drill

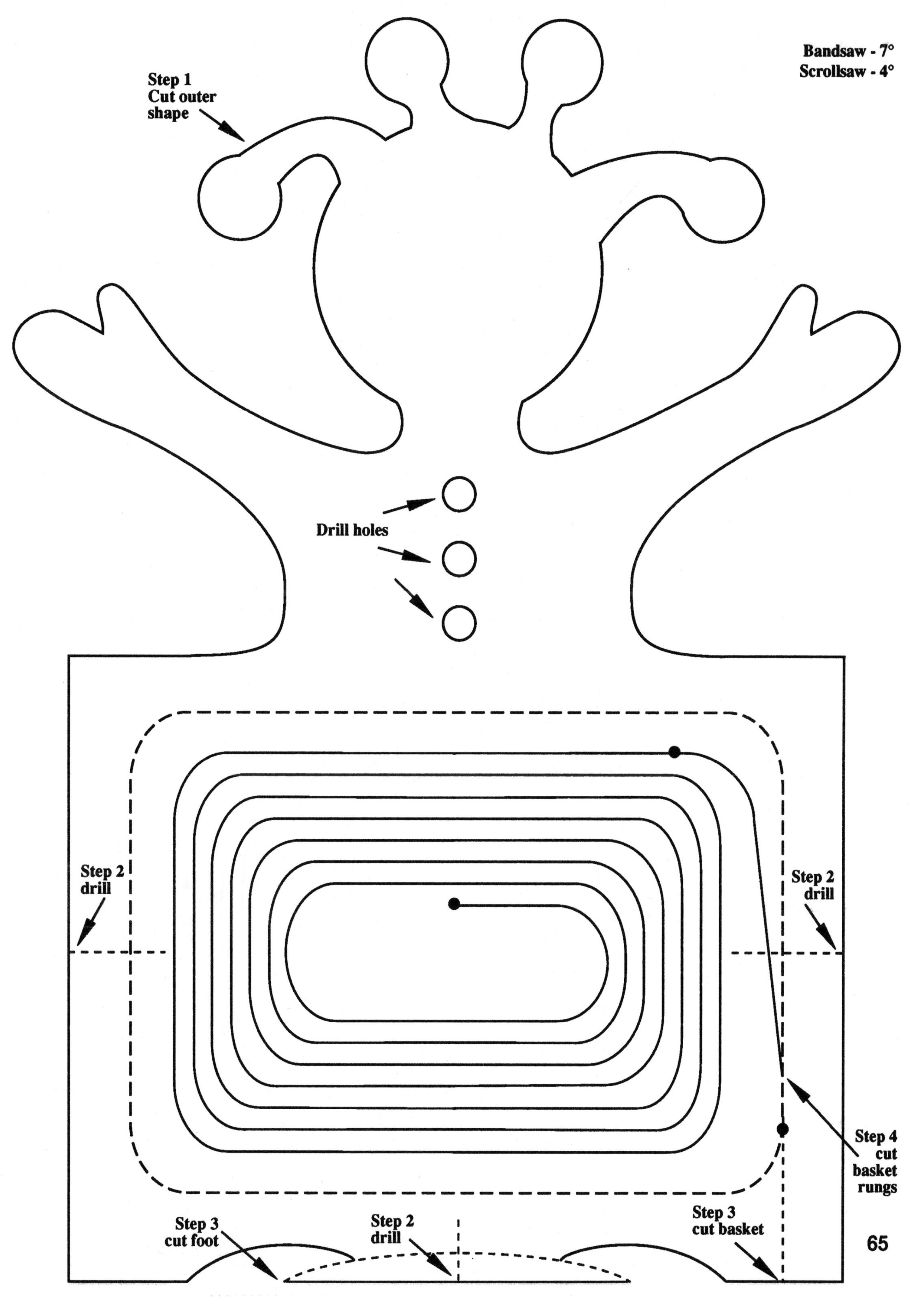
Bandsaw - 7°
Scrollsaw - 4°
Step 1
Cut outer
shape
Drill holes
Step 2
drill
Step 2
drill
Step 4
cut
basket
rungs
Step 3
cut foot
Step 2
drill
Step 3
cut basket

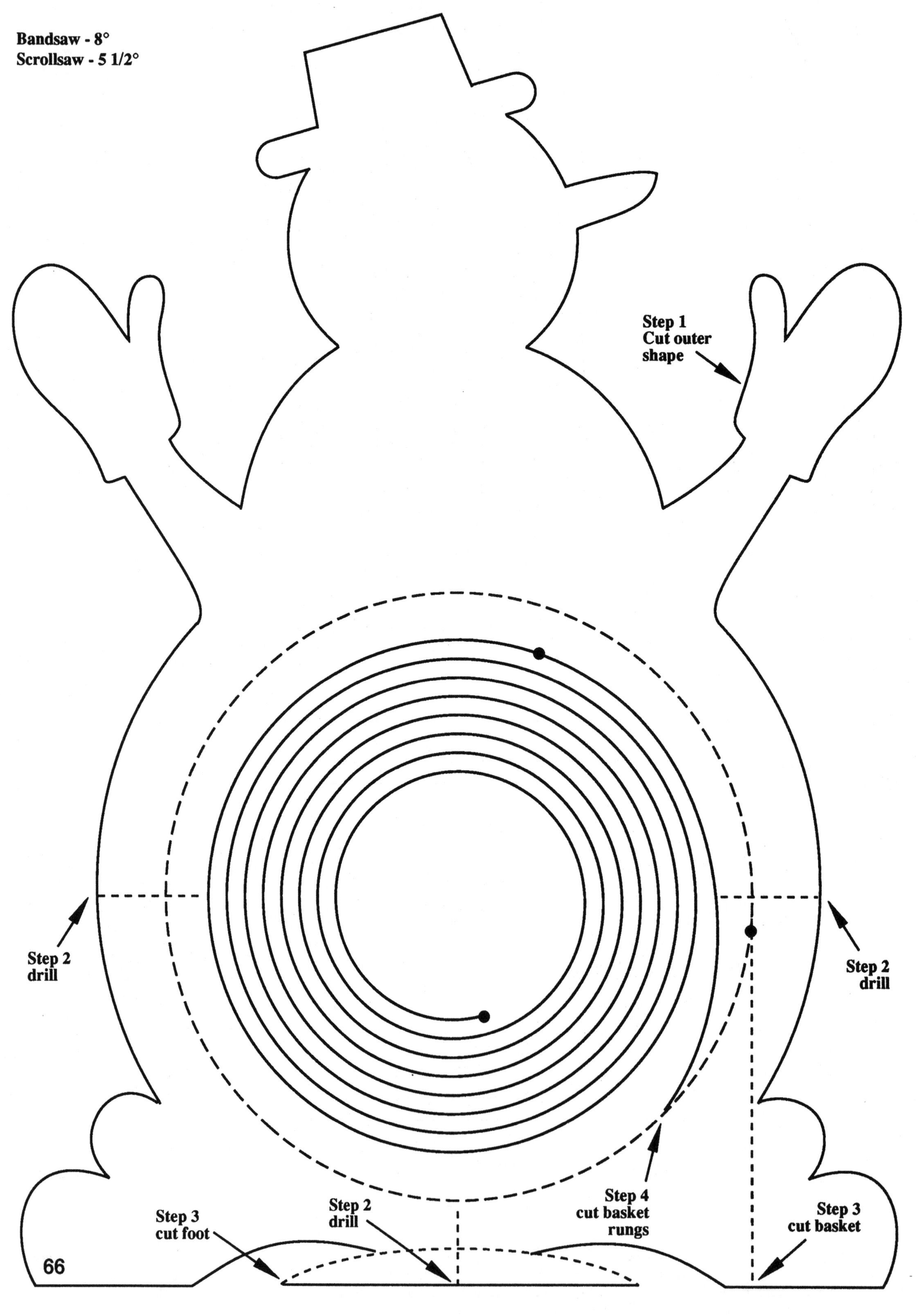

Bandsaw - 8°
Scrollsaw - 5 1/2°
Step 1
Cut outer
shape
Step 2
drill
Step 2
drill
Step 4
cut basket
rungs
Step 3
cut foot
Step 2
drill
Step 3
cut basket

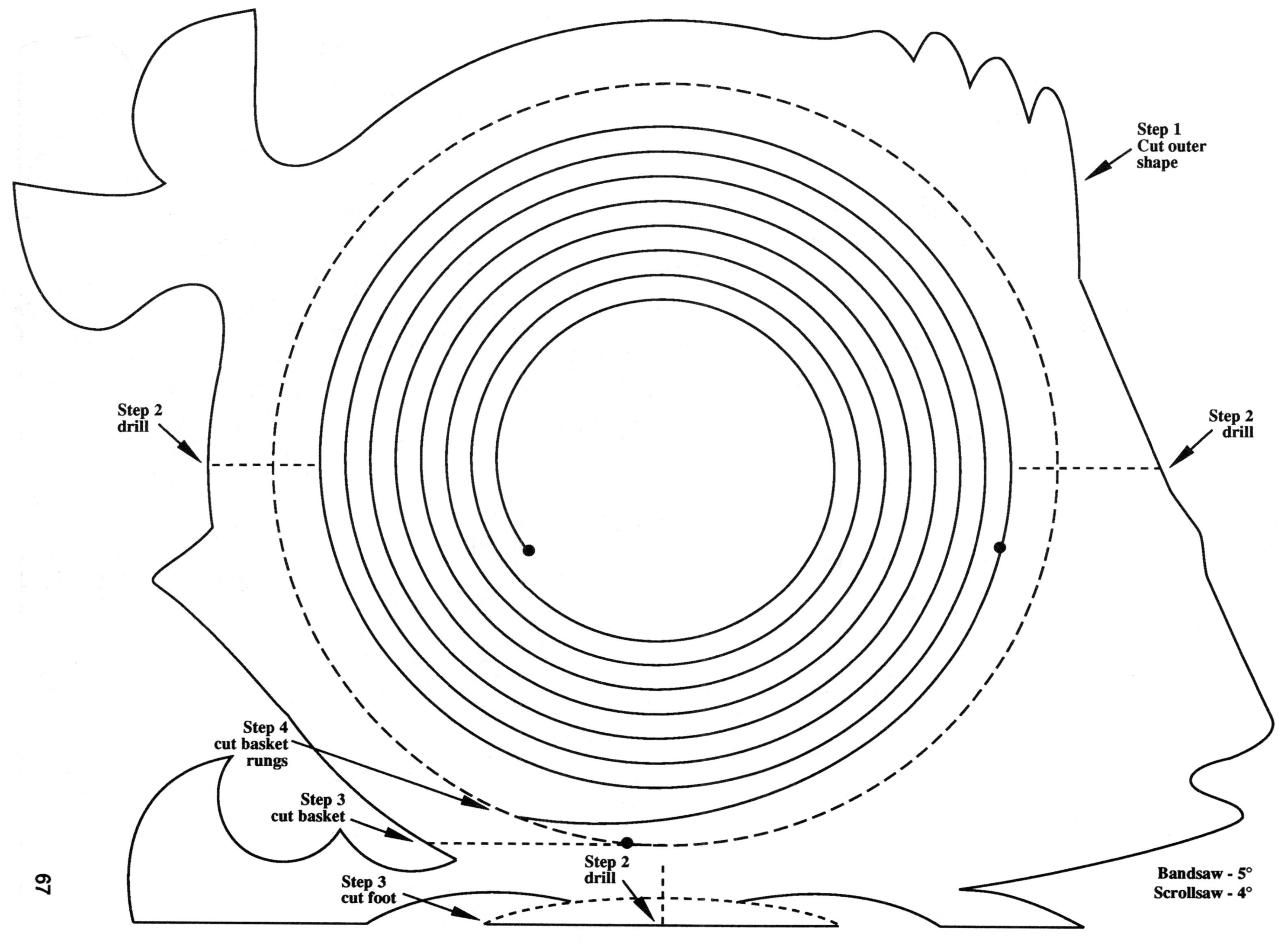
Step 1
Cut outer
shape
Step 2
drill
Step 2
drill
Step 4
cut basket
rungs
Step 3
cut basket
Step 2
drill
Step 3
cut foot
Bandsaw - 5°
Scrollsaw - 4°

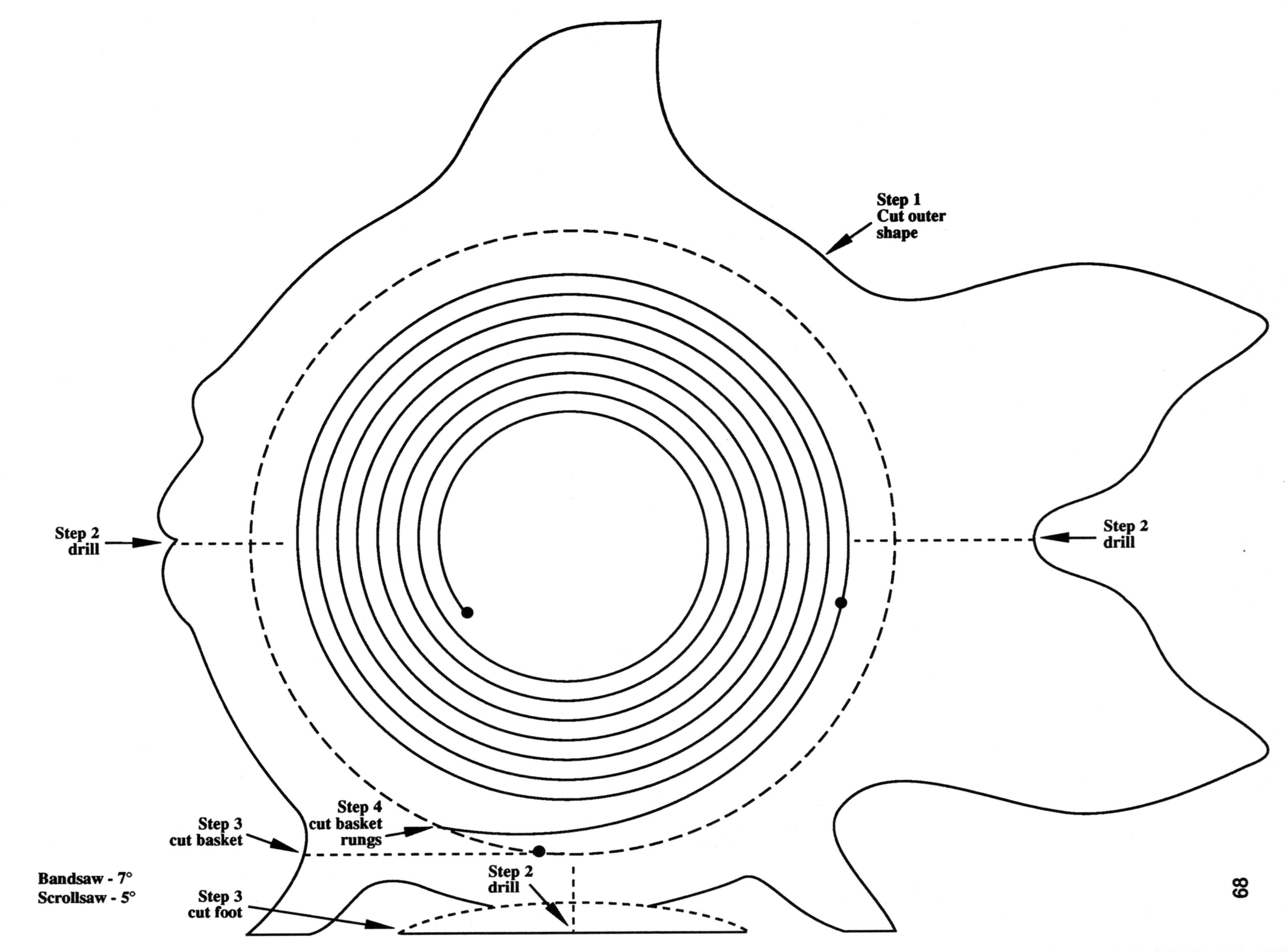
Step 1
Cut outer
shape
Step 2
drill
Step 2
drill
Step 4
cut basket
rungs
Step 3
cut basket
Step 2
drill
Step 3
cut foot
Bandsaw - 7°
Scrollsaw - 5°

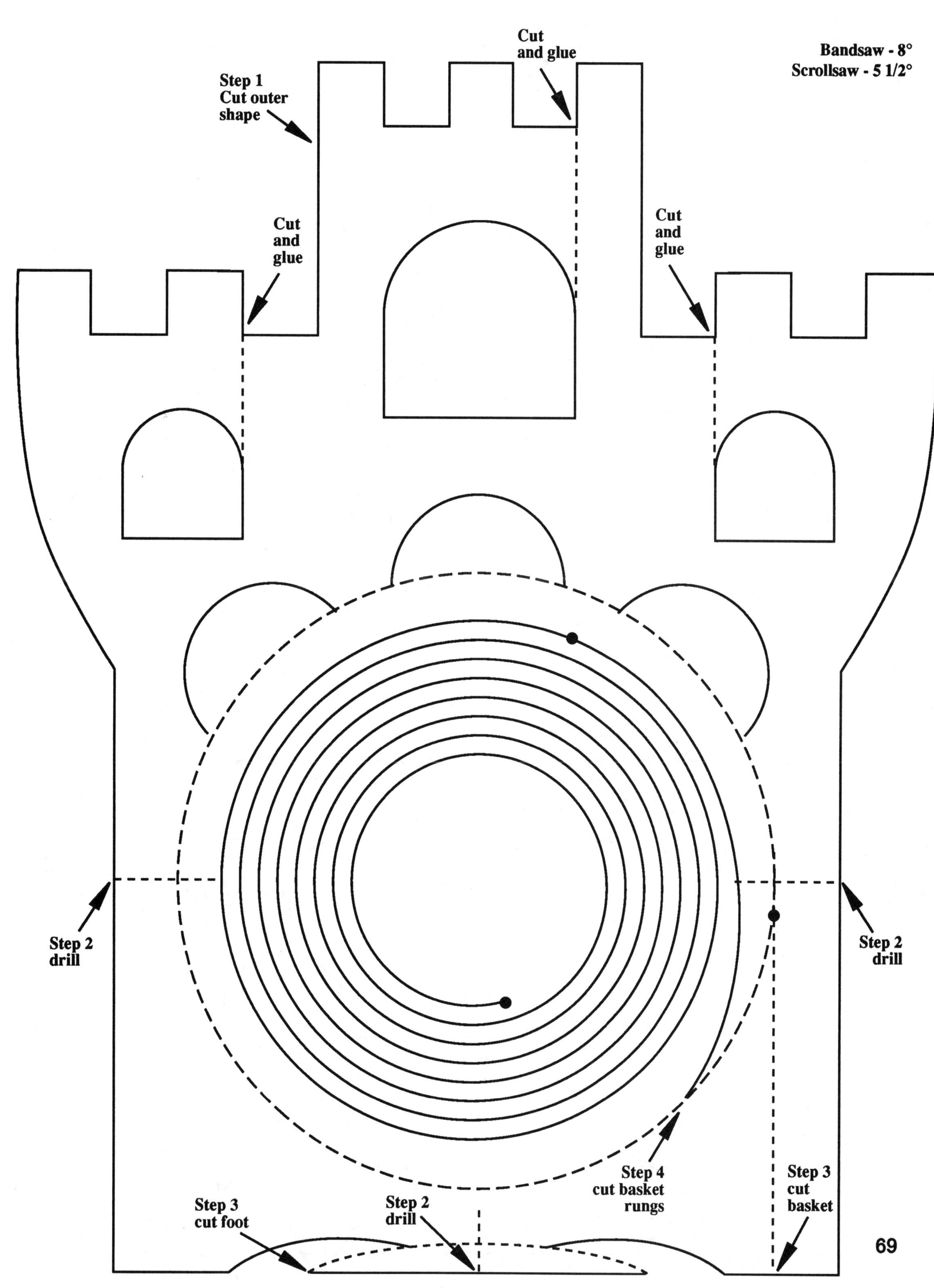
Bandsaw - 8°
Scrollsaw - 5 1/2°
Cut
and glue
Step 1
Cut outer
shape
Cut
and
glue
Cut
and
glue
Step 2
drill
Step 2
drill
Step 4
cut basket
rungs
Step 3
cut
basket
Step 3
cut foot
Step 2
drill

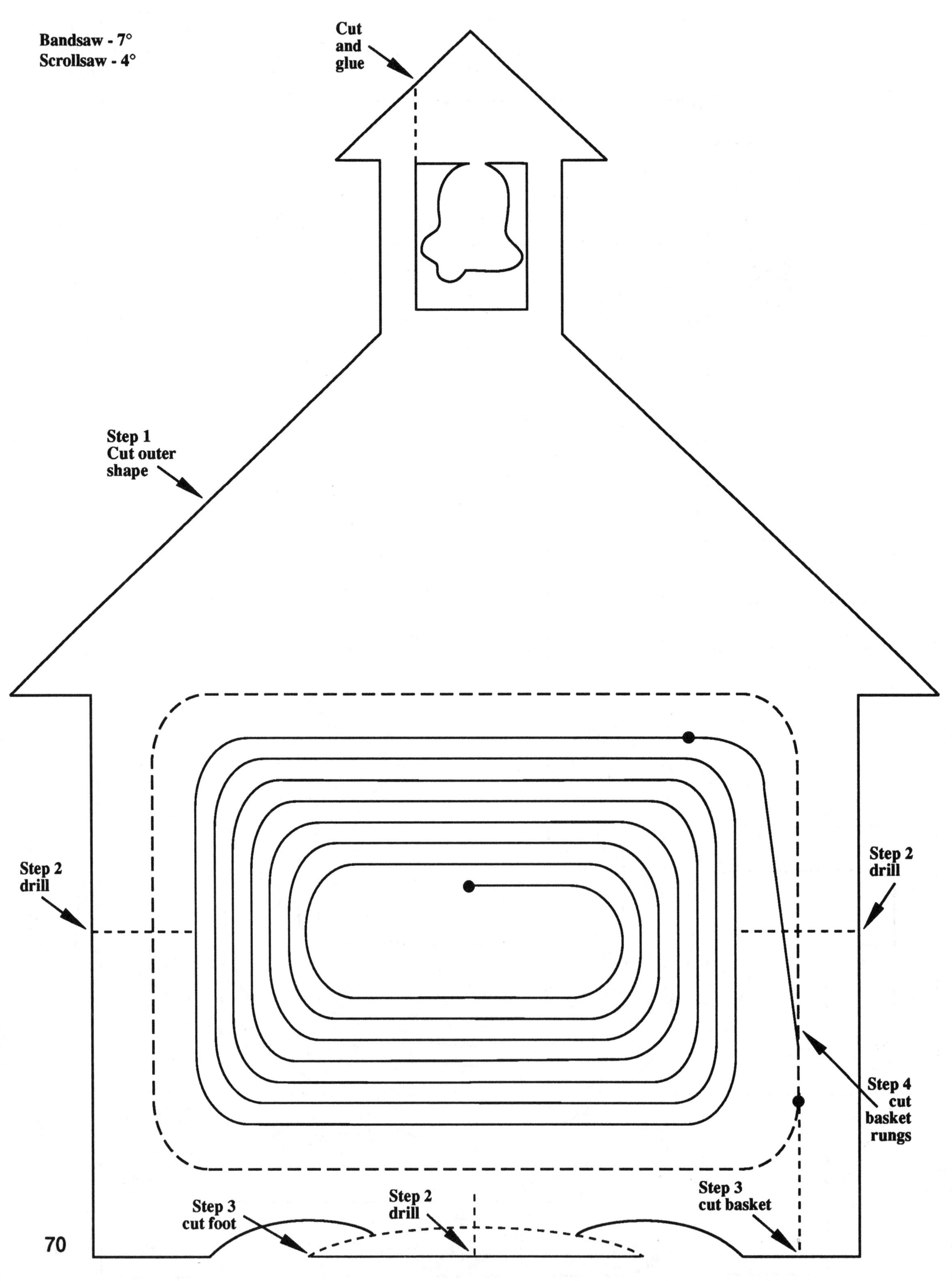
Bandsaw - 7°
Scrollsaw - 4°
Cut
and
glue
Step 1
Cut outer
shape
Step 2
drill
Step 2
drill
Step 4
cut
basket
rungs
Step 3
cut foot
Step 2
drill
Step 3
cut basket

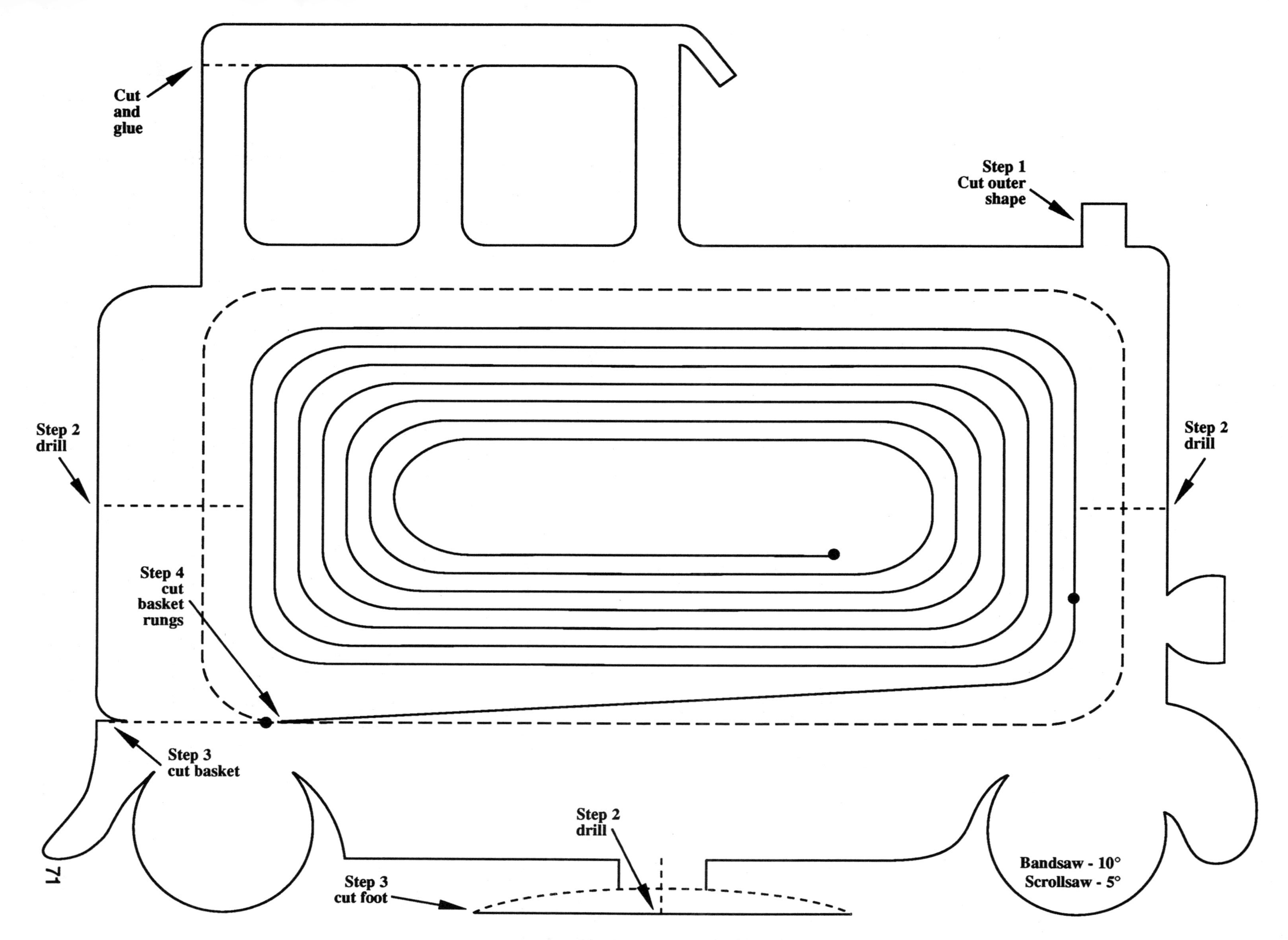
Cut
and
glue
Step 1
Cut outer
shape
Step 2
drill
Step 2
drill
Step 4
cut
basket
rungs
Step 3
cut basket
Step 2
drill
Step 3
cut foot
Bandsaw - 10°
Scrollsaw - 5°

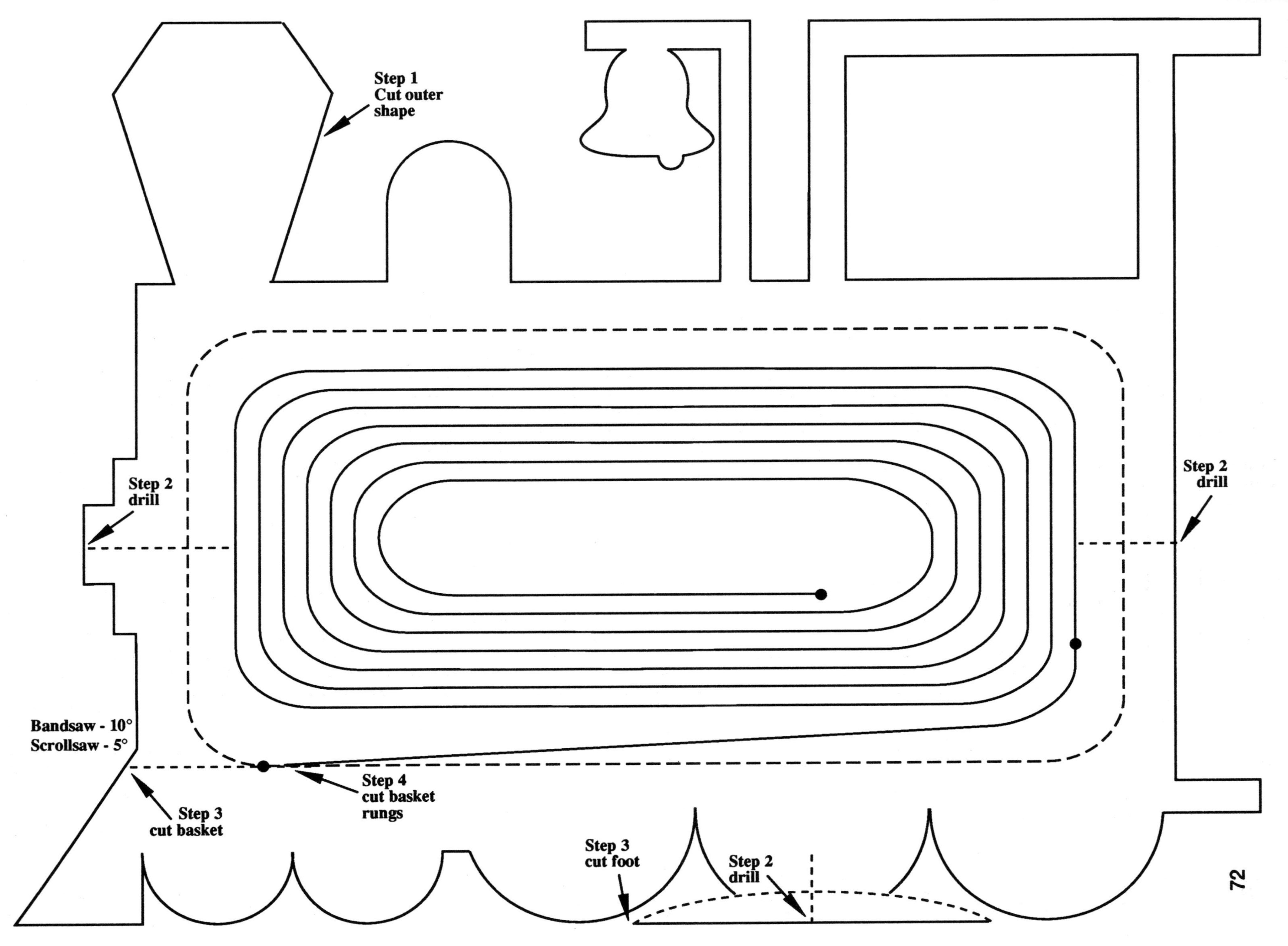
Step 1
Cut outer
shape
Step 2
drill
Step 2
drill
Bandsaw - 10°
Scrollsaw - 5°
Step 4
cut basket
rungs
Step 3
cut basket
Step 3
cut foot
Step 2
drill

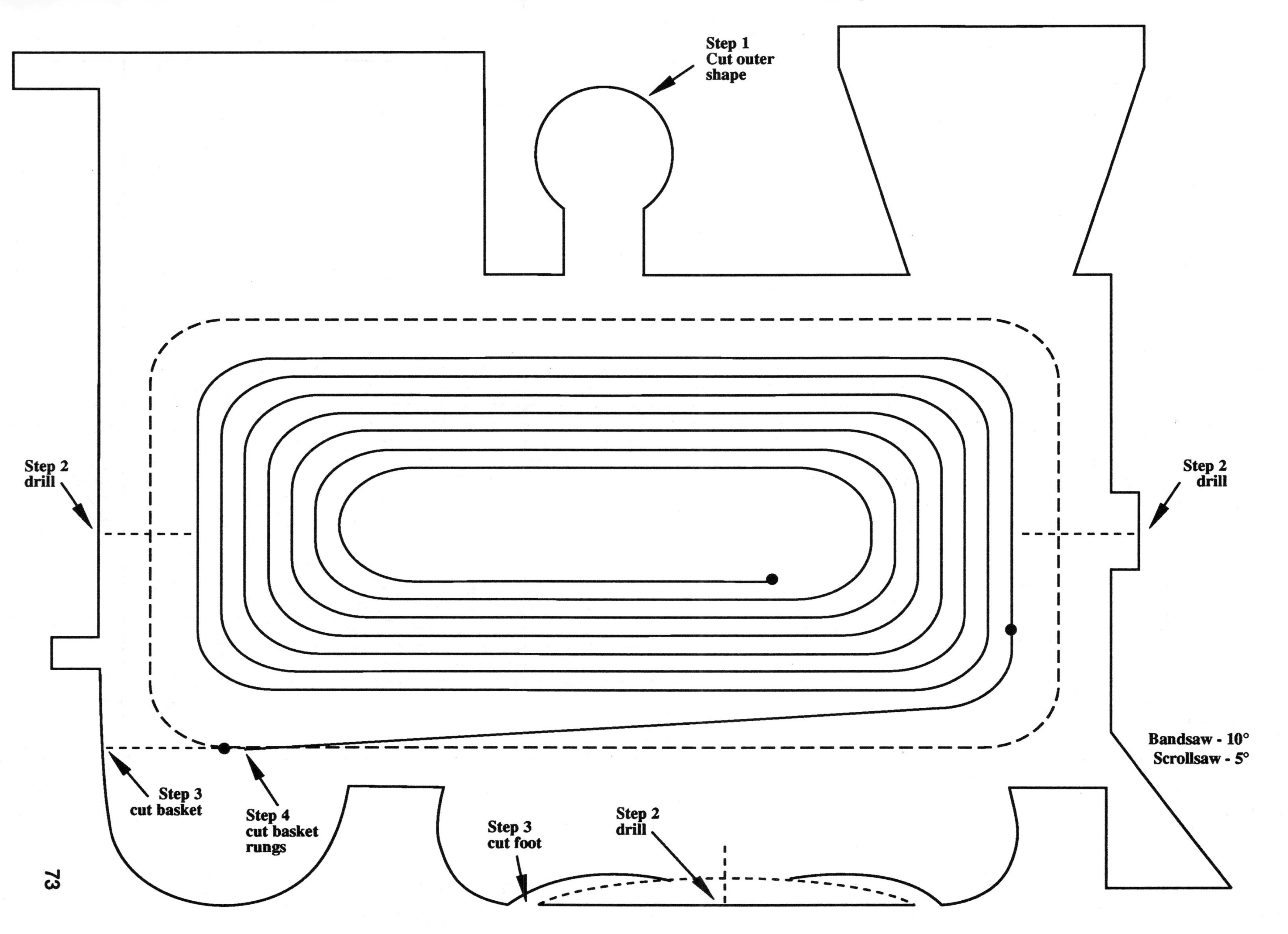
Step 1
Cut outer
shape
Step 2
drill
Step 2
drill
Bandsaw - 10°
Scrollsaw - 5°
Step 3
cut basket
Step 4
cut basket
rungs
Step 3
cut foot
Step 2
drill

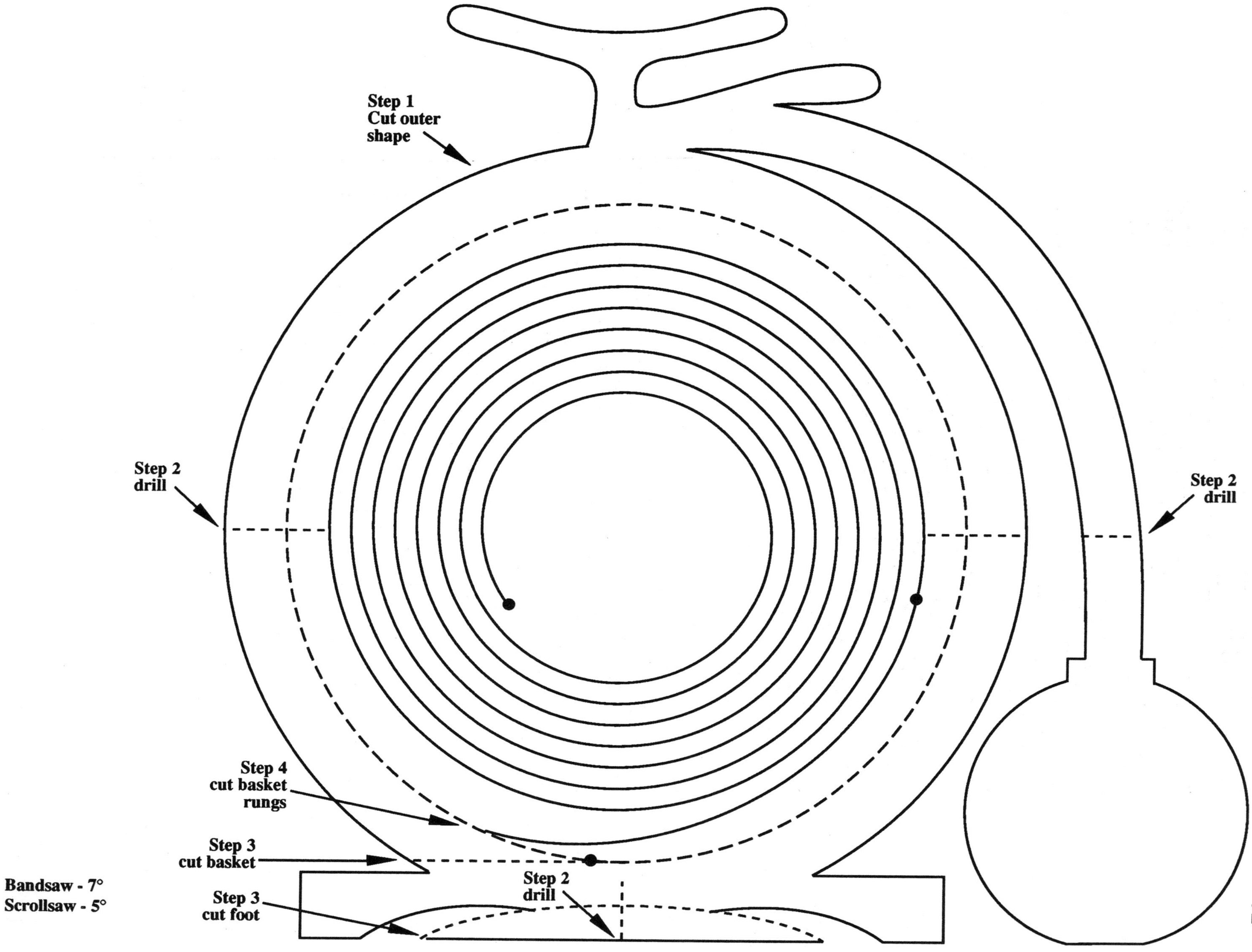

Step 1
Cut outer
shape

Step 2
drill

Step 2
drill

Step 4
cut basket
rungs

Step 3
cut basket

Step 2
drill

Bandsaw - 7°
Scrollsaw - 5°

Step 3
cut foot

Bandsaw - 8°
Scrollsaw - 5 1/2°

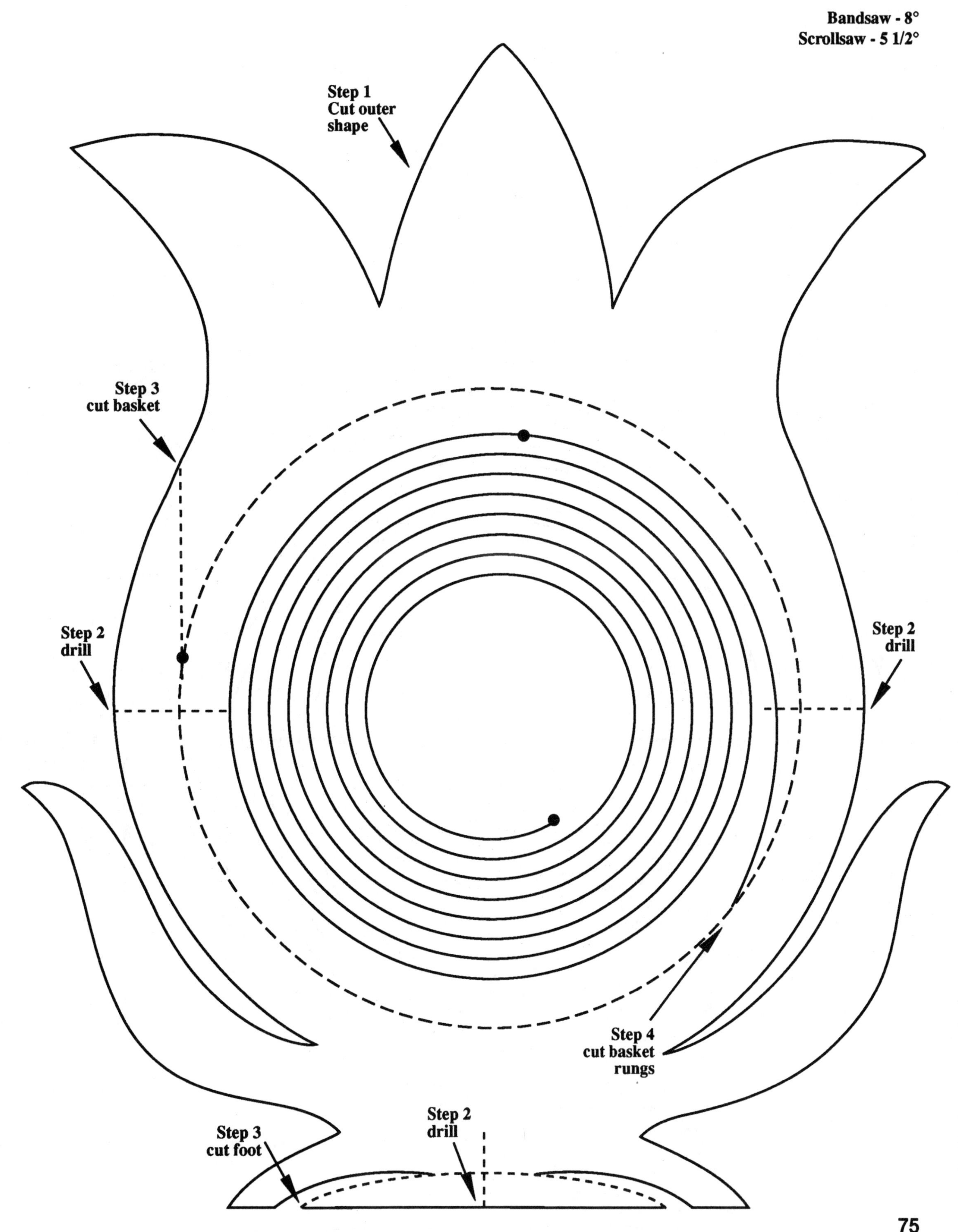

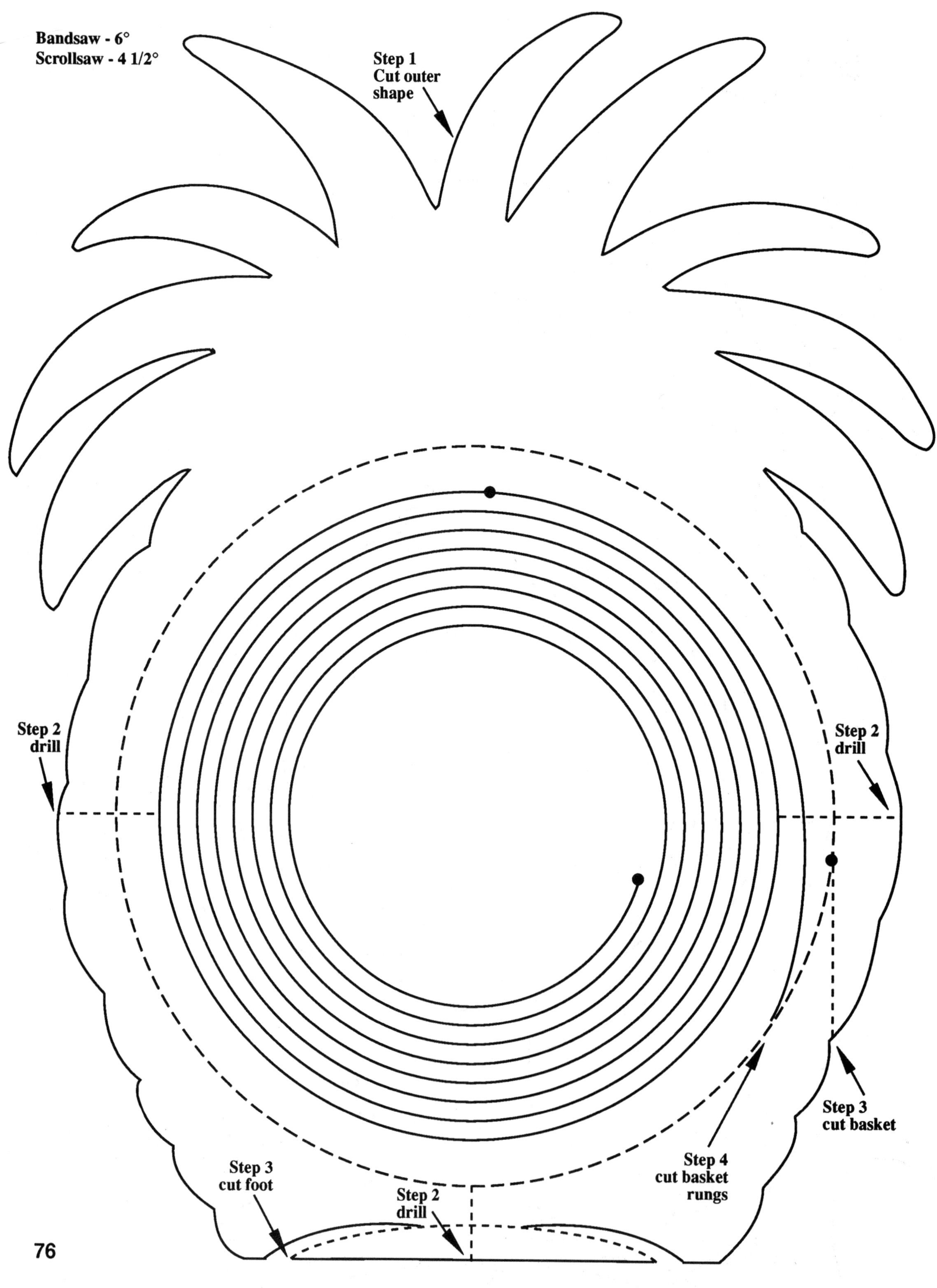
Bandsaw - 6°
Scrollsaw - 4 1/2°
Step 1
Cut outer
shape
Step 2
drill
Step 2
drill
Step 3
cut basket
Step 4
cut basket
rungs
Step 3
cut foot
Step 2
drill

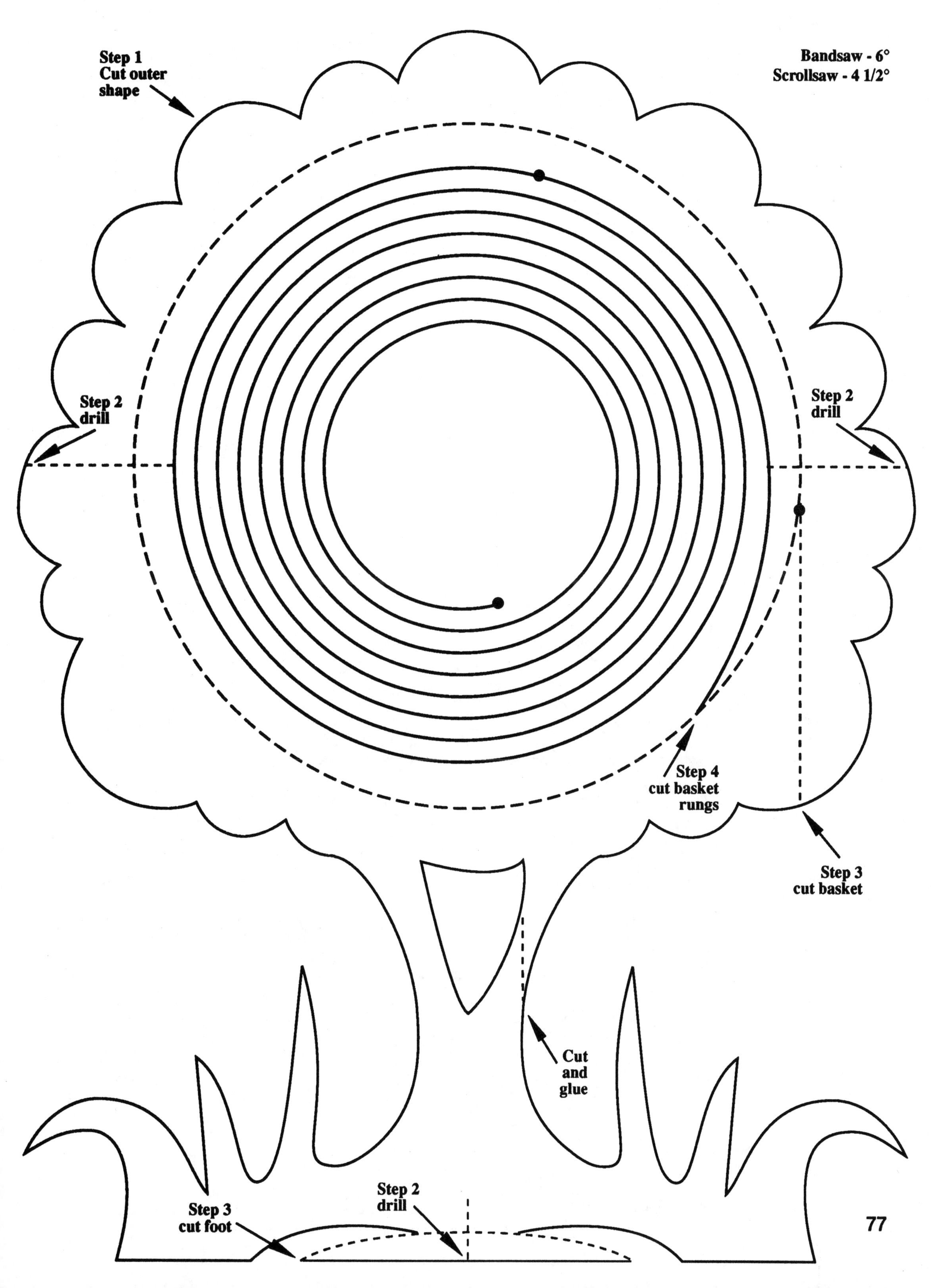
Step 1
Cut outer
shape
Bandsaw - 6°
Scrollsaw - 4 1/2°
Step 2
drill
Step 2
drill
Step 4
cut basket
rungs
Step 3
cut basket
Cut
and
glue
Step 2
drill
Step 3
cut foot

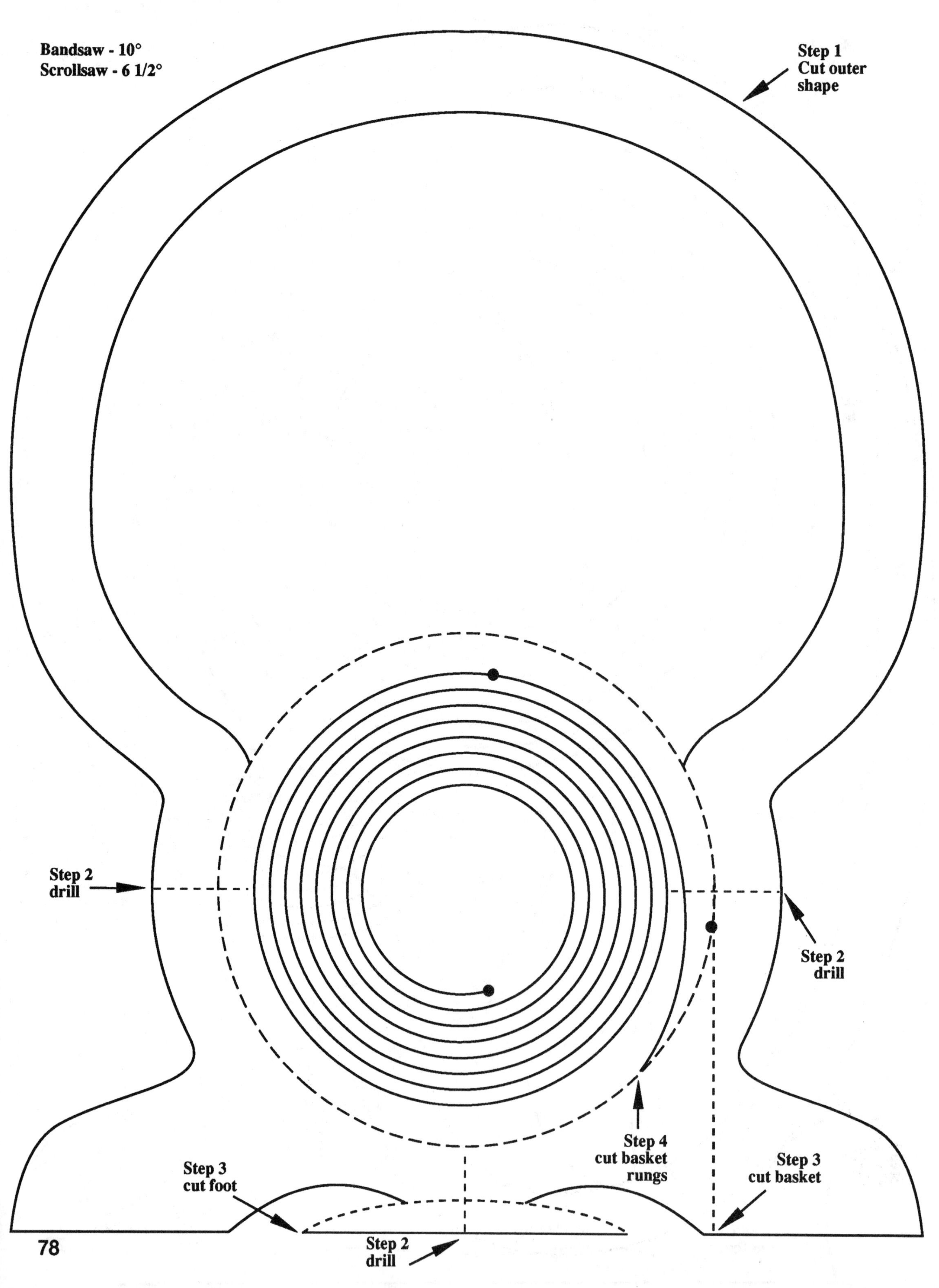

Bandsaw - 10°
Scrollsaw - 6 1/2°
Step 1
Cut outer
shape
Step 2
drill
Step 2
drill
Step 4
cut basket
rungs
Step 3
cut basket
Step 3
cut foot
Step 2
drill

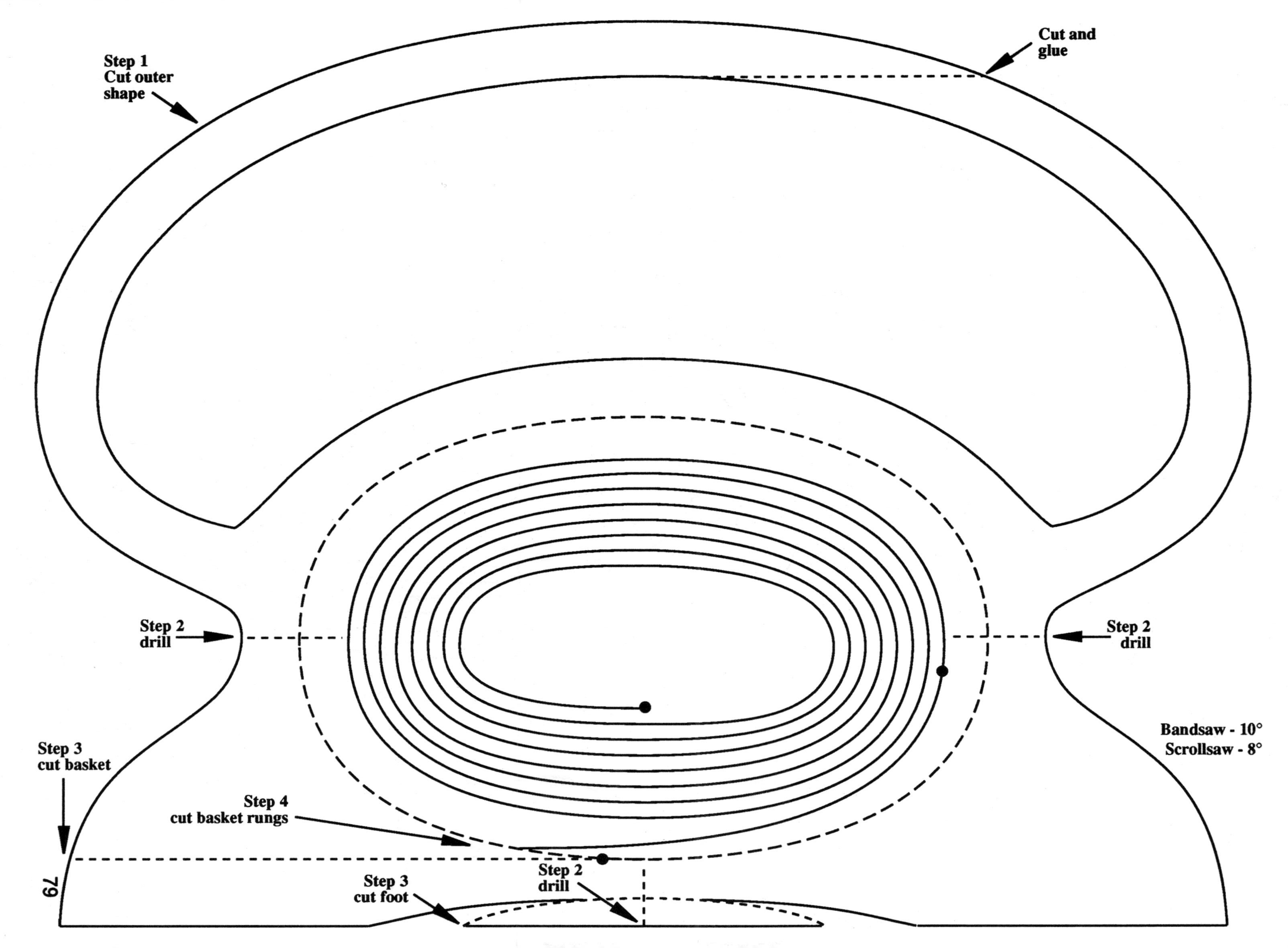
Step 1
Cut outer
shape
Cut and
glue
Step 2
drill
Step 2
drill
Step 3
cut basket
Step 4
cut basket rungs
Step 2
drill
Step 3
cut foot
Bandsaw - 10°
Scrollsaw - 8°

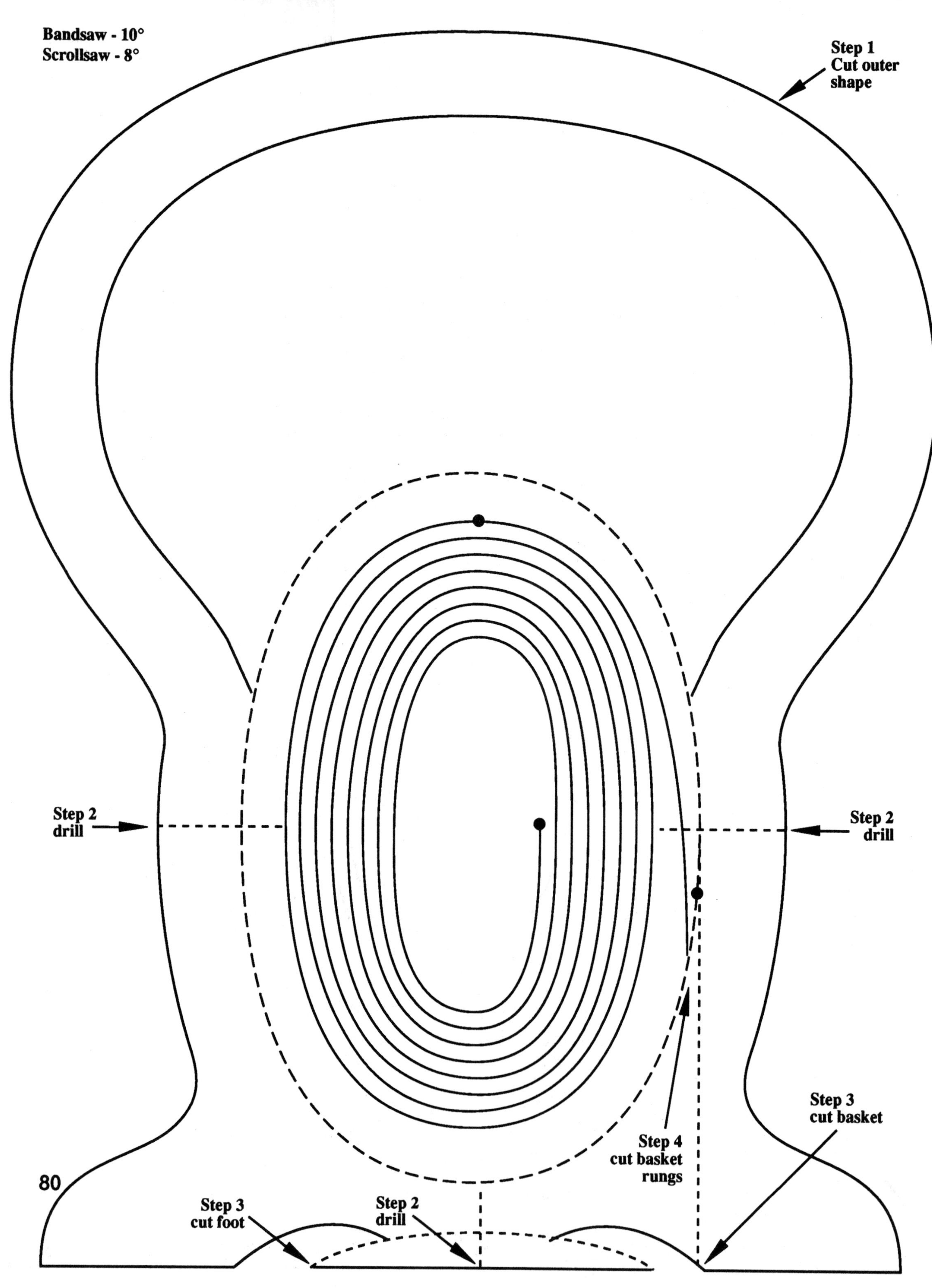

Bandsaw - 10°
Scrollsaw - 8°
Step 1
Cut outer
shape
Step 2
drill
Step 2
drill
Step 3
cut basket
Step 4
cut basket
rungs
Step 3
cut foot
Step 2
drill

Bandsaw - 6°
Scrollsaw - 4°

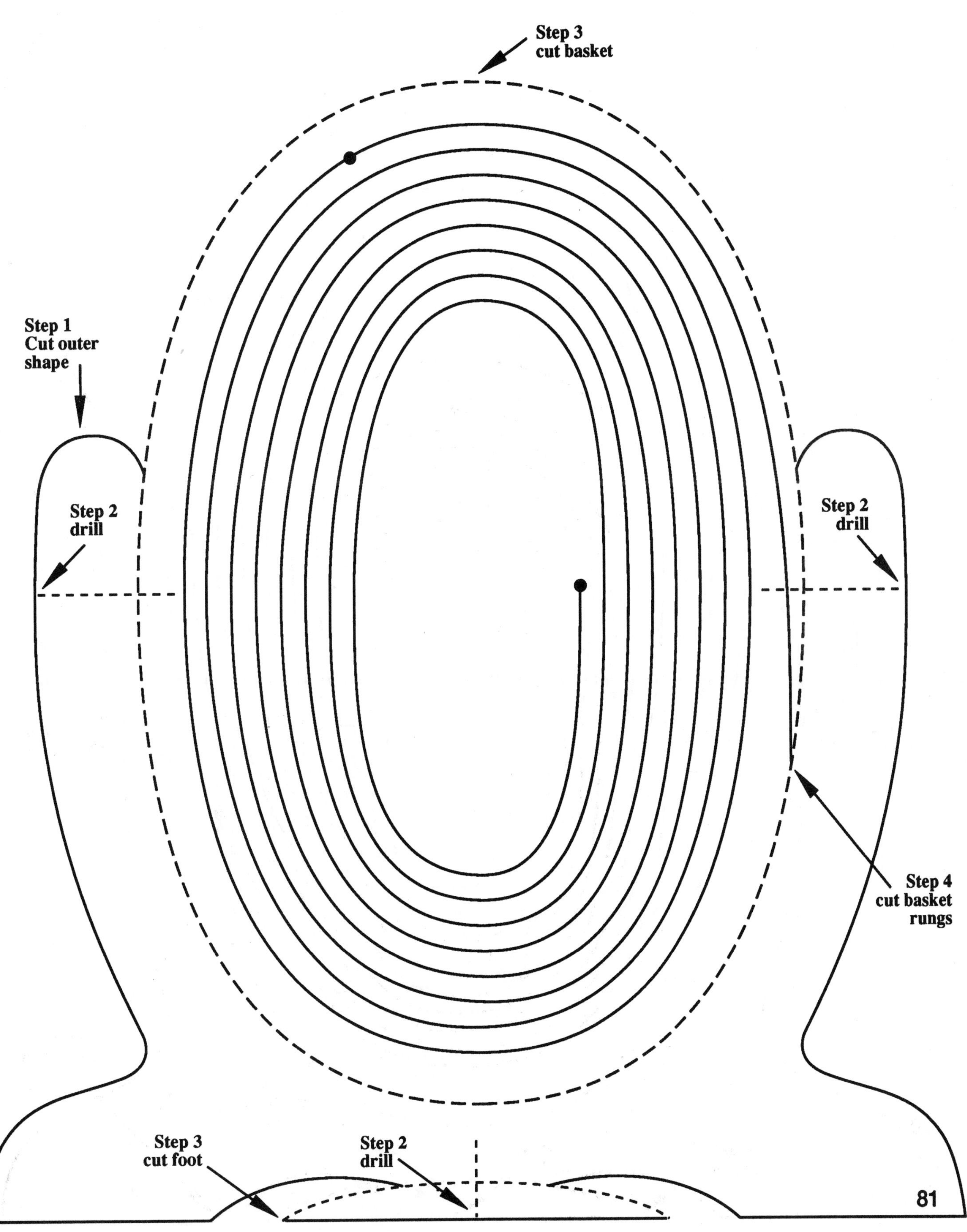

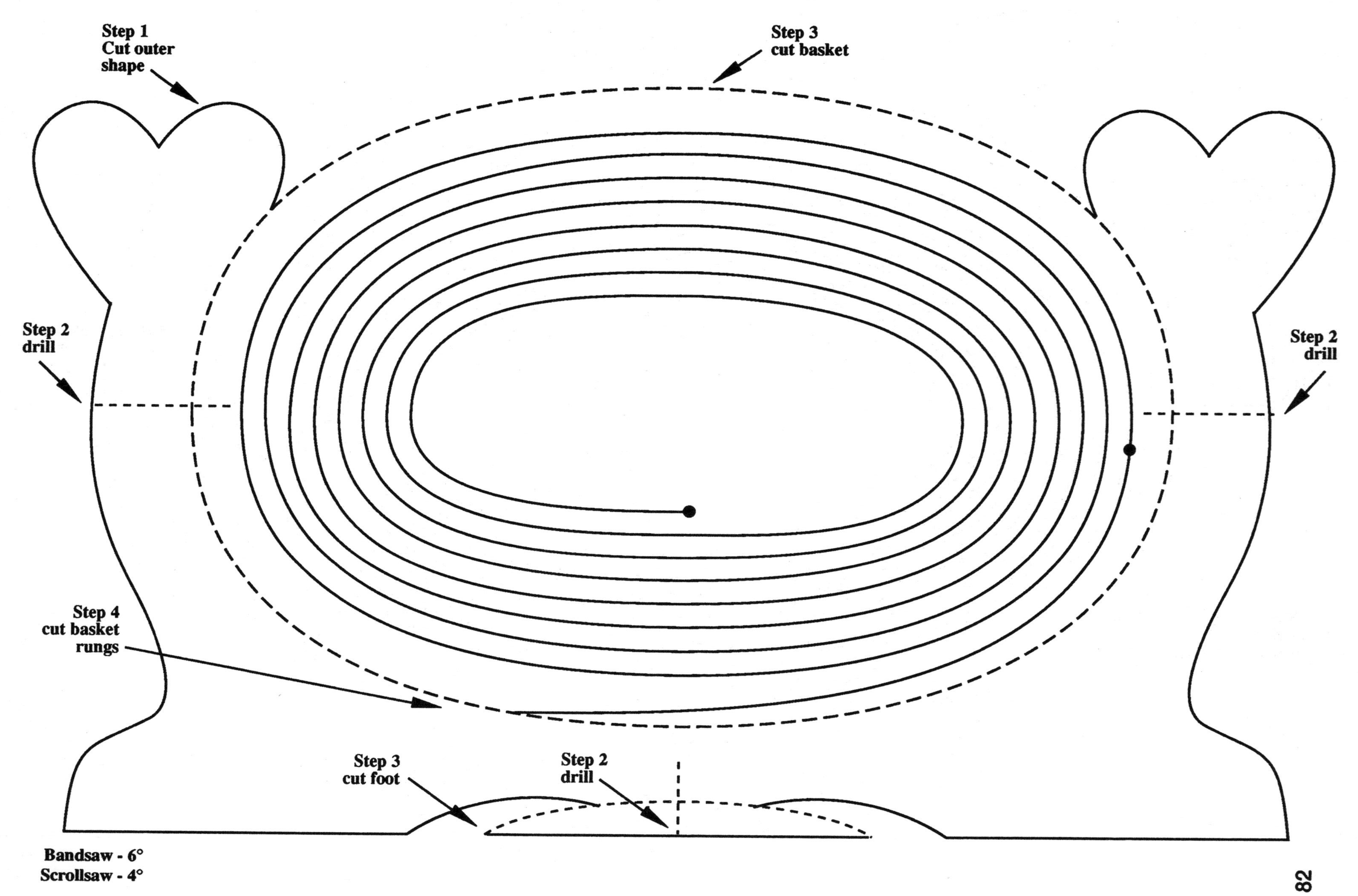

Step 1
Cut outer
shape
Step 3
cut basket
Step 2
drill
Step 2
drill
Step 4
cut basket
rungs
Step 3
cut foot
Step 2
drill
Bandsaw - 6°
Scrollsaw - 4°

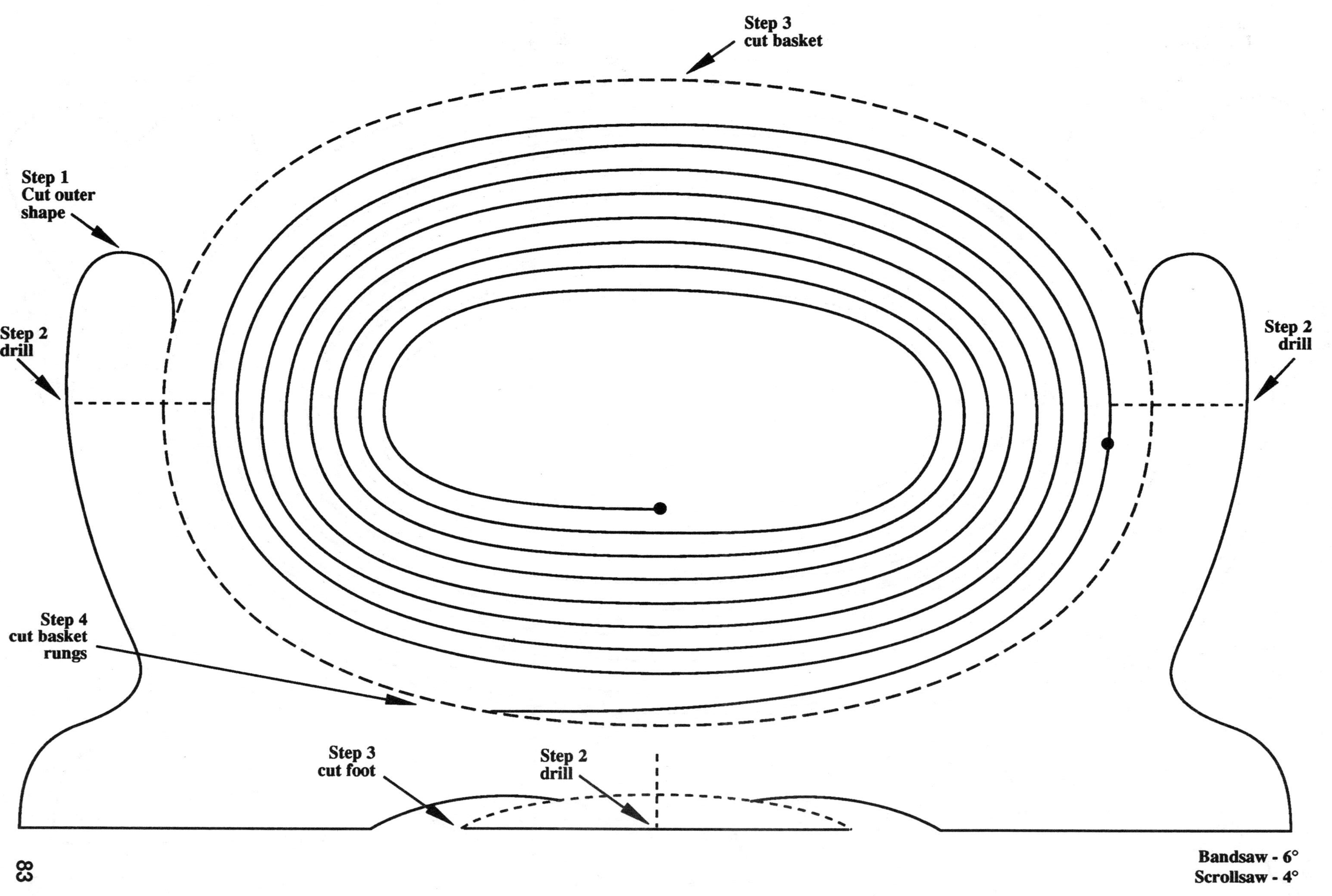
Step 3
cut basket
Step 1
Cut outer
shape
Step 2
drill
Step 2
drill
Step 4
cut basket
rungs
Step 3
cut foot
Step 2
drill
Bandsaw - 6°
Scrollsaw - 4°

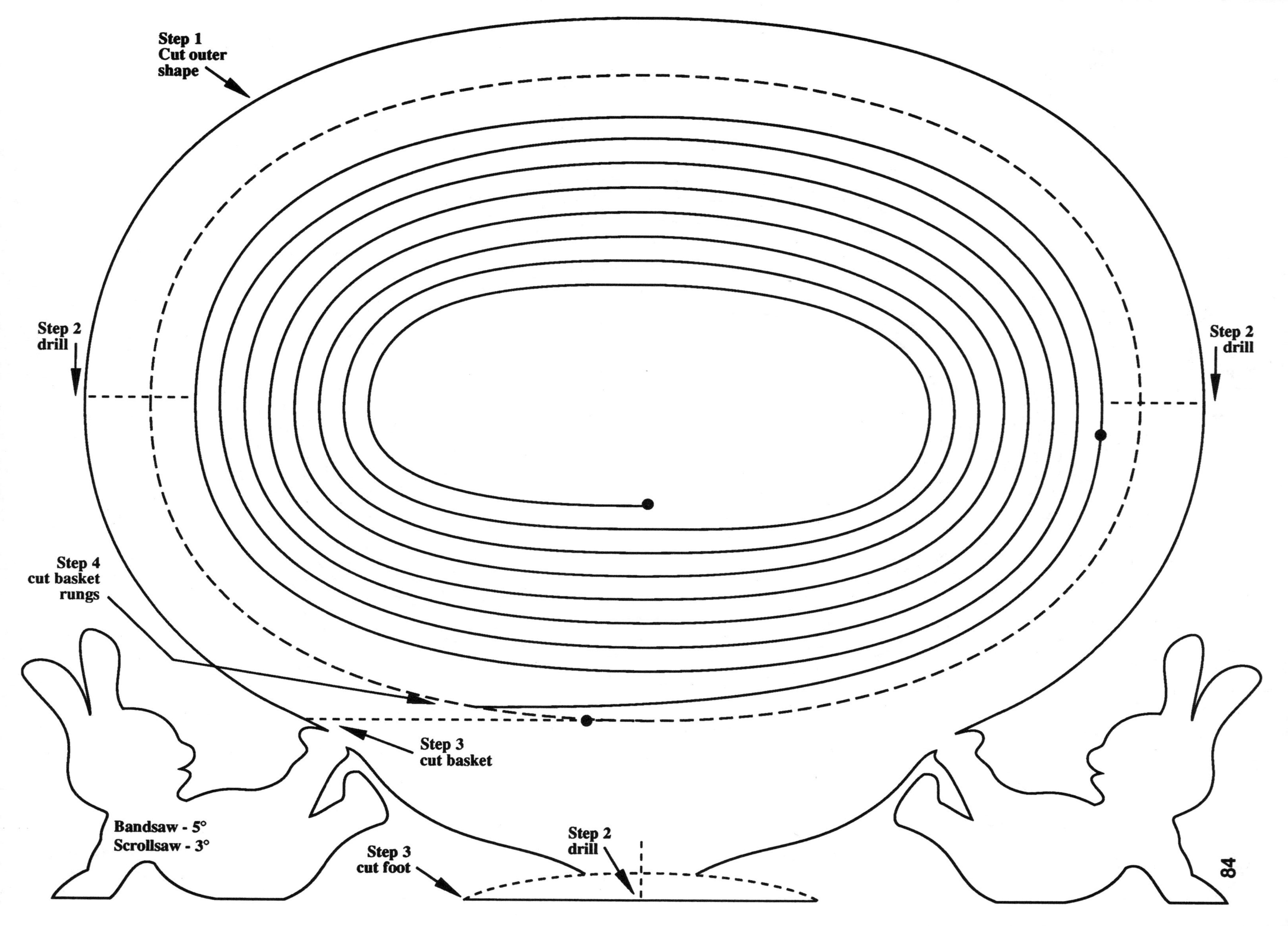
Step 1
Cut outer
shape
Step 2
drill
Step 2
drill
Step 4
cut basket
rungs
Step 3
cut basket
Bandsaw - 5°
Scrollsaw - 3°
Step 3
cut foot
Step 2
drill

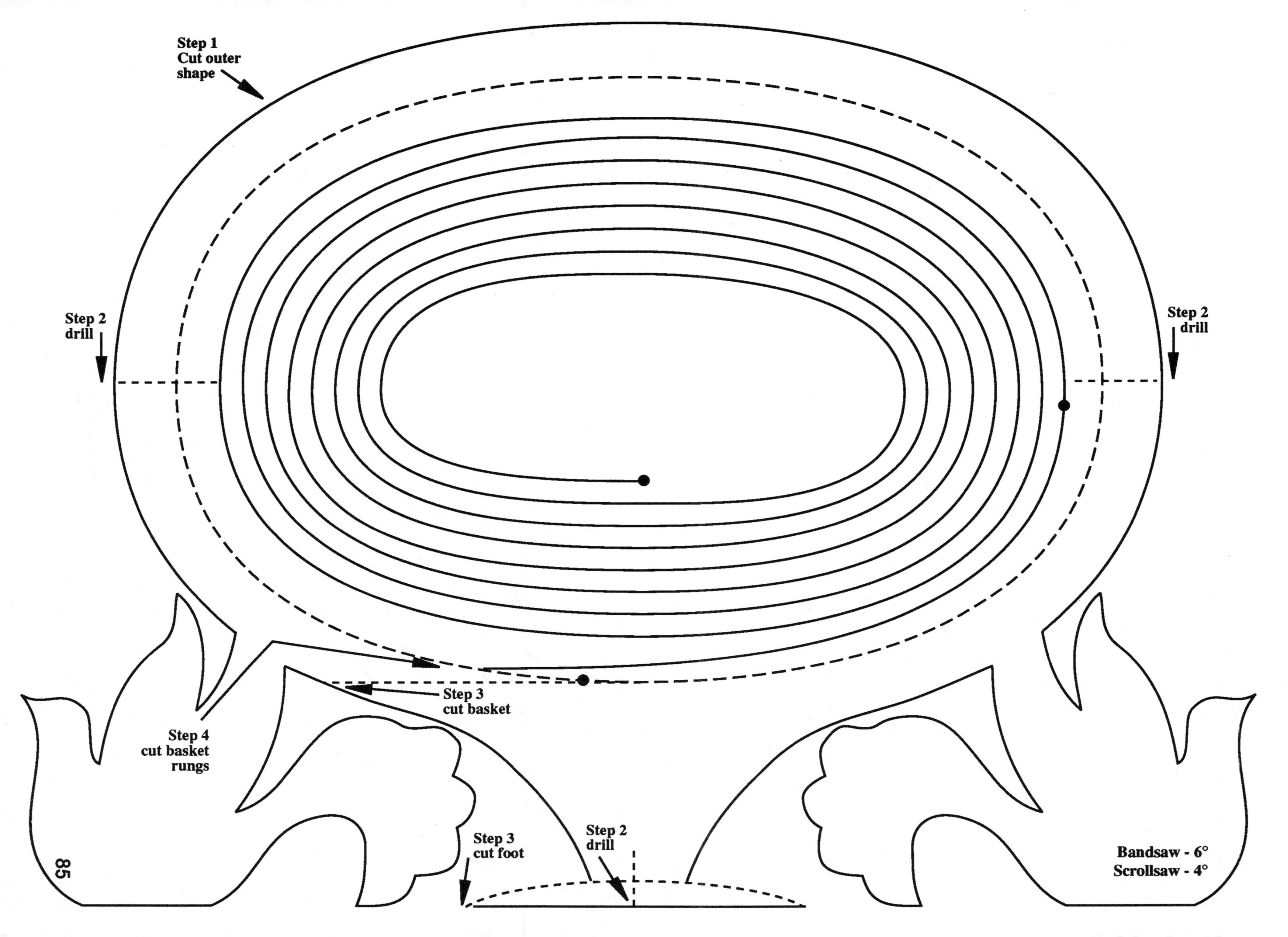
Step 1
Cut outer shape
Step 2
drill
Step 2
drill
Step 3
cut basket
Step 4
cut basket rungs
Step 3
cut foot
Step 2
drill
Bandsaw - 6°
Scrollsaw - 4°

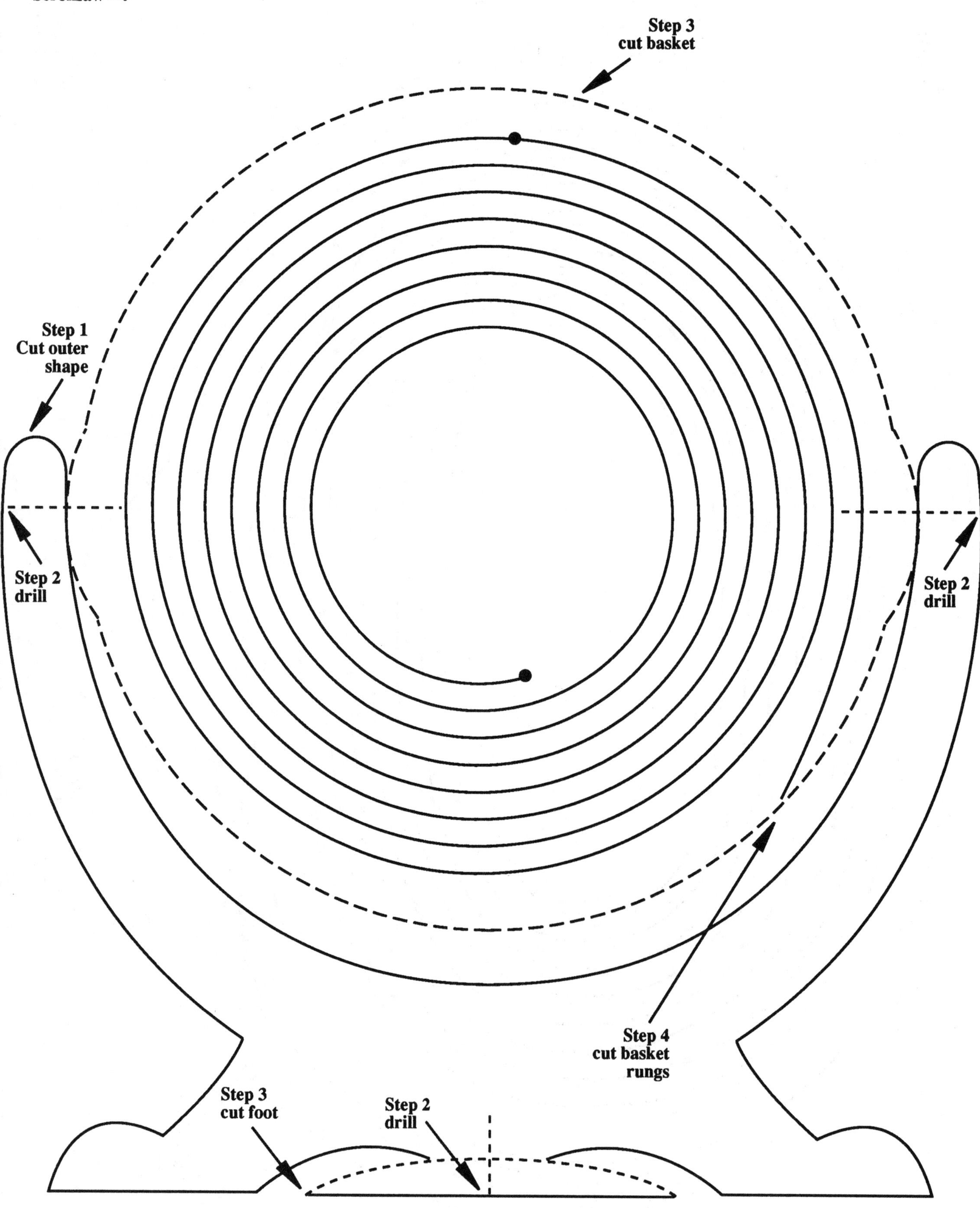
Bandsaw - 5°
Scrollsaw - 4°
Step 3
cut basket
Step 1
Cut outer
shape
Step 2
drill
Step 2
drill
Step 4
cut basket
rungs
Step 3
cut foot
Step 2
drill

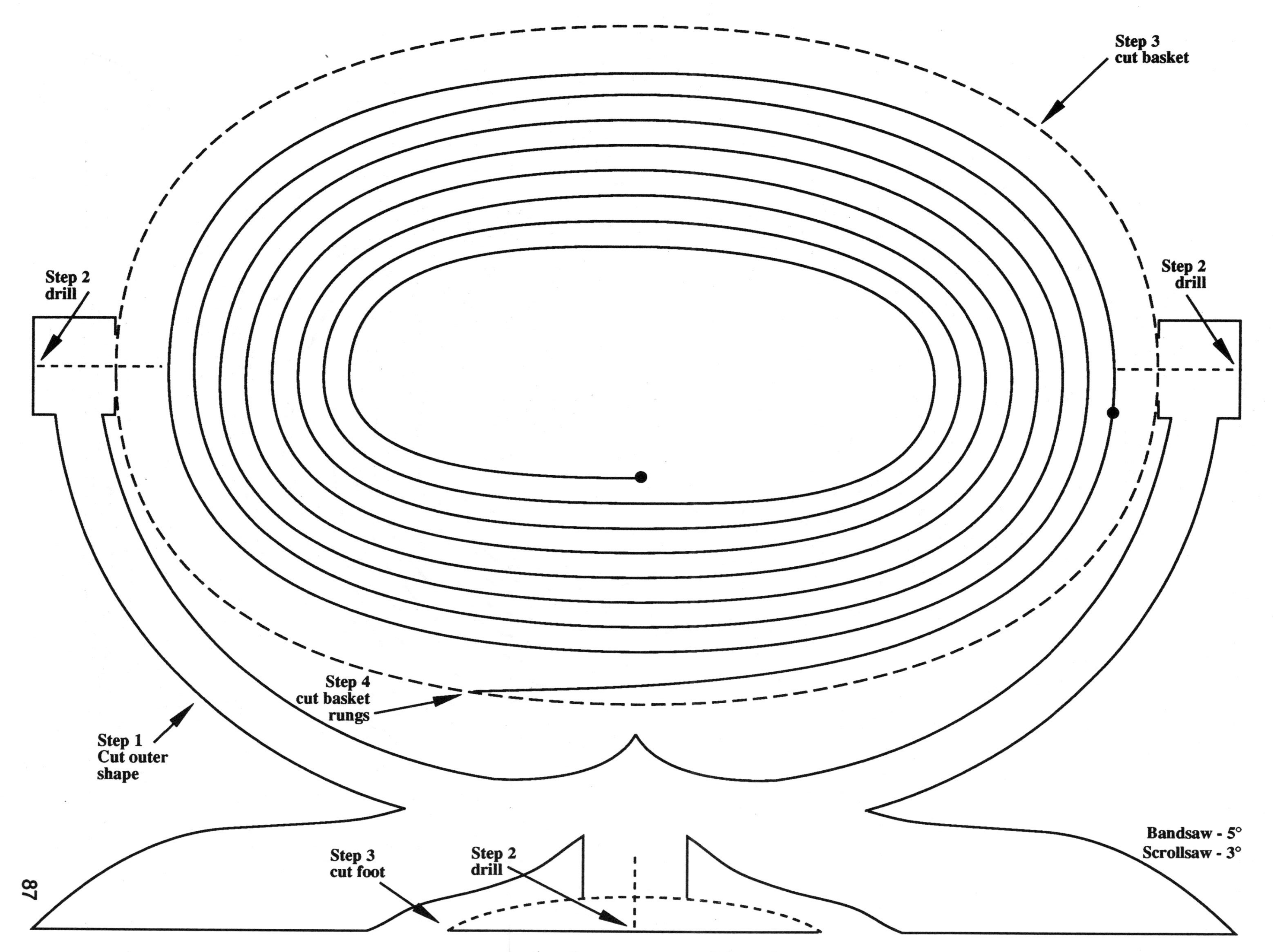

Step 3
cut basket
Step 2
drill
Step 2
drill
Step 4
cut basket
rungs
Step 1
Cut outer
shape
Step 3
cut foot
Step 2
drill
Bandsaw - 5°
Scrollsaw - 3°

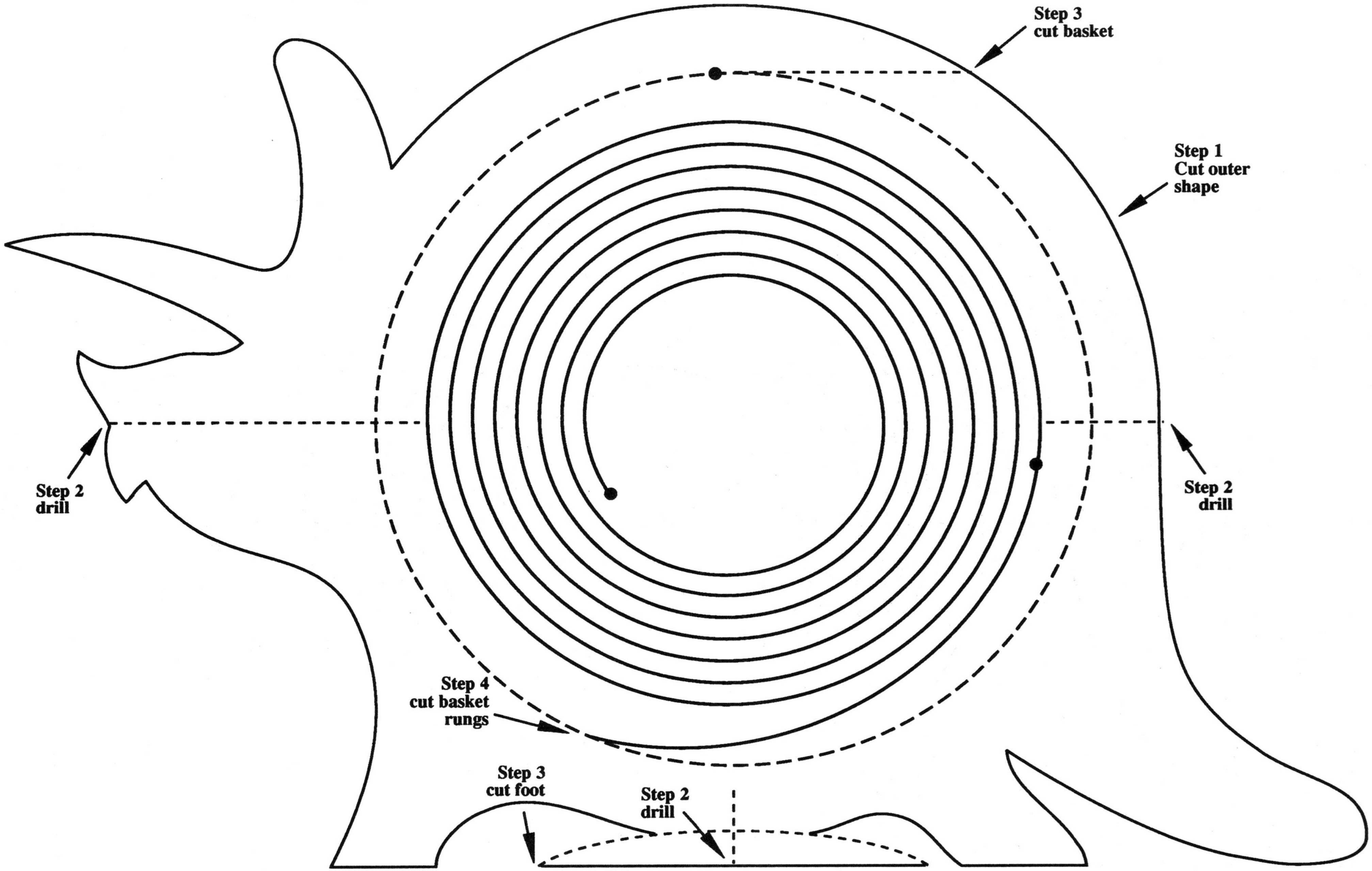

Step 3
cut basket

Step 1
Cut outer
shape

Step 2
drill

Step 2
drill

Step 4
cut basket
rungs

Step 3
cut foot

Step 2
drill

Bandsaw - 7°
Scrollsaw - 5°

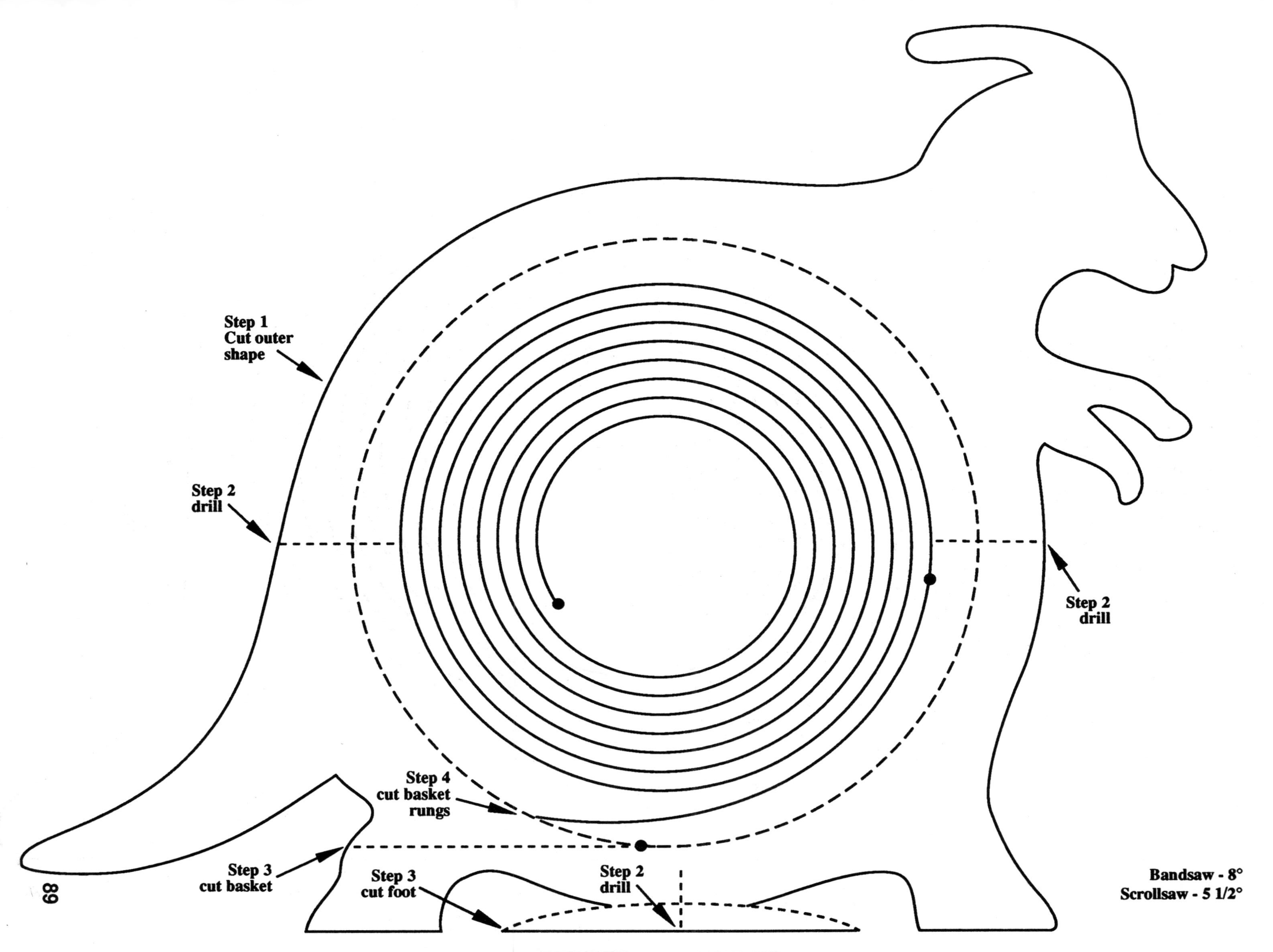
Step 1
Cut outer
shape
Step 2
drill
Step 2
drill
Step 4
cut basket
rungs
Step 3
cut basket
Step 3
cut foot
Step 2
drill
Bandsaw - 8°
Scrollsaw - 5 1/2°

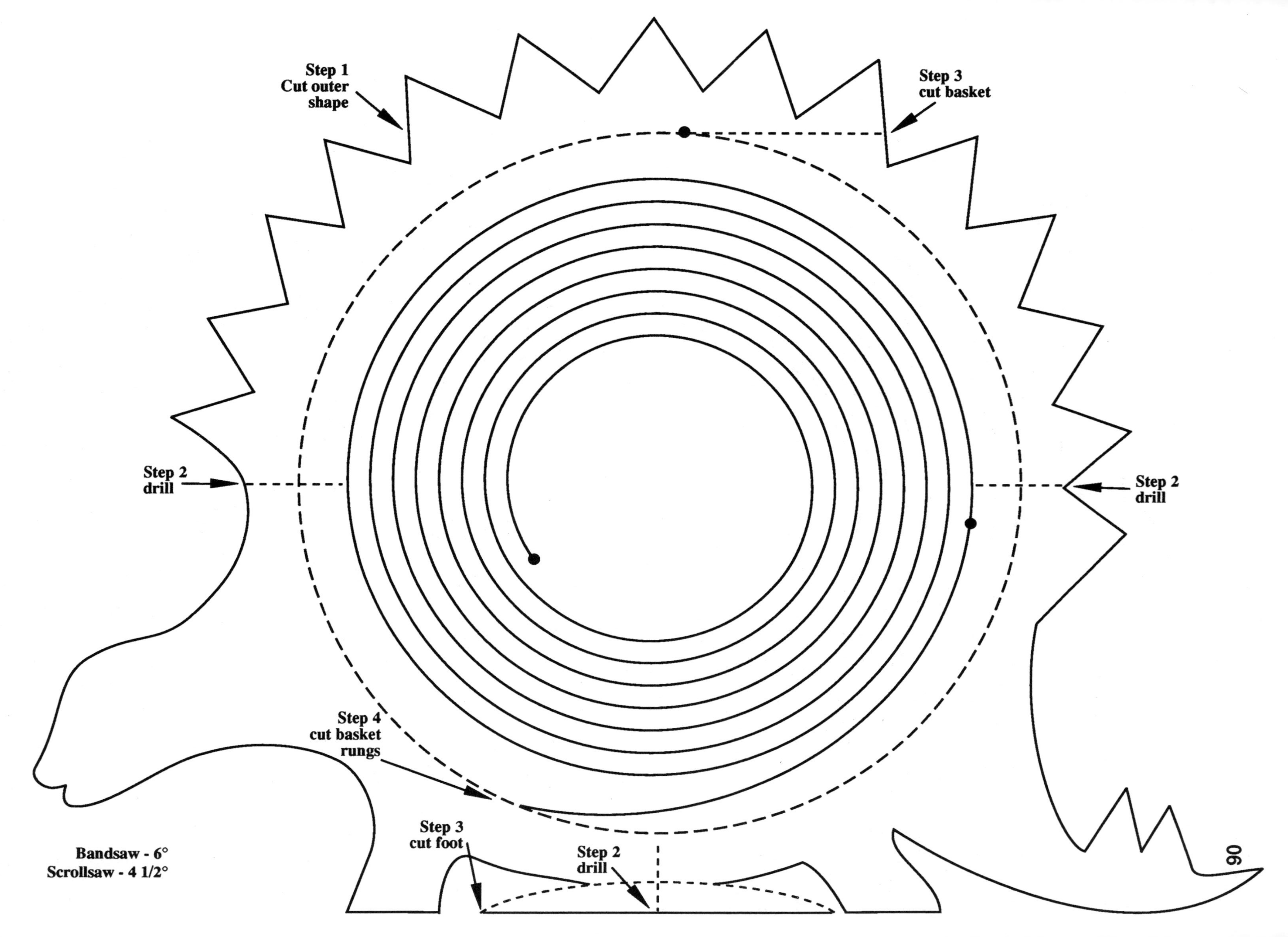
Step 1
Cut outer
shape
Step 3
cut basket
Step 2
drill
Step 2
drill
Step 4
cut basket
rungs
Step 3
cut foot
Step 2
drill
Bandsaw - 6°
Scrollsaw - 4 1/2°

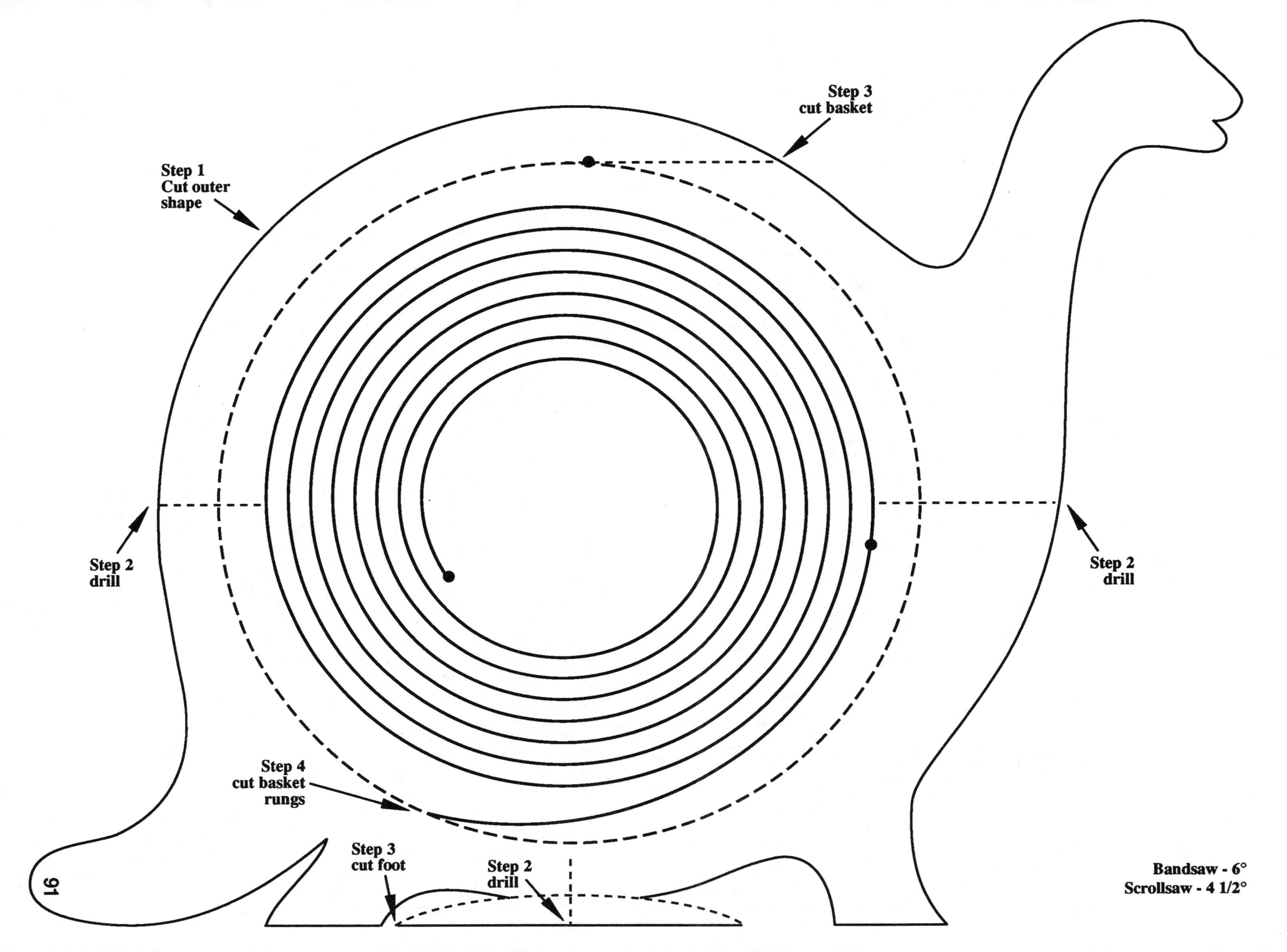
Step 3
cut basket
Step 1
Cut outer
shape
Step 2
drill
Step 2
drill
Step 4
cut basket
rungs
Step 3
cut foot
Step 2
drill
Bandsaw - 6°
Scrollsaw - 4 1/2°

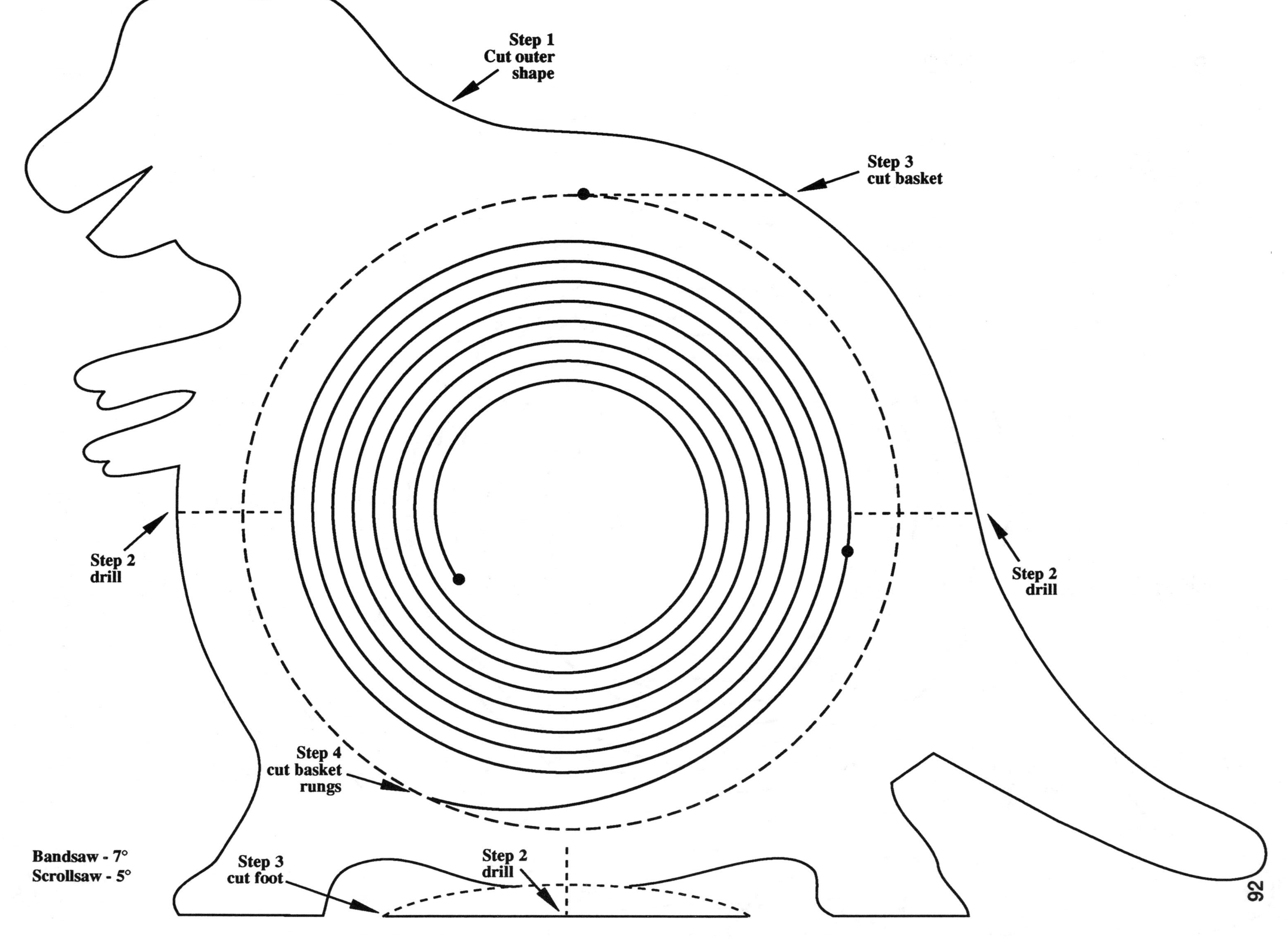
Step 1
Cut outer shape
Step 3
cut basket
Step 2
drill
Step 2
drill
Step 4
cut basket rungs
Step 3
cut foot
Step 2
drill
Bandsaw - 7°
Scrollsaw - 5°

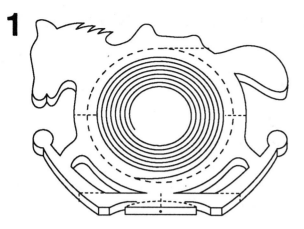

Bandsaw Instructions

For the Rocking Patterns

Step 1 Adhere pattern to work piece. Cut outer shape of basket.

Step 2 Mark the drill points using a hammer and center punch. Drill basket and foot pivot points the length of their dotted lines.

Step 3 Cut along dashed lines (with table flat) to separate inner basket and foot. Glue outer shape where cut was made, and clamp.

Step 4 Using the bevel indicated on the pattern, cut basket rungs following the solid line, shut off saw and back out blade. Glue 1"-2" at start of cut, and clamp.

Step 5 Assemble basket and foot with screws at drilled pivot points.

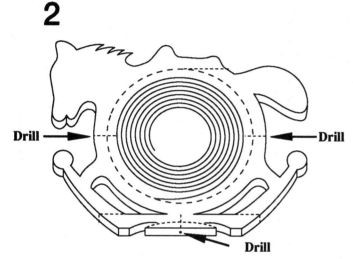

1

2

Drill

Drill

Drill

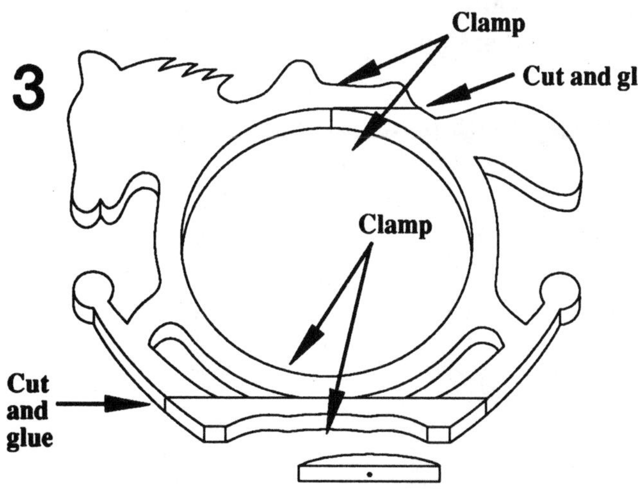

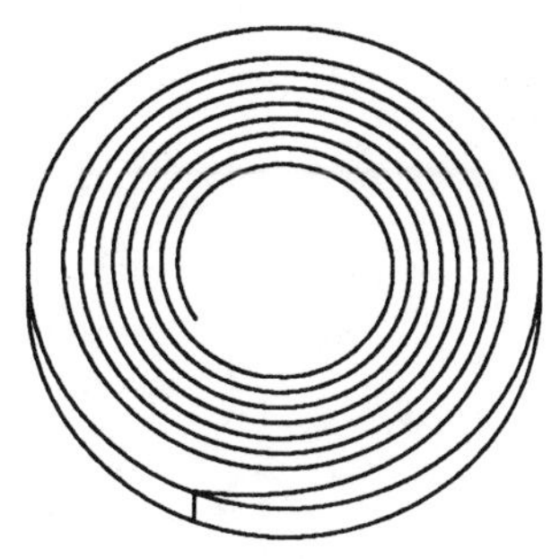

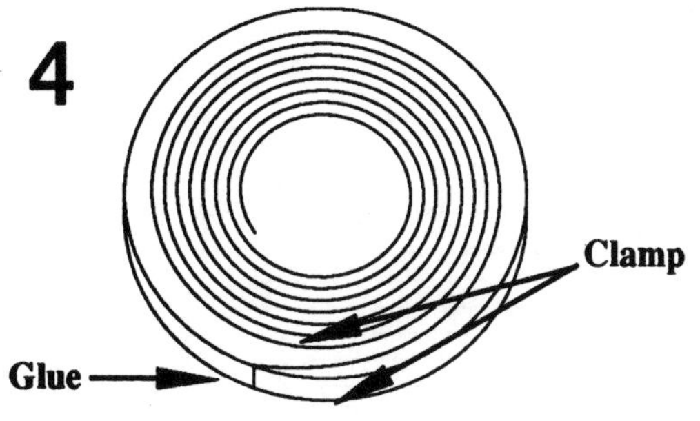

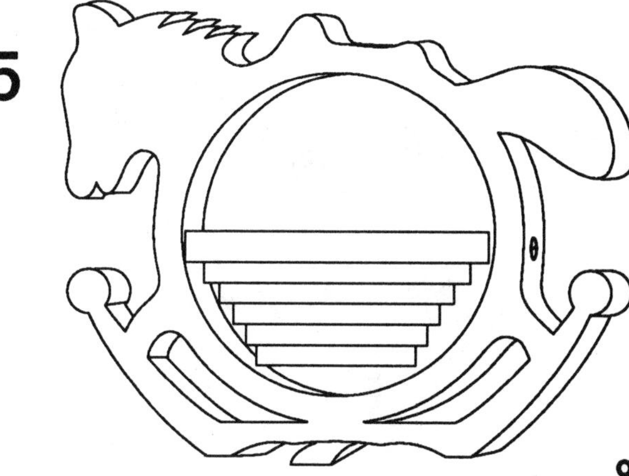

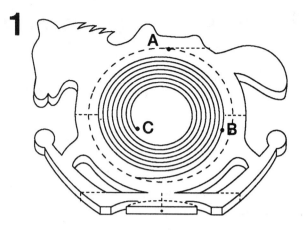

Scrollsaw Instructions

For the Rocking Patterns

Step 1 Adhere pattern to work piece. Cut outer shape of basket.

Step 2 Mark the drill points using a hammer and center punch. Drill basket and foot pivot points the length of their dotted lines.

Step 3 With table flat, cut along dashed lines to separate foot. Drill at points A, B, C using a 1/16" drill bit. Beginning at Point A, cut along dashed lines (with table flat) to separate inner basket from the outer shape.

Step 4 Using the bevel indicated on the pattern, cut basket rungs following the solid line. If your table tilts to the left begin your cut at Point C and finish at Point B. If your table tilts to the right begin your cut at Point B and finish at Point C. **Note:** It is easier to begin at Point C and end at Point B.

Step 5 Assemble basket and foot with screws at drilled pivot points.

1

A

C

B

2

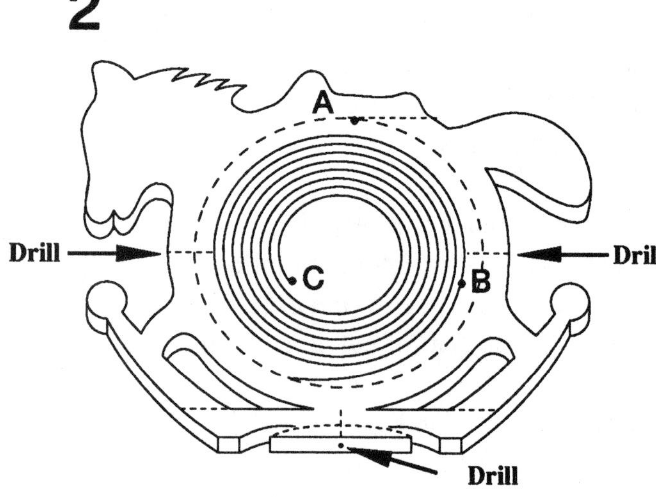

3

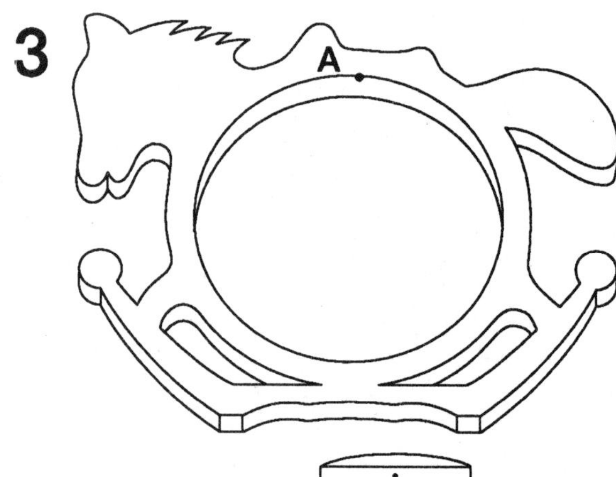

4

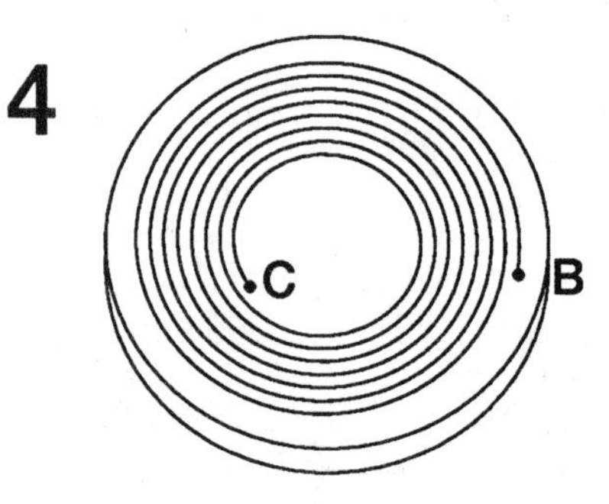

5

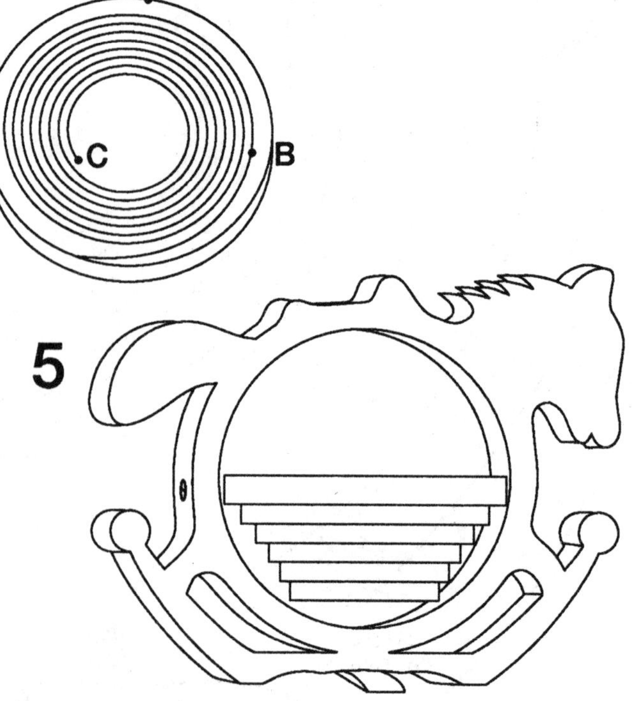

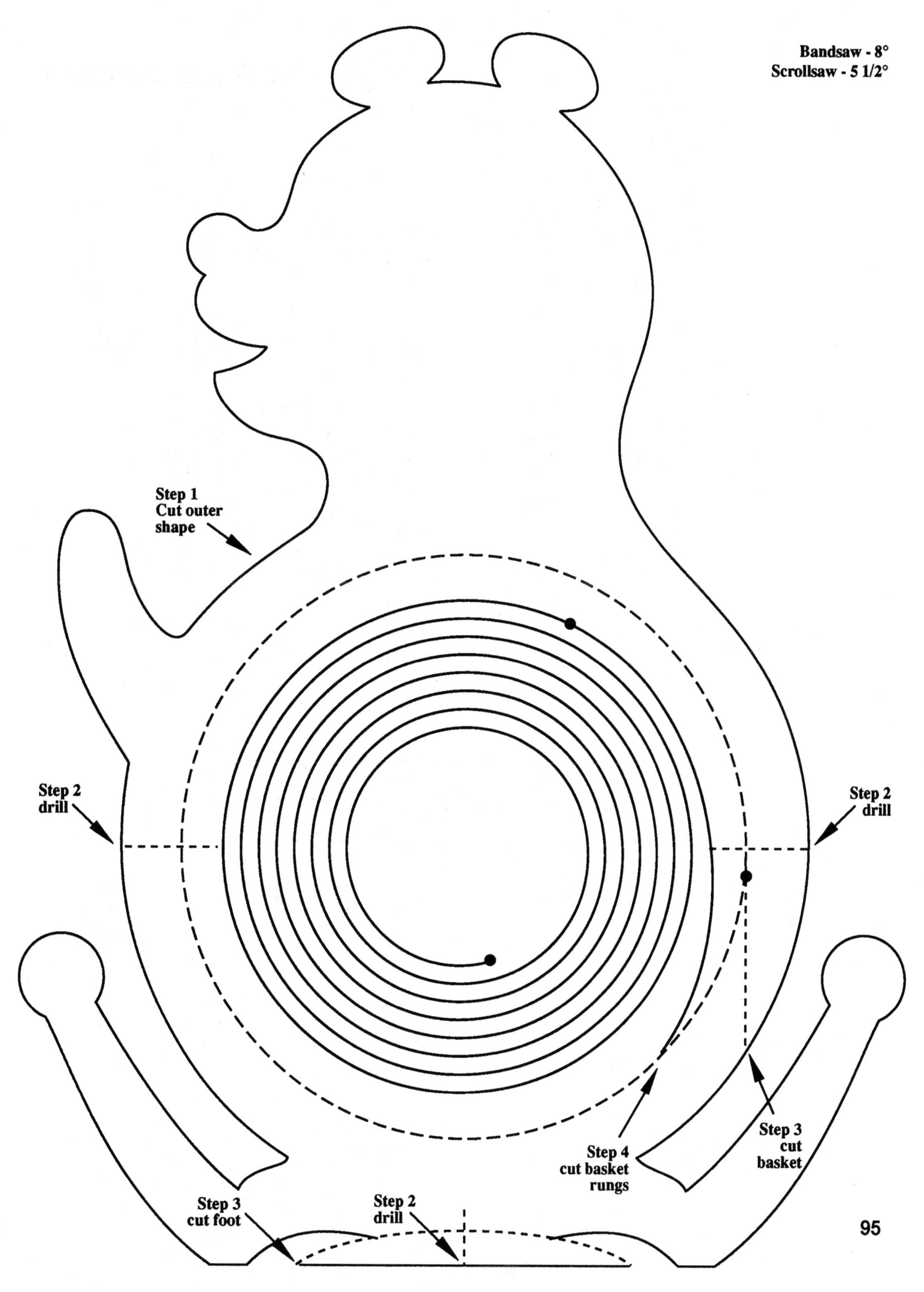
Bandsaw - 8°
Scrollsaw - 5 1/2°
Step 1
Cut outer
shape
Step 2
drill
Step 2
drill
Step 3
cut
basket
Step 4
cut basket
rungs
Step 3
cut foot
Step 2
drill

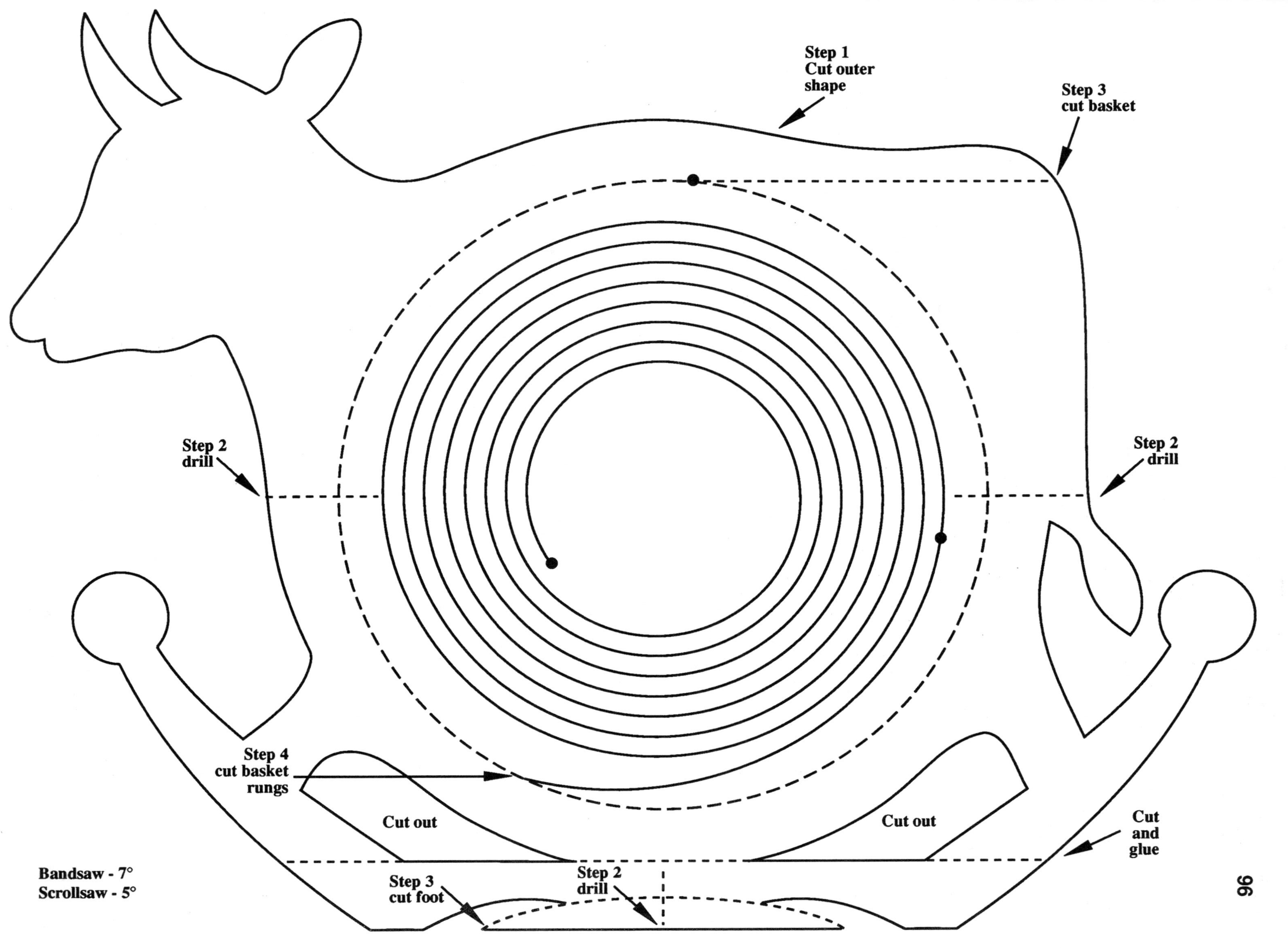
Step 1
Cut outer
shape
Step 3
cut basket
Step 2
drill
Step 2
drill
Step 4
cut basket
rungs
Cut out
Cut out
Cut
and
glue
Bandsaw - 7°
Scrollsaw - 5°
Step 3
cut foot
Step 2
drill

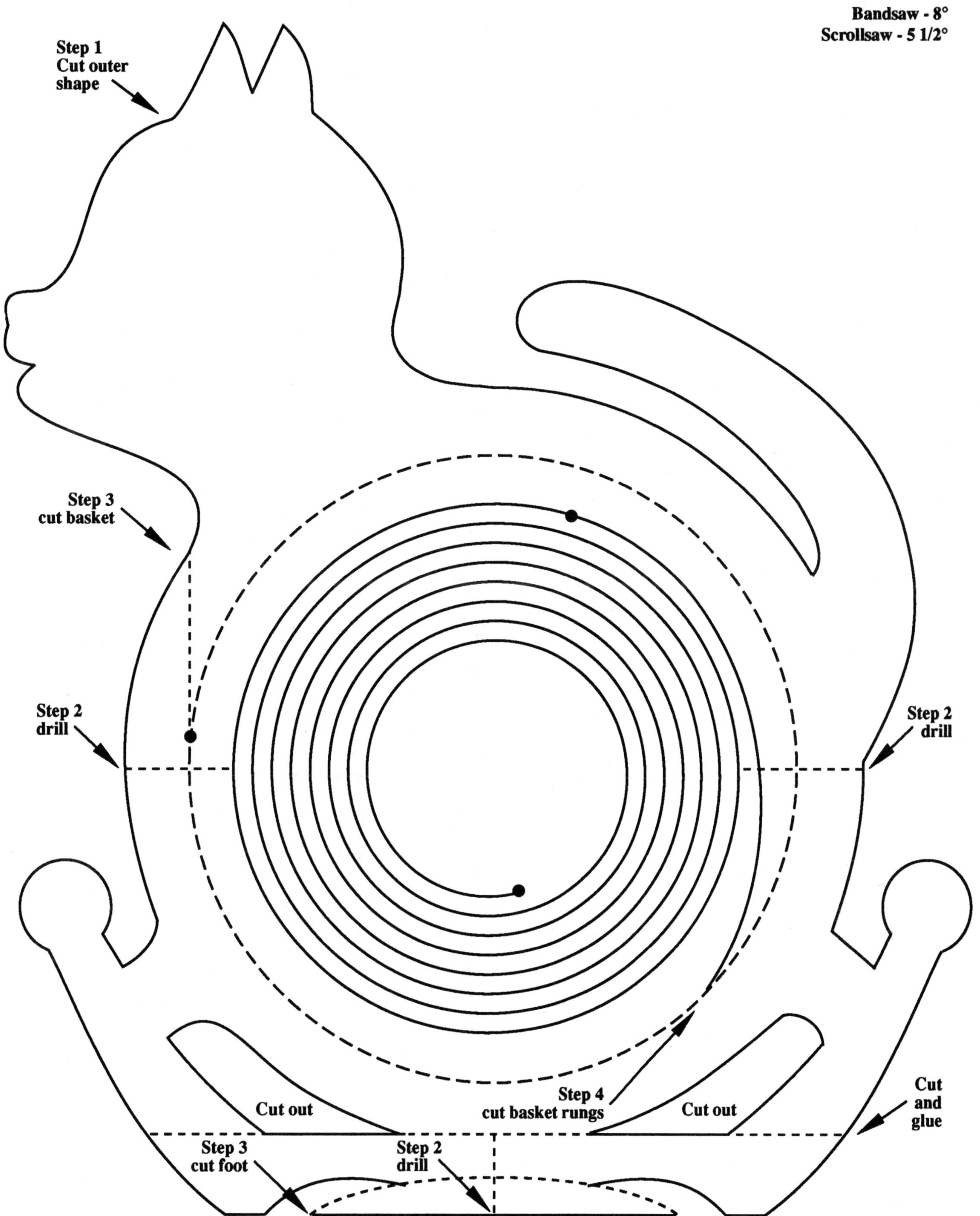
Bandsaw - 8°
Scrollsaw - 5 1/2°
Step 1
Cut outer
shape
Step 3
cut basket
Step 2
drill
Step 2
drill
Cut out
Step 4
cut basket rungs
Cut out
Cut
and
glue
Step 3
cut foot
Step 2
drill

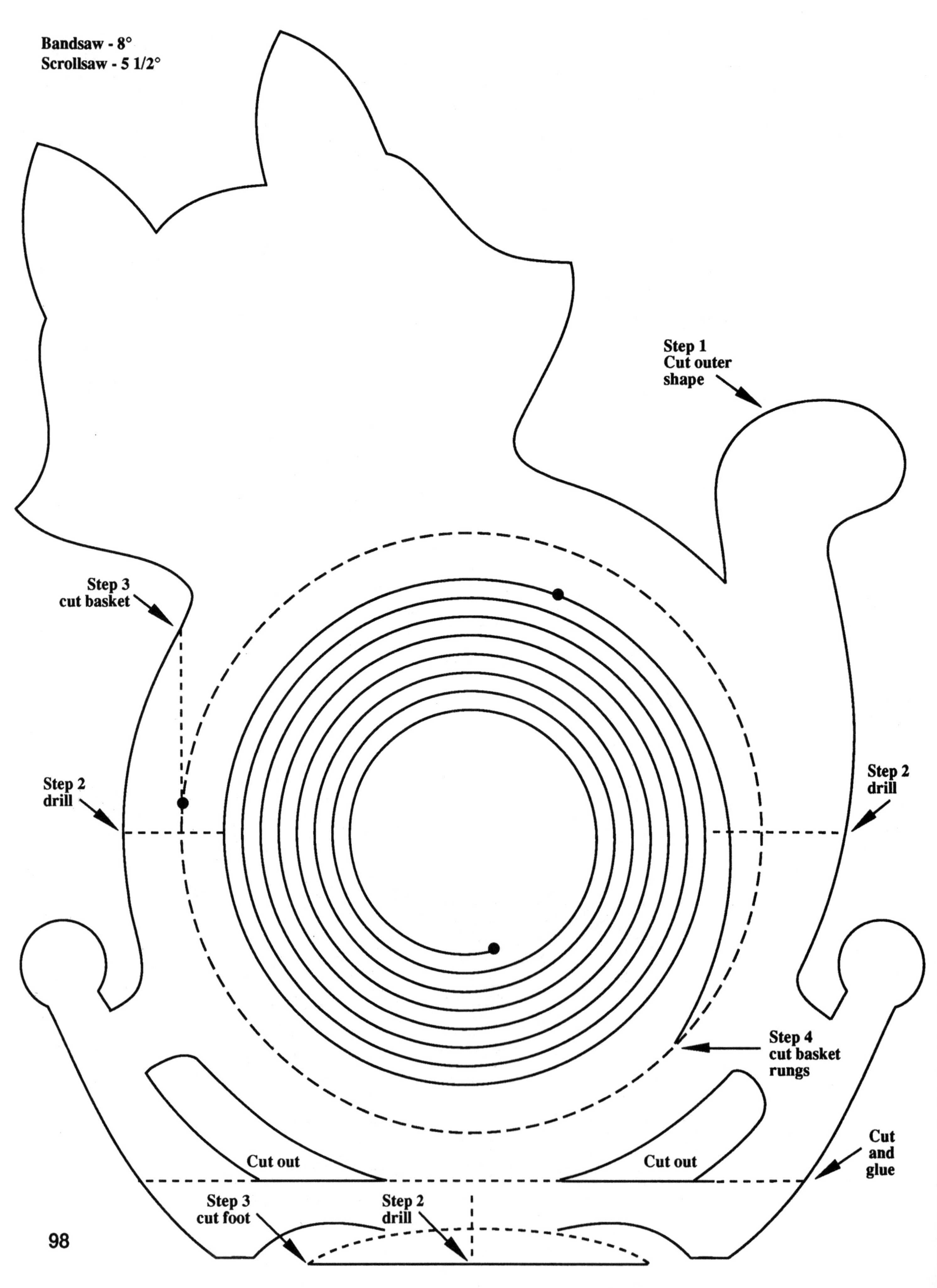
Bandsaw - 8°
Scrollsaw - 5 1/2°
Step 1
Cut outer
shape
Step 3
cut basket
Step 2
drill
Step 2
drill
Step 4
cut basket
rungs
Cut out
Cut out
Cut
and
glue
Step 3
cut foot
Step 2
drill

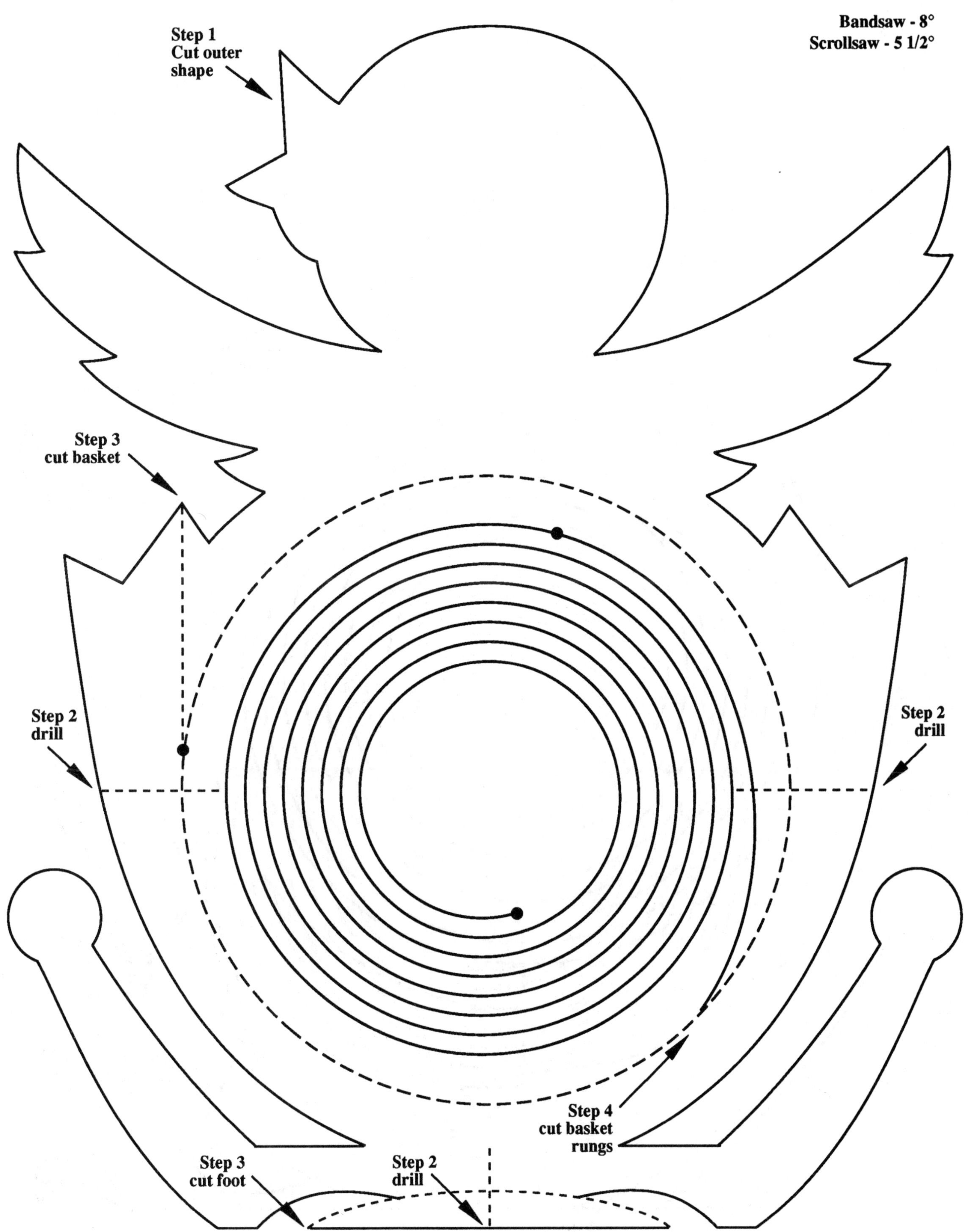
Bandsaw - 8°
Scrollsaw - 5 1/2°
Step 1
Cut outer
shape
Step 3
cut basket
Step 2
drill
Step 2
drill
Step 4
cut basket
rungs
Step 3
cut foot
Step 2
drill

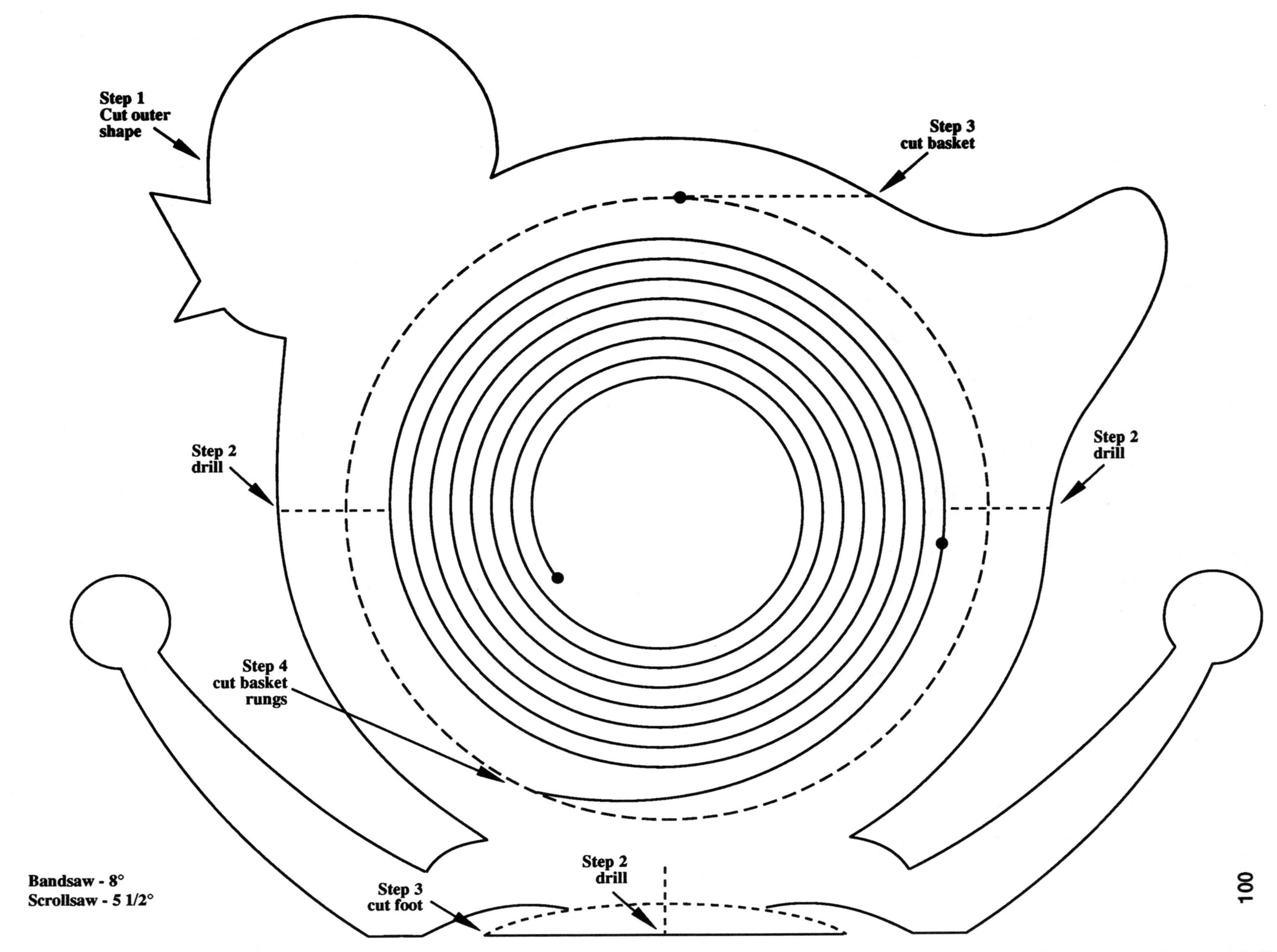

Step 1
Cut outer
shape
Step 3
cut basket
Step 2
drill
Step 2
drill
Step 4
cut basket
rungs
Step 2
drill
Step 3
cut foot
Bandsaw - 8°
Scrollsaw - 5 1/2°

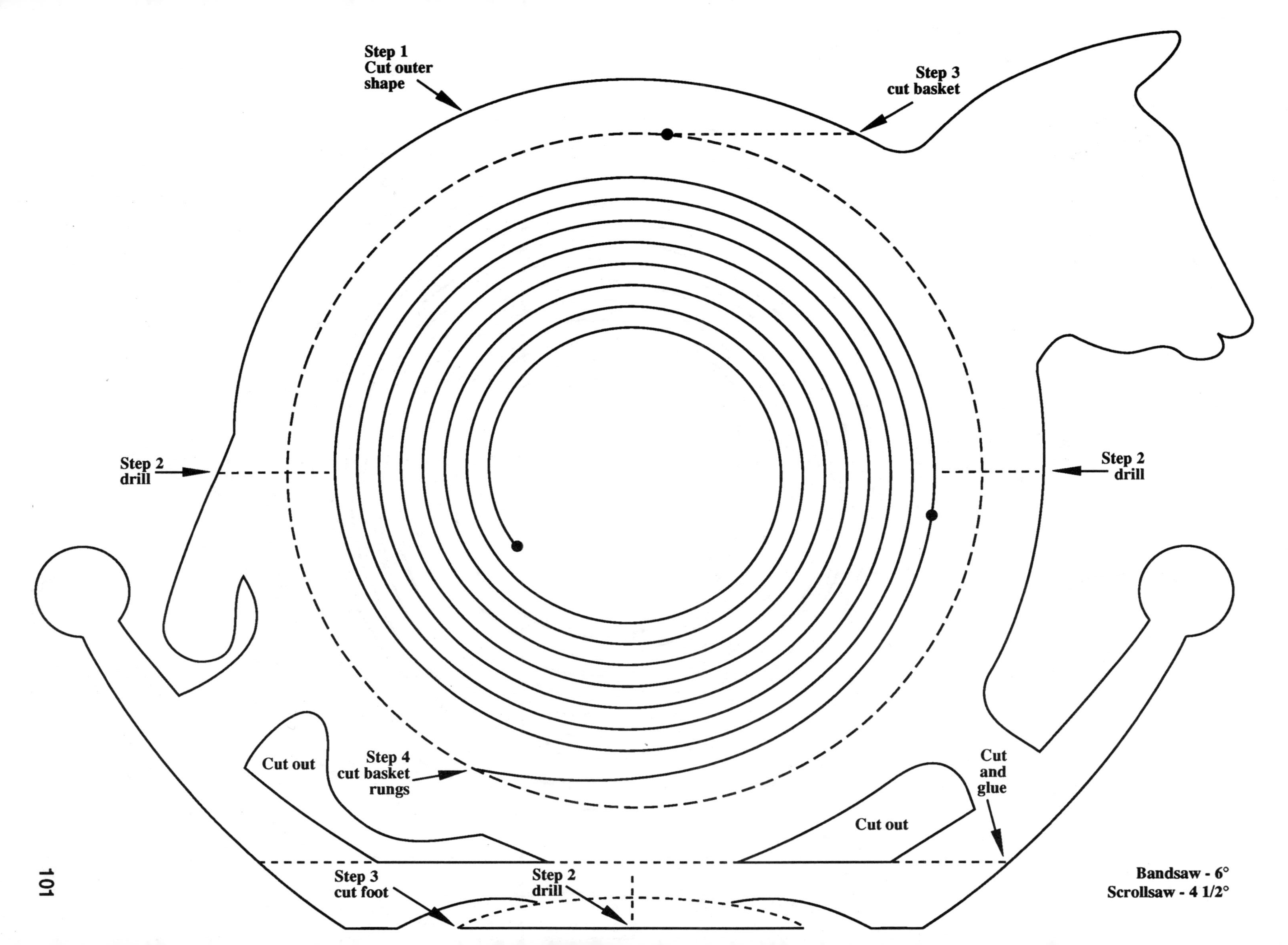
Step 1
Cut outer
shape
Step 3
cut basket
Step 2
drill
Step 2
drill
Cut out
Step 4
cut basket
rungs
Cut
and
glue
Cut out
Step 3
cut foot
Step 2
drill
Bandsaw - 6°
Scrollsaw - 4 1/2°

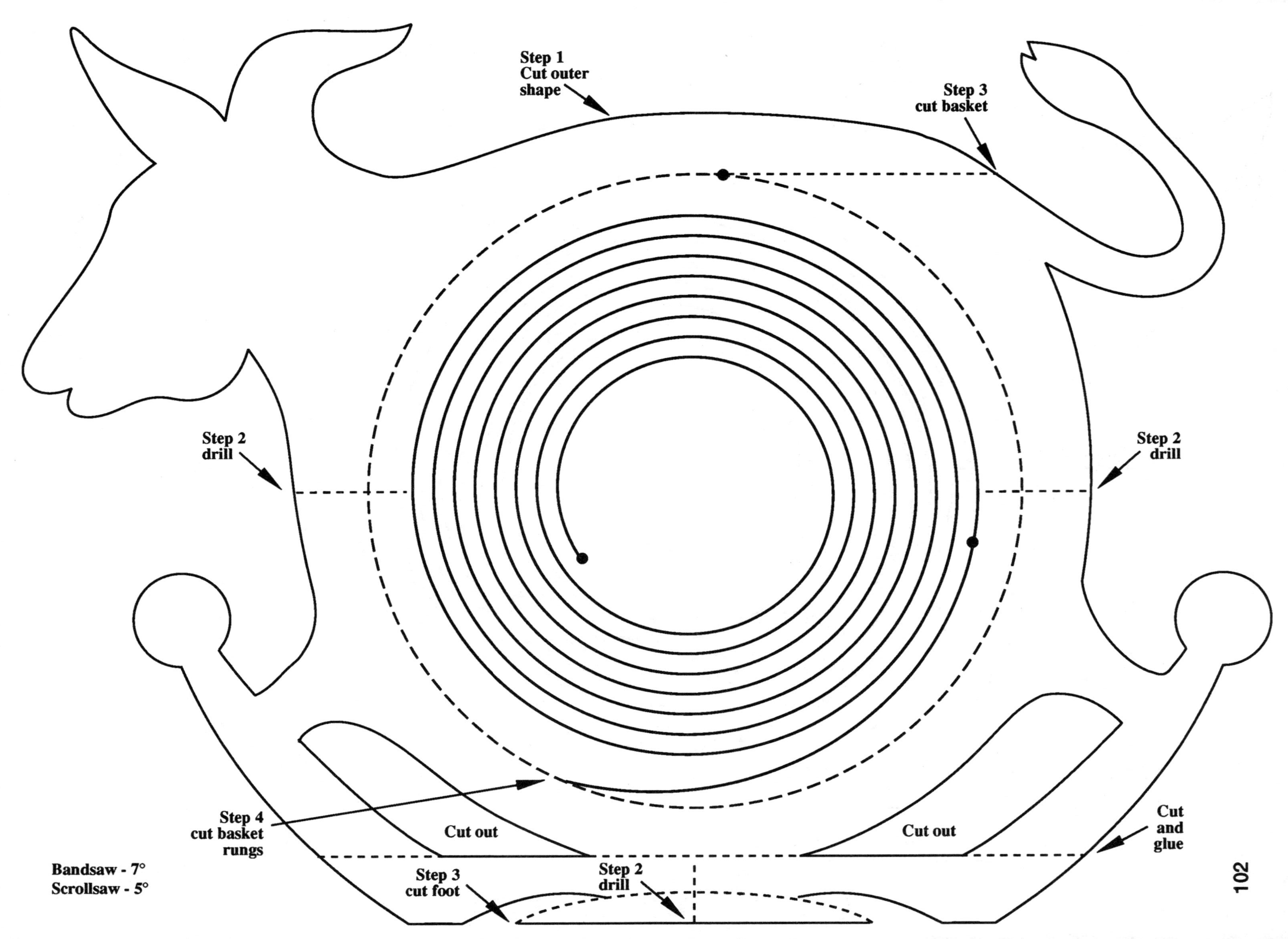

Step 1
Cut outer
shape
Step 3
cut basket
Step 2
drill
Step 2
drill
Step 4
cut basket
rungs
Cut out
Cut out
Cut
and
glue
Bandsaw - 7°
Scrollsaw - 5°
Step 3
cut foot
Step 2
drill

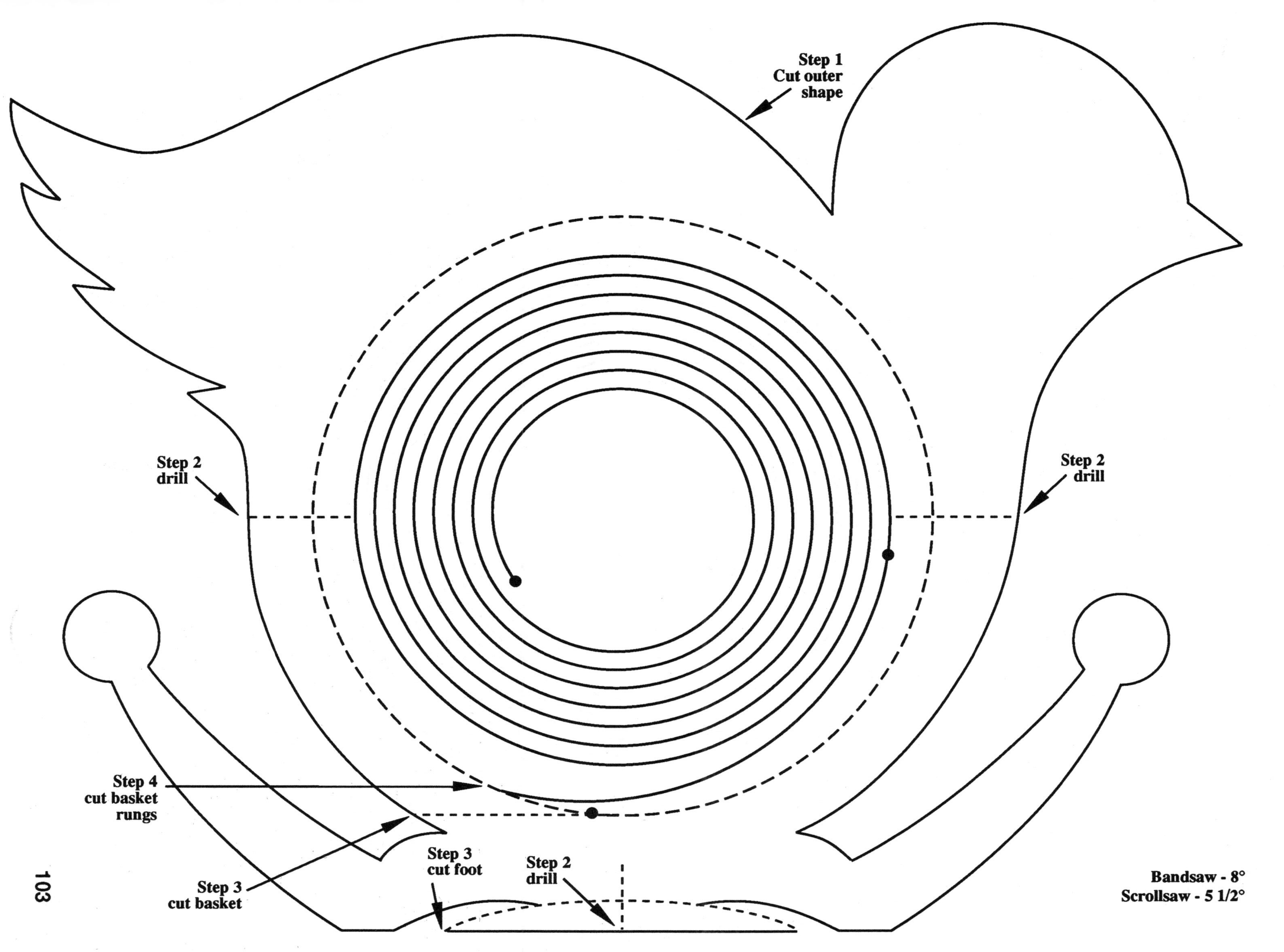
Step 1
Cut outer
shape
Step 2
drill
Step 2
drill
Step 4
cut basket
rungs
Step 3
cut basket
Step 3
cut foot
Step 2
drill
Bandsaw - 8°
Scrollsaw - 5 1/2°

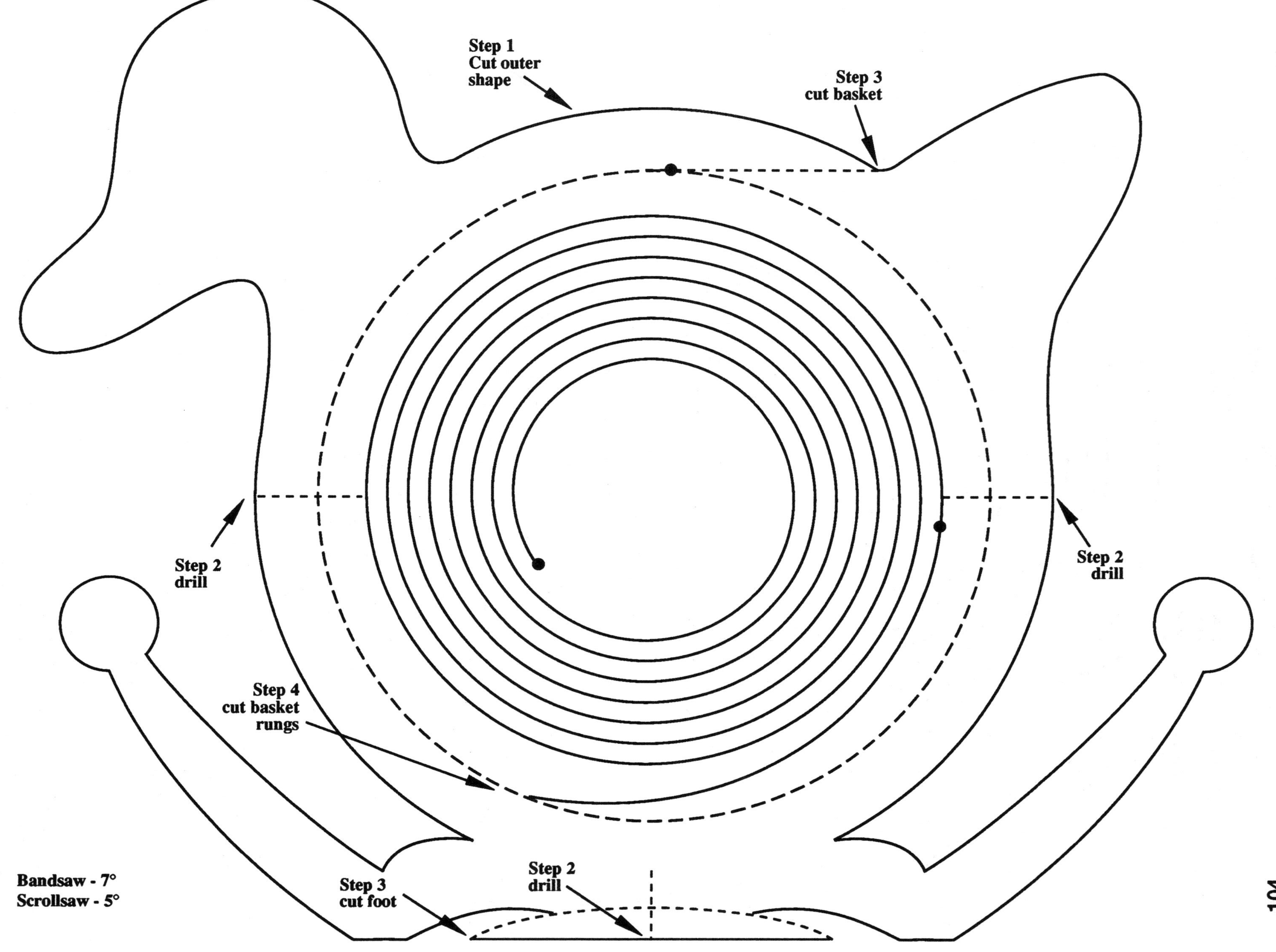
Step 1
Cut outer
shape
Step 3
cut basket
Step 2
drill
Step 2
drill
Step 4
cut basket
rungs
Bandsaw - 7°
Scrollsaw - 5°
Step 3
cut foot
Step 2
drill

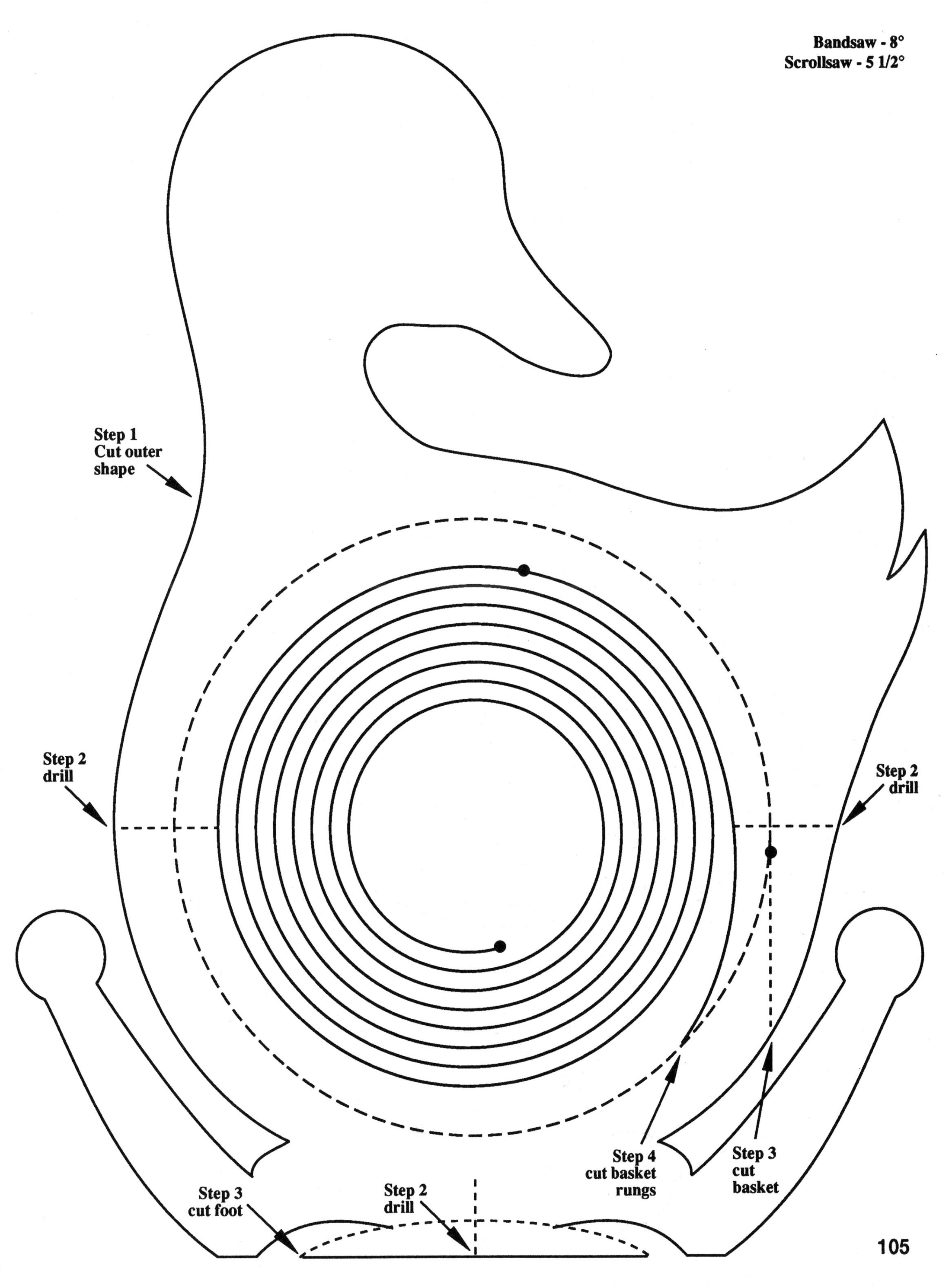
Bandsaw - 8°
Scrollsaw - 5 1/2°
Step 1
Cut outer
shape
Step 2
drill
Step 2
drill
Step 4
cut basket
rungs
Step 3
cut
basket
Step 3
cut foot
Step 2
drill

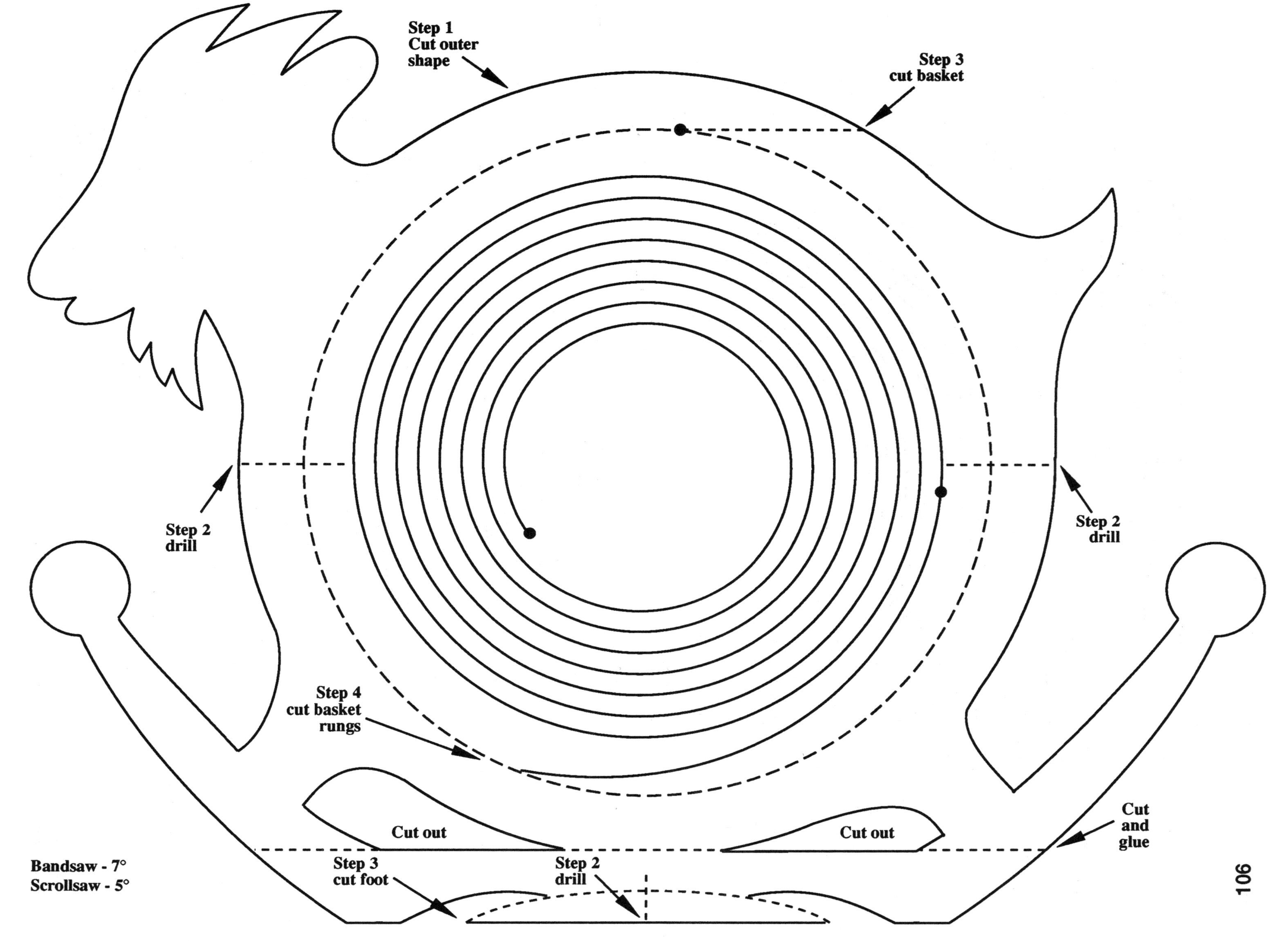
Step 1
Cut outer
shape
Step 3
cut basket
Step 2
drill
Step 2
drill
Step 4
cut basket
rungs
Cut out
Cut out
Cut
and
glue
Bandsaw - 7°
Scrollsaw - 5°
Step 3
cut foot
Step 2
drill

Bandsaw - 8°
Scrollsaw - 5 1/2°

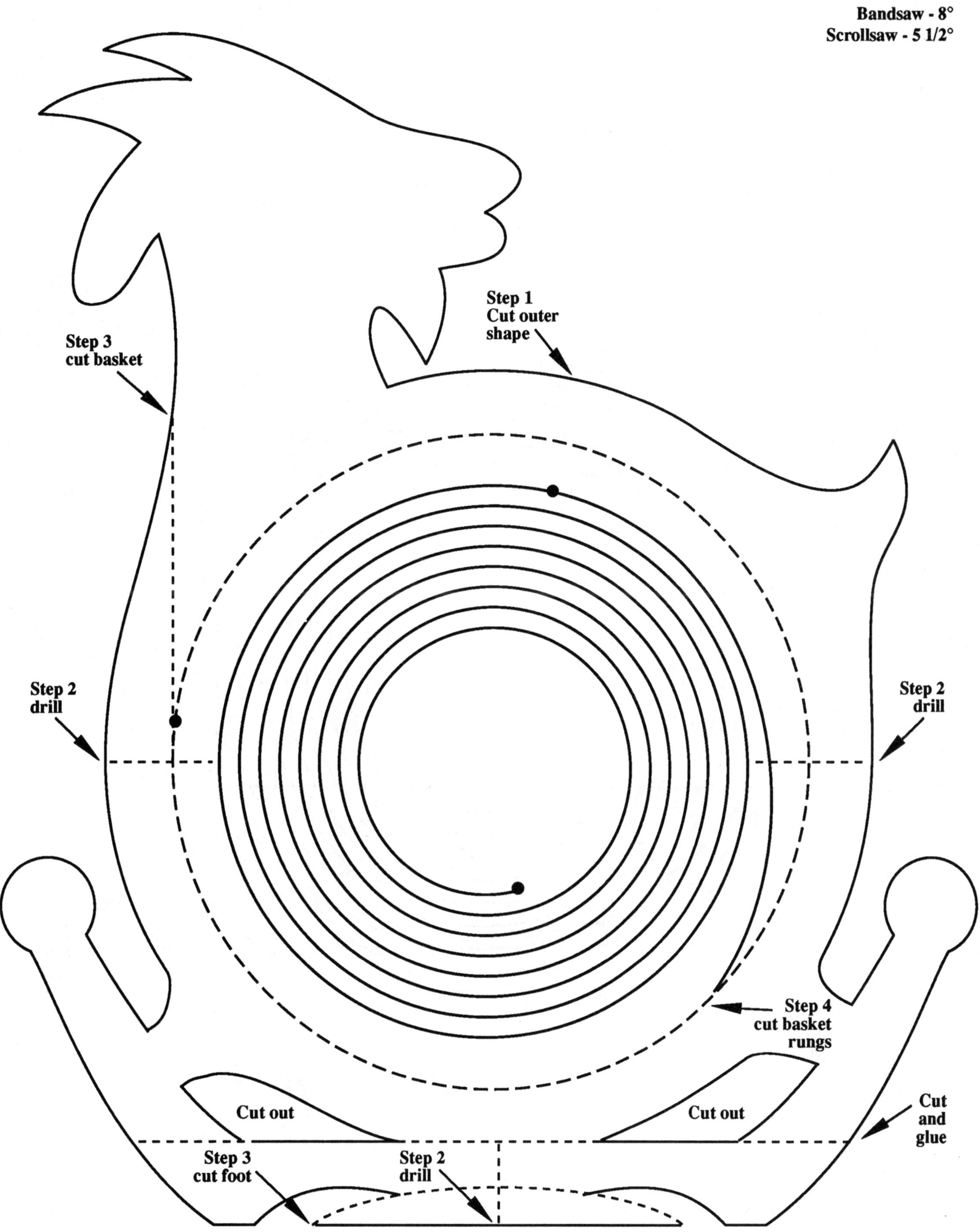

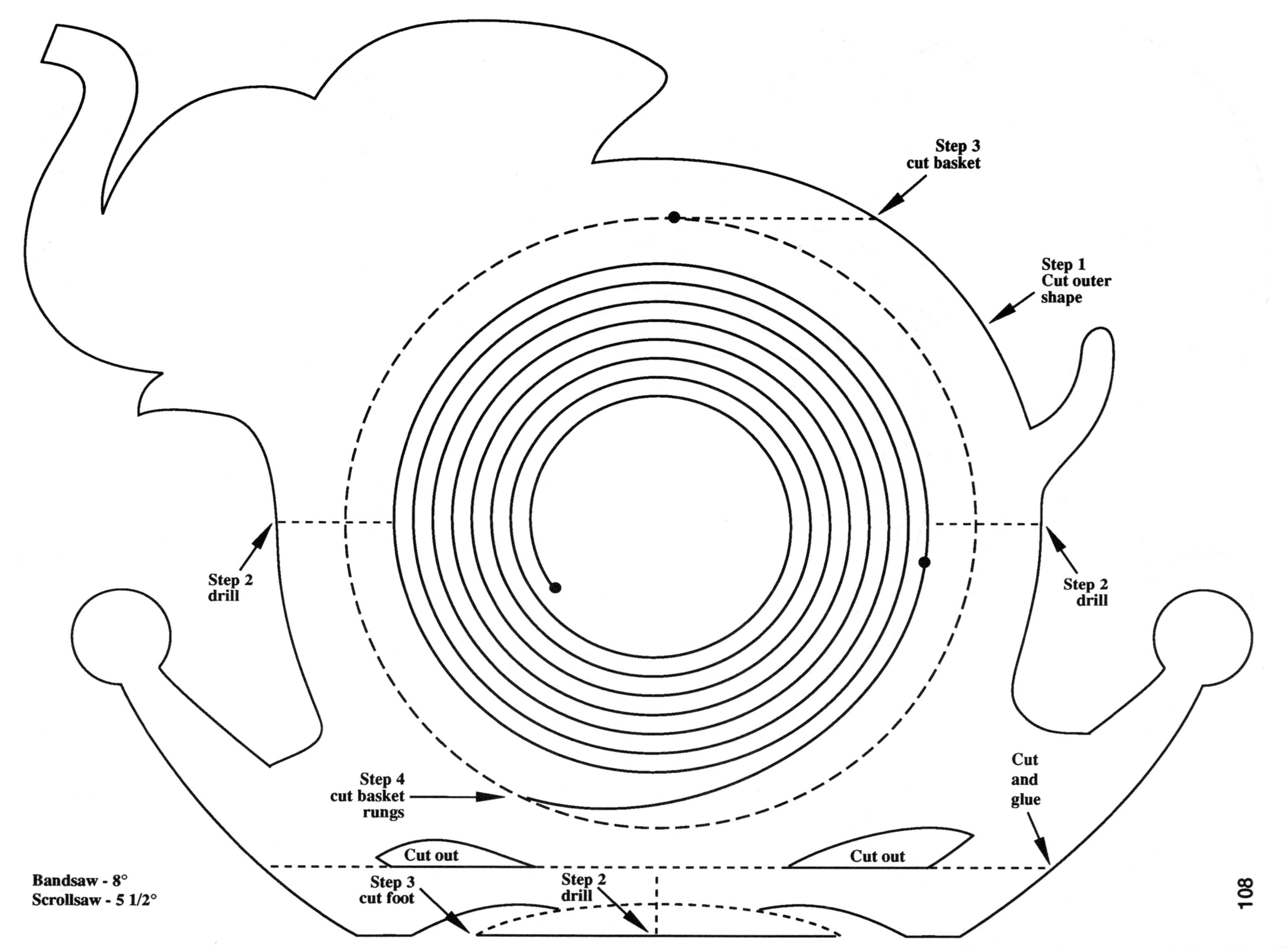
Step 3
cut basket
Step 1
Cut outer
shape
Step 2
drill
Step 2
drill
Step 4
cut basket
rungs
Cut
and
glue
Cut out
Cut out
Step 3
cut foot
Step 2
drill
Bandsaw - 8°
Scrollsaw - 5 1/2°

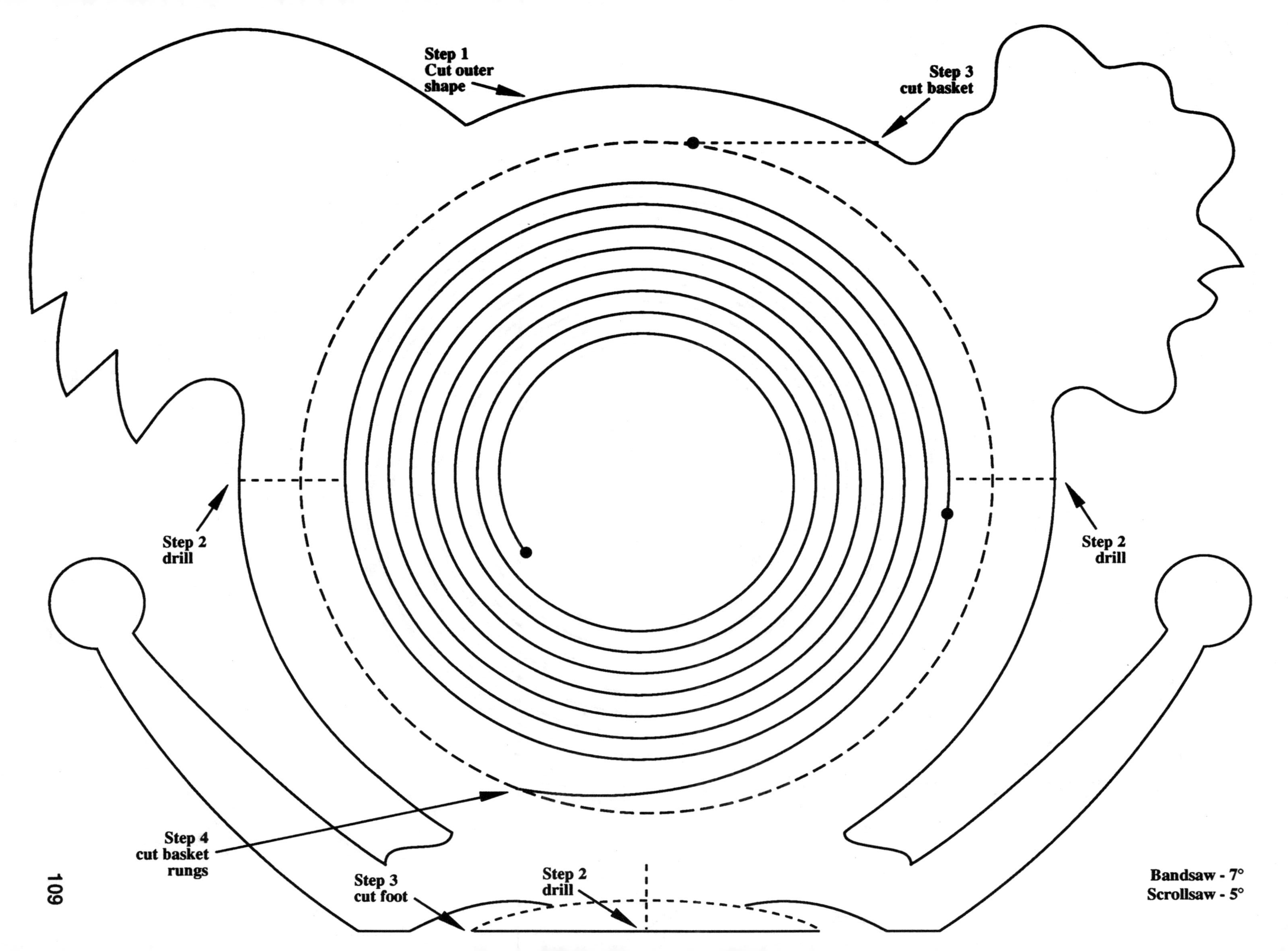
Step 1
Cut outer
shape
Step 3
cut basket
Step 2
drill
Step 2
drill
Step 4
cut basket
rungs
Step 3
cut foot
Step 2
drill
Bandsaw - 7°
Scrollsaw - 5°

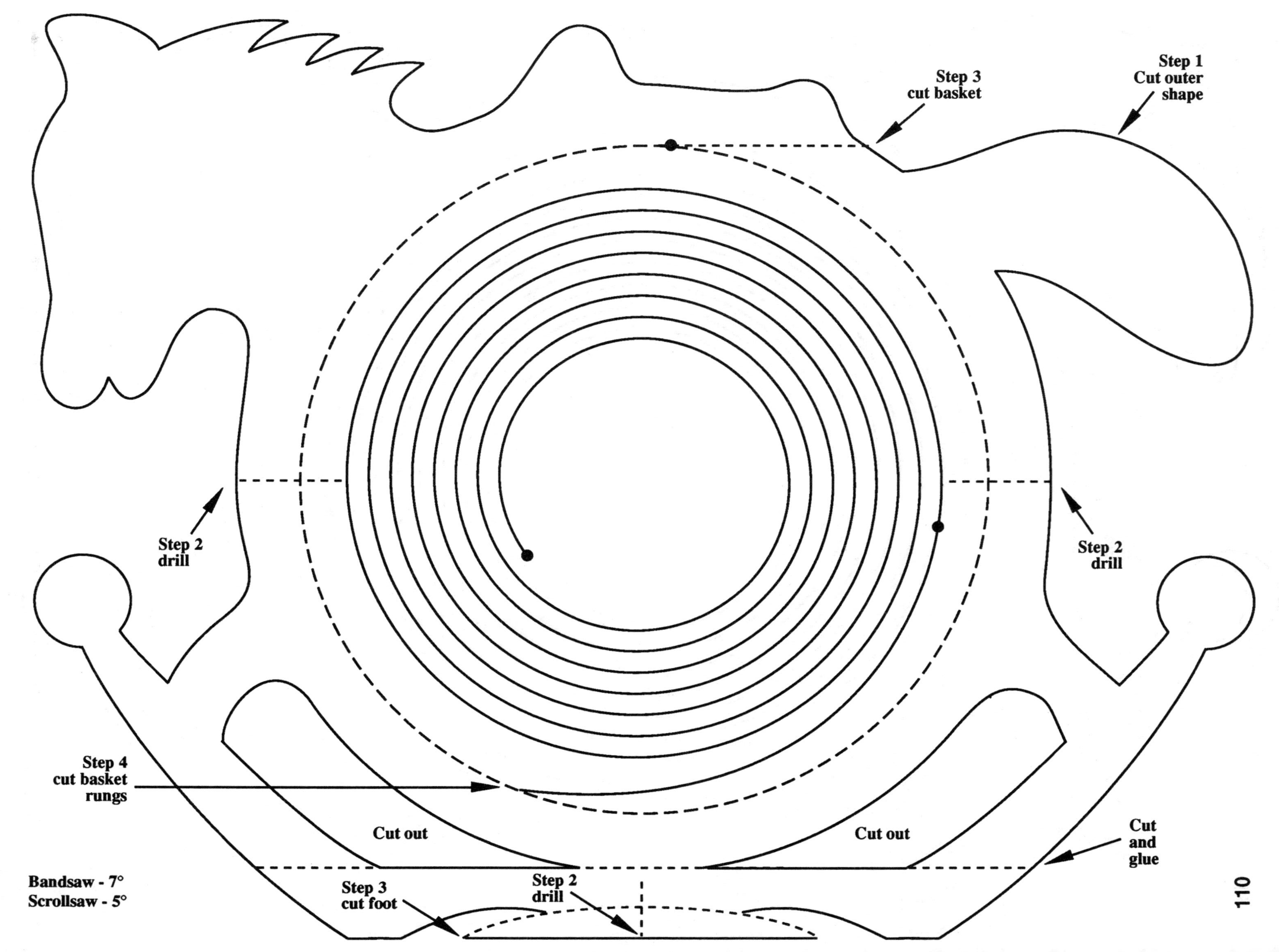
Step 3
cut basket
Step 1
Cut outer
shape
Step 2
drill
Step 2
drill
Step 4
cut basket
rungs
Cut out
Cut out
Cut
and
glue
Bandsaw - 7°
Scrollsaw - 5°
Step 3
cut foot
Step 2
drill

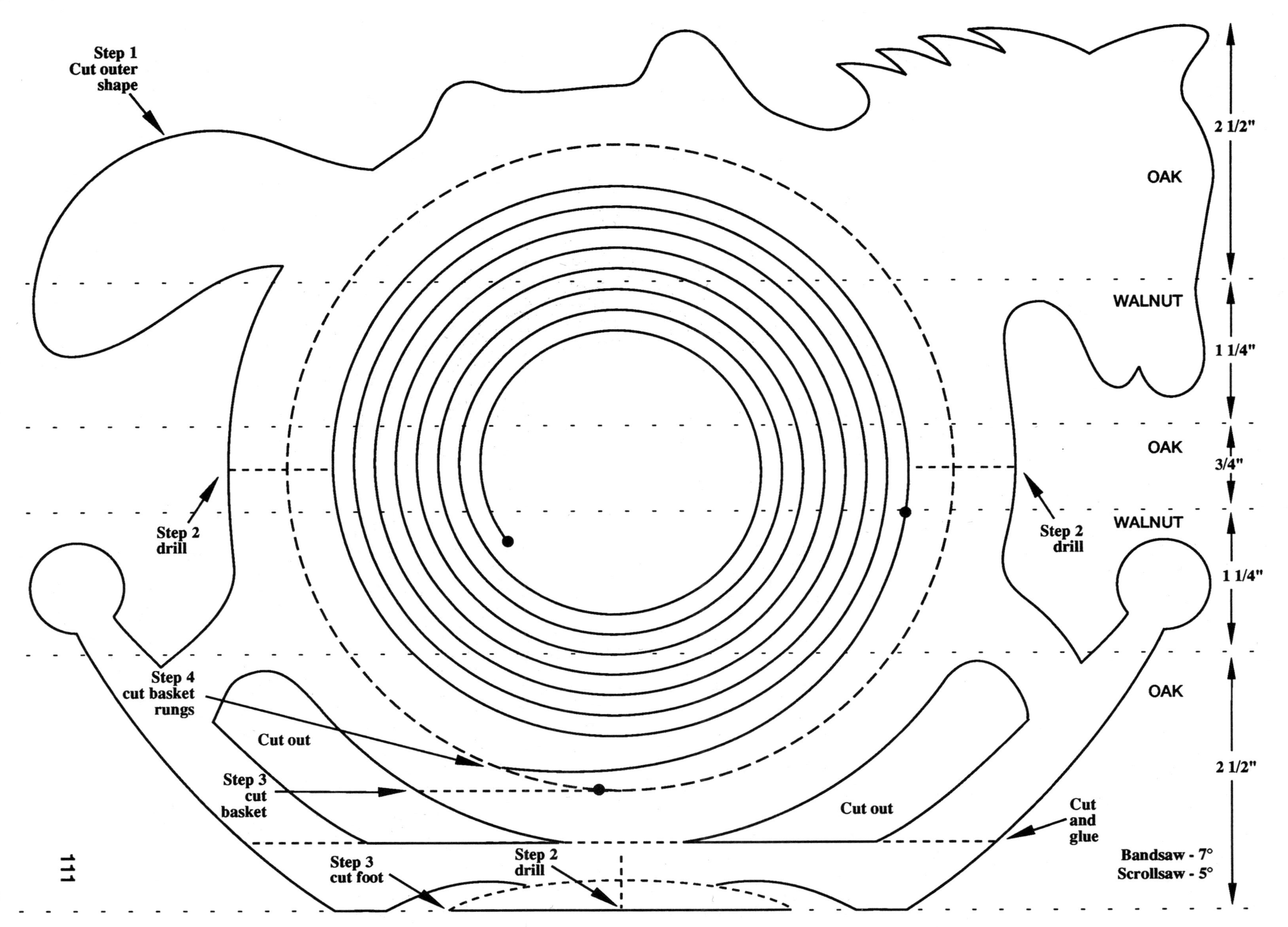
Step 1
Cut outer
shape
OAK
WALNUT
OAK
WALNUT
OAK
2 1/2"
1 1/4"
3/4"
1 1/4"
2 1/2"
Step 2
drill
Step 2
drill
Step 4
cut basket
rungs
Cut out
Step 3
cut
basket
Cut out
Cut
and
glue
Step 3
cut foot
Step 2
drill
Bandsaw - 7°
Scrollsaw - 5°

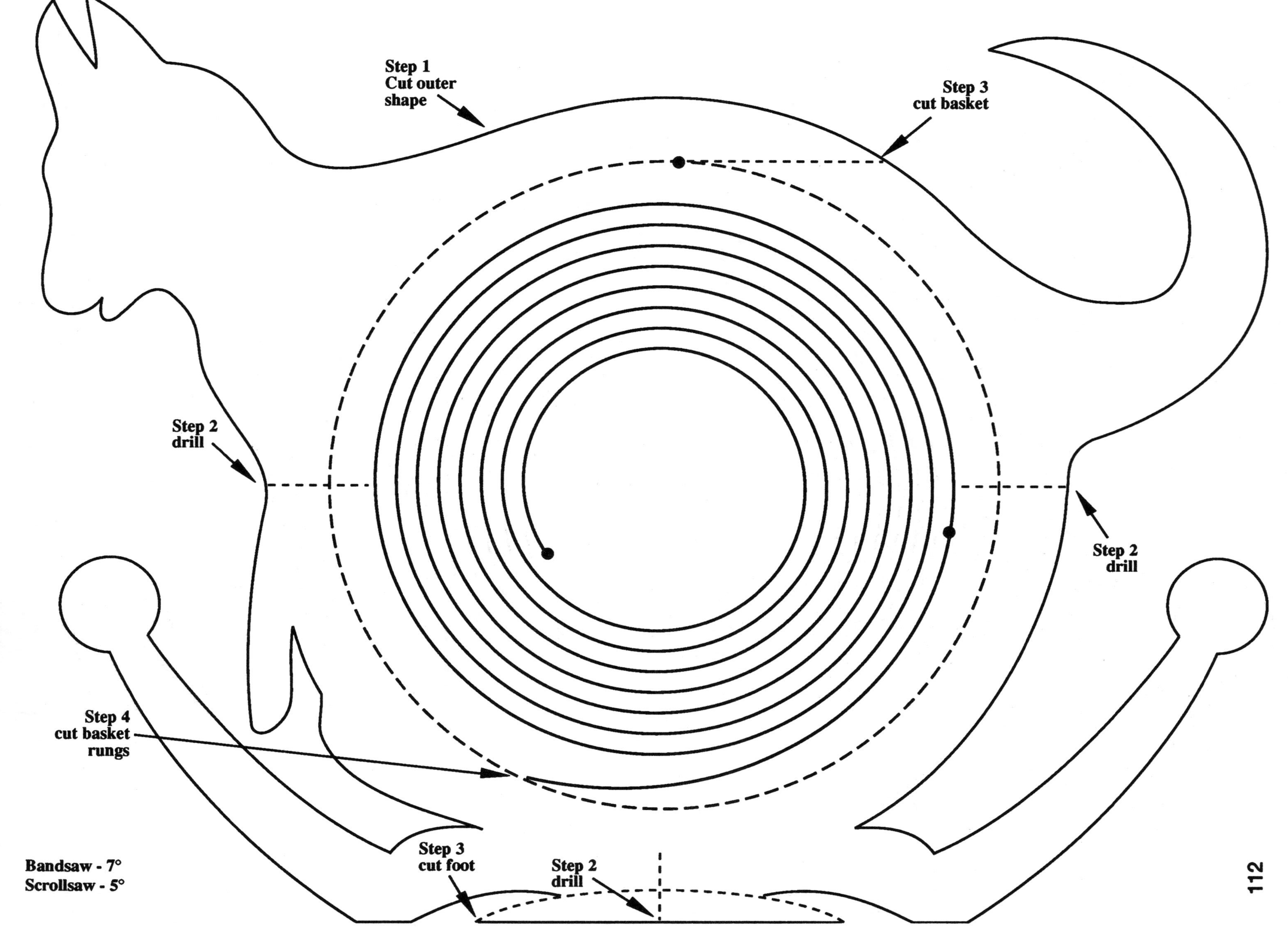
Step 1
Cut outer
shape
Step 3
cut basket
Step 2
drill
Step 2
drill
Step 4
cut basket
rungs
Step 3
cut foot
Step 2
drill
Bandsaw - 7°
Scrollsaw - 5°

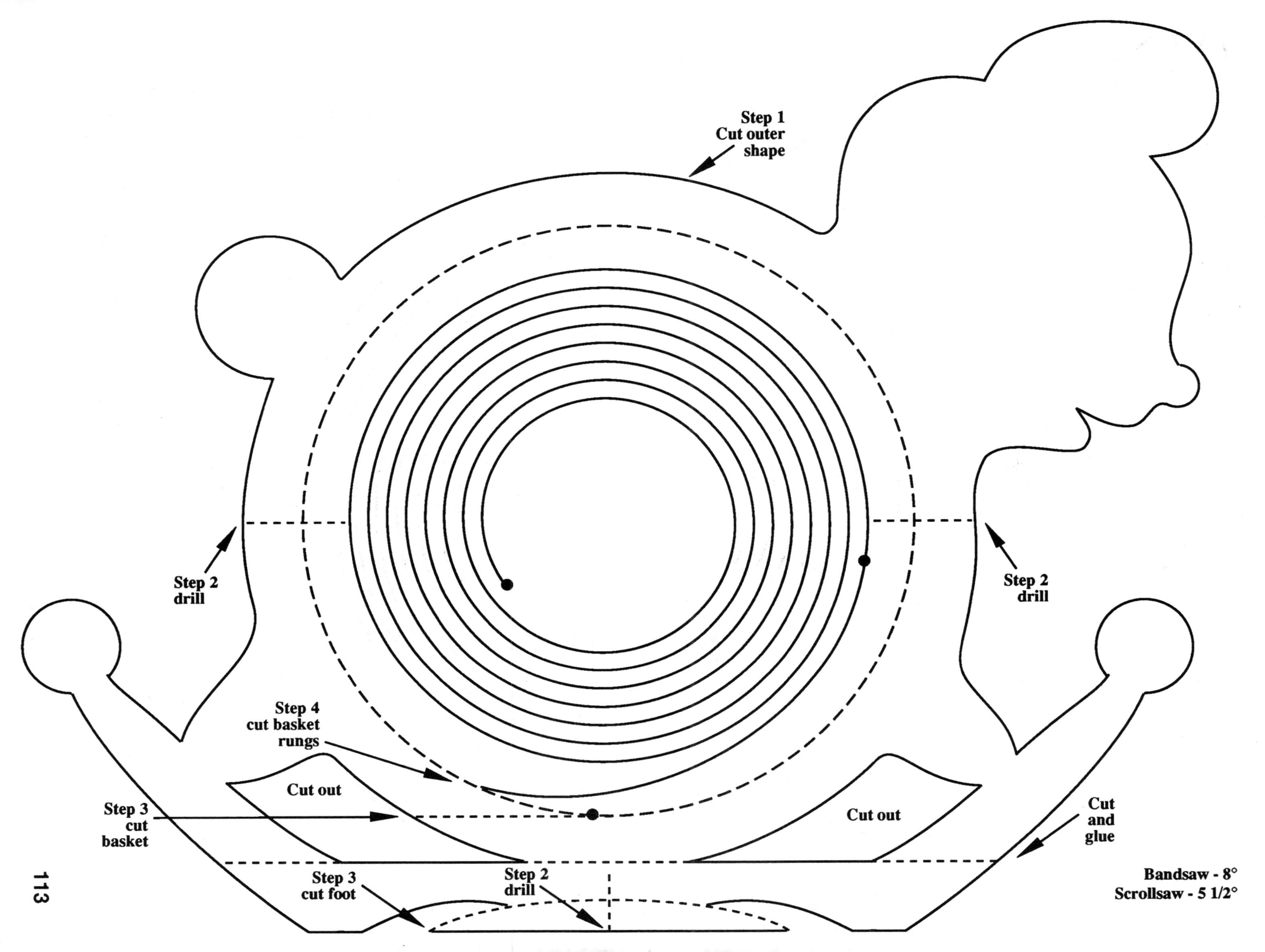
Step 1
Cut outer
shape
Step 2
drill
Step 2
drill
Step 4
cut basket
rungs
Cut out
Cut out
Step 3
cut
basket
Cut
and
glue
Step 3
cut foot
Step 2
drill
Bandsaw - 8°
Scrollsaw - 5 1/2°

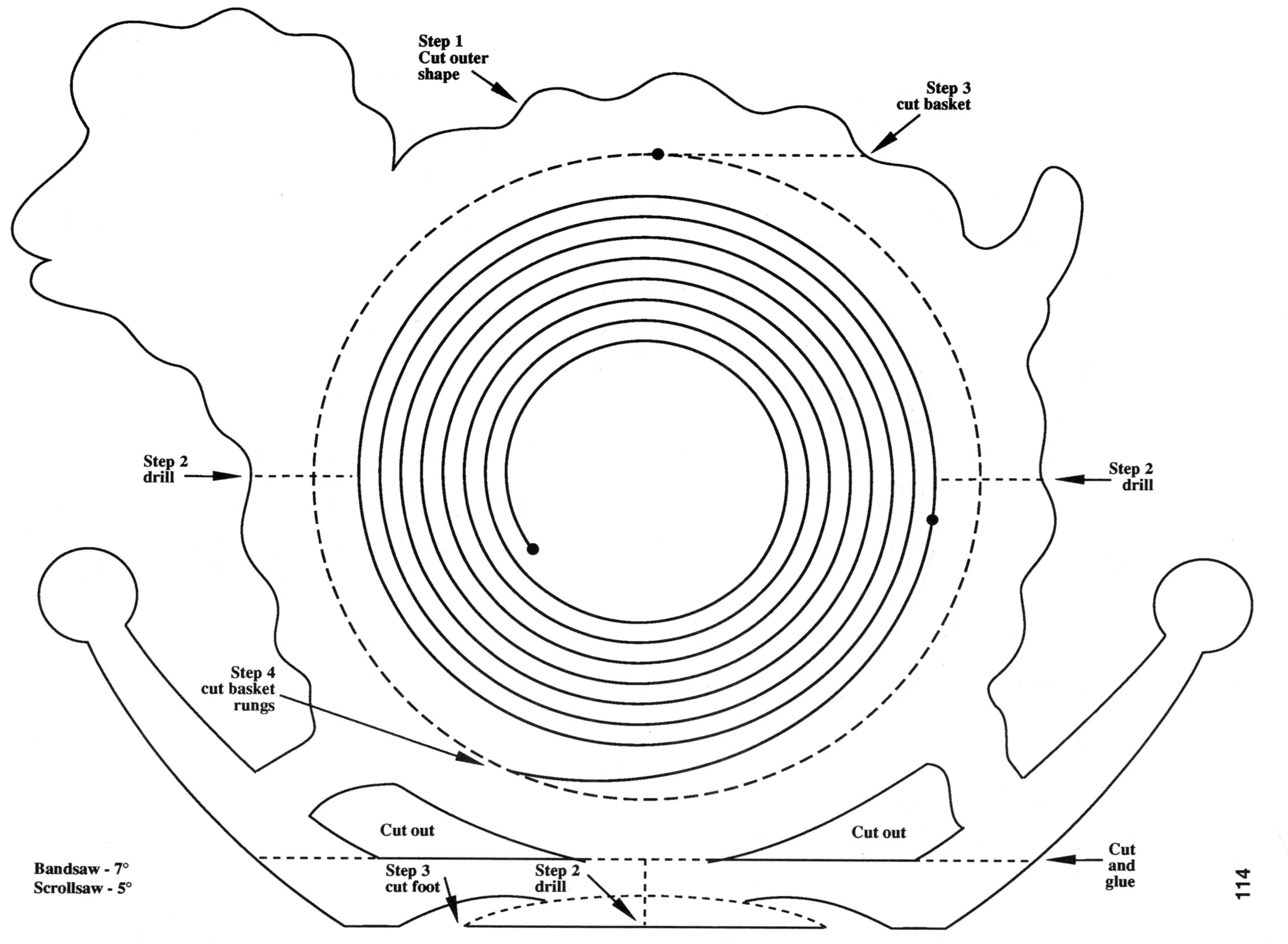
Step 1
Cut outer
shape
Step 3
cut basket
Step 2
drill
Step 2
drill
Step 4
cut basket
rungs
Cut out
Cut out
Bandsaw - 7°
Scrollsaw - 5°
Step 3
cut foot
Step 2
drill
Cut
and
glue

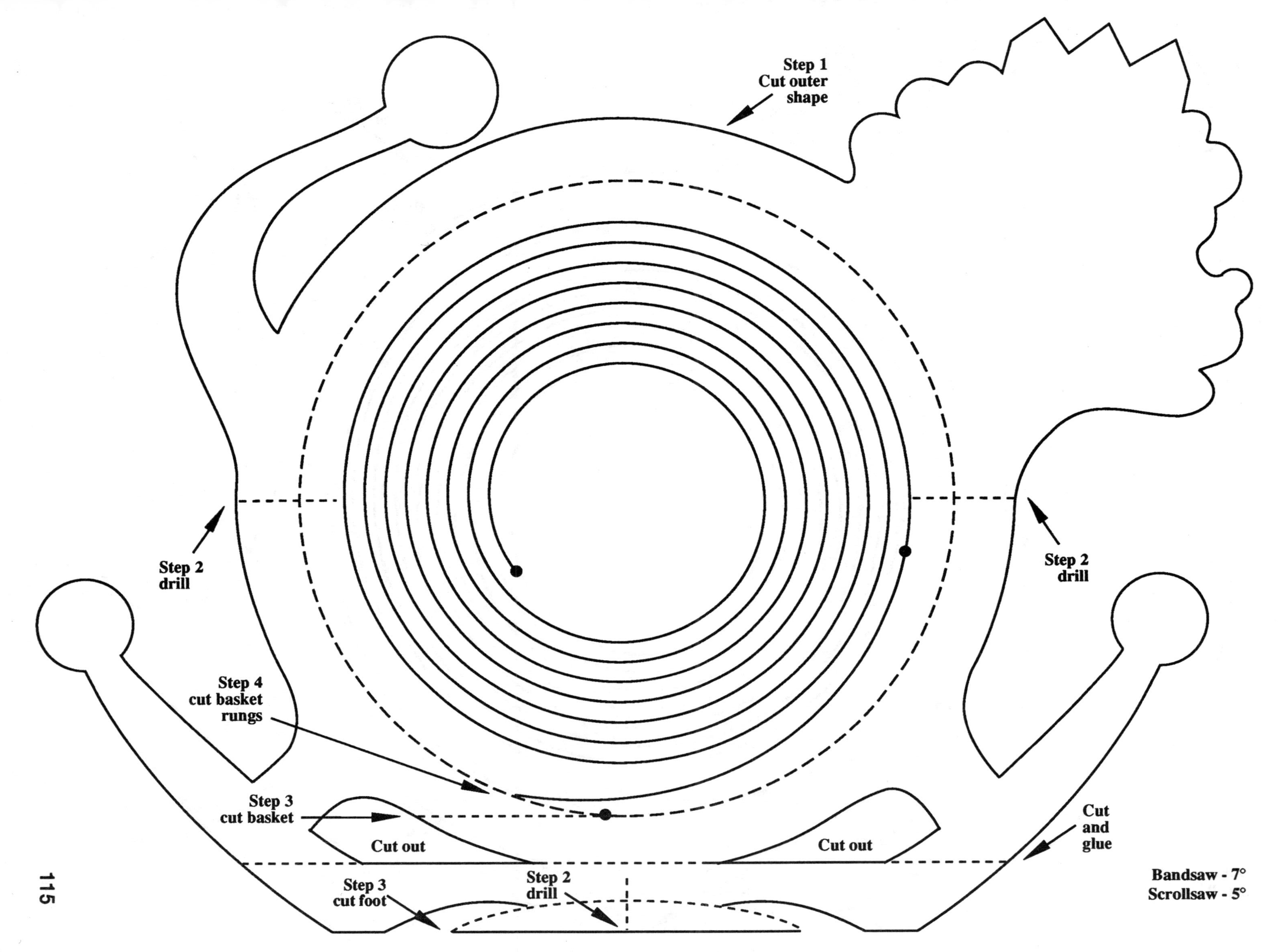
Step 1
Cut outer
shape
Step 2
drill
Step 2
drill
Step 4
cut basket
rungs
Step 3
cut basket
Cut out
Cut out
Cut
and
glue
Step 3
cut foot
Step 2
drill
Bandsaw - 7°
Scrollsaw - 5°

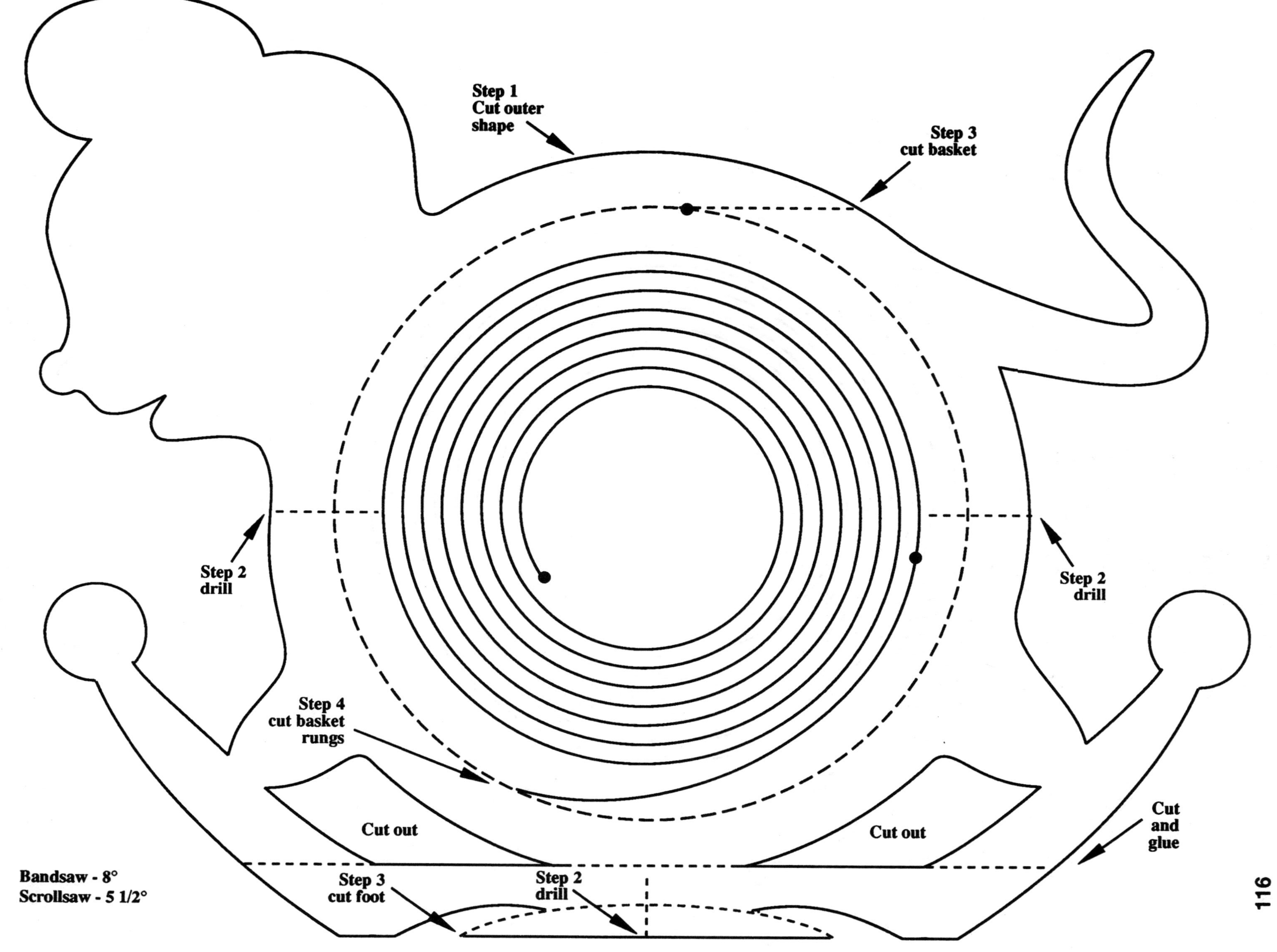
Step 1
Cut outer
shape
Step 3
cut basket
Step 2
drill
Step 2
drill
Step 4
cut basket
rungs
Cut out
Cut out
Cut
and
glue
Bandsaw - 8°
Scrollsaw - 5 1/2°
Step 3
cut foot
Step 2
drill

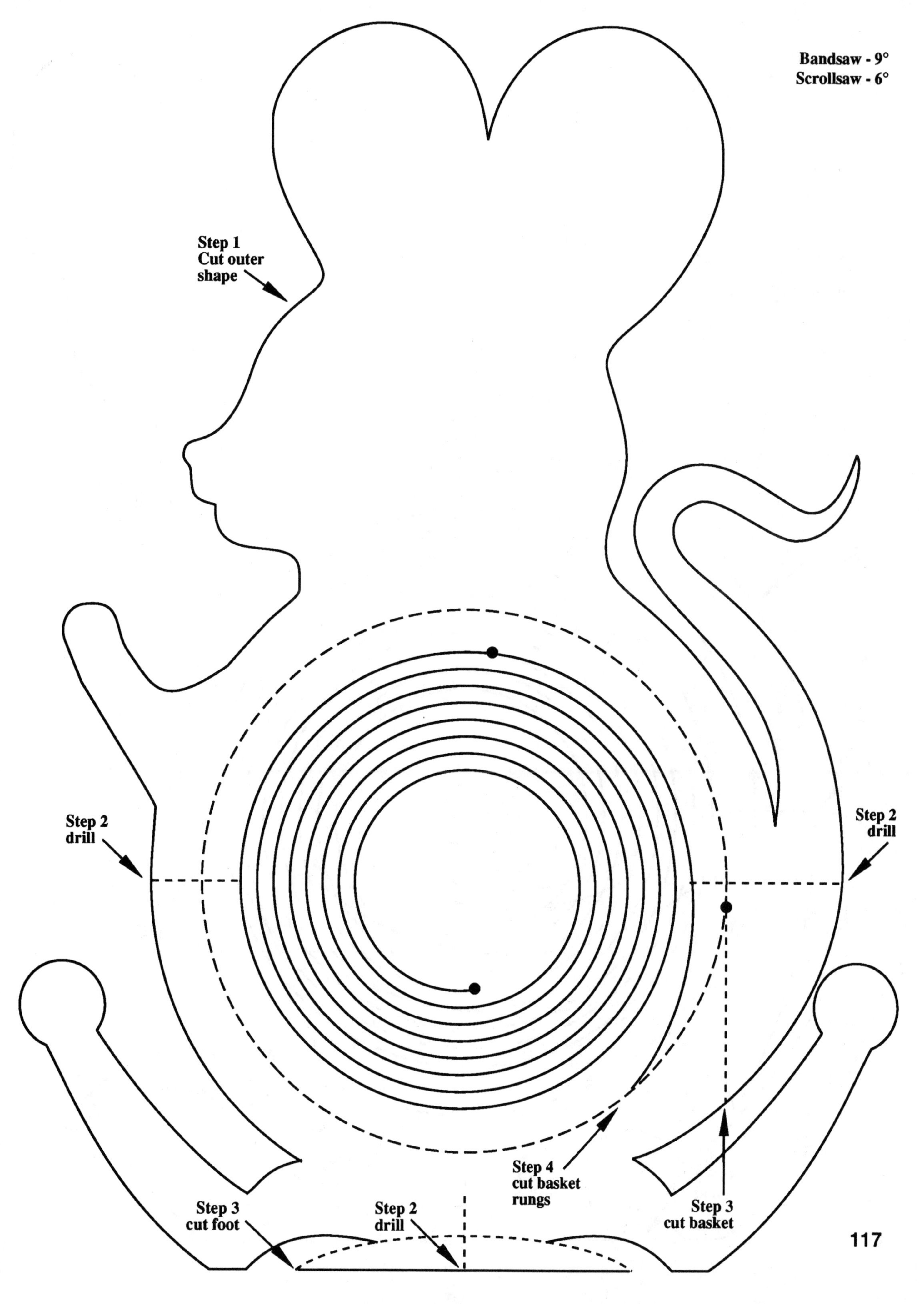
Bandsaw - 9°
Scrollsaw - 6°
Step 1
Cut outer
shape
Step 2
drill
Step 2
drill
Step 4
cut basket
rungs
Step 3
cut foot
Step 2
drill
Step 3
cut basket

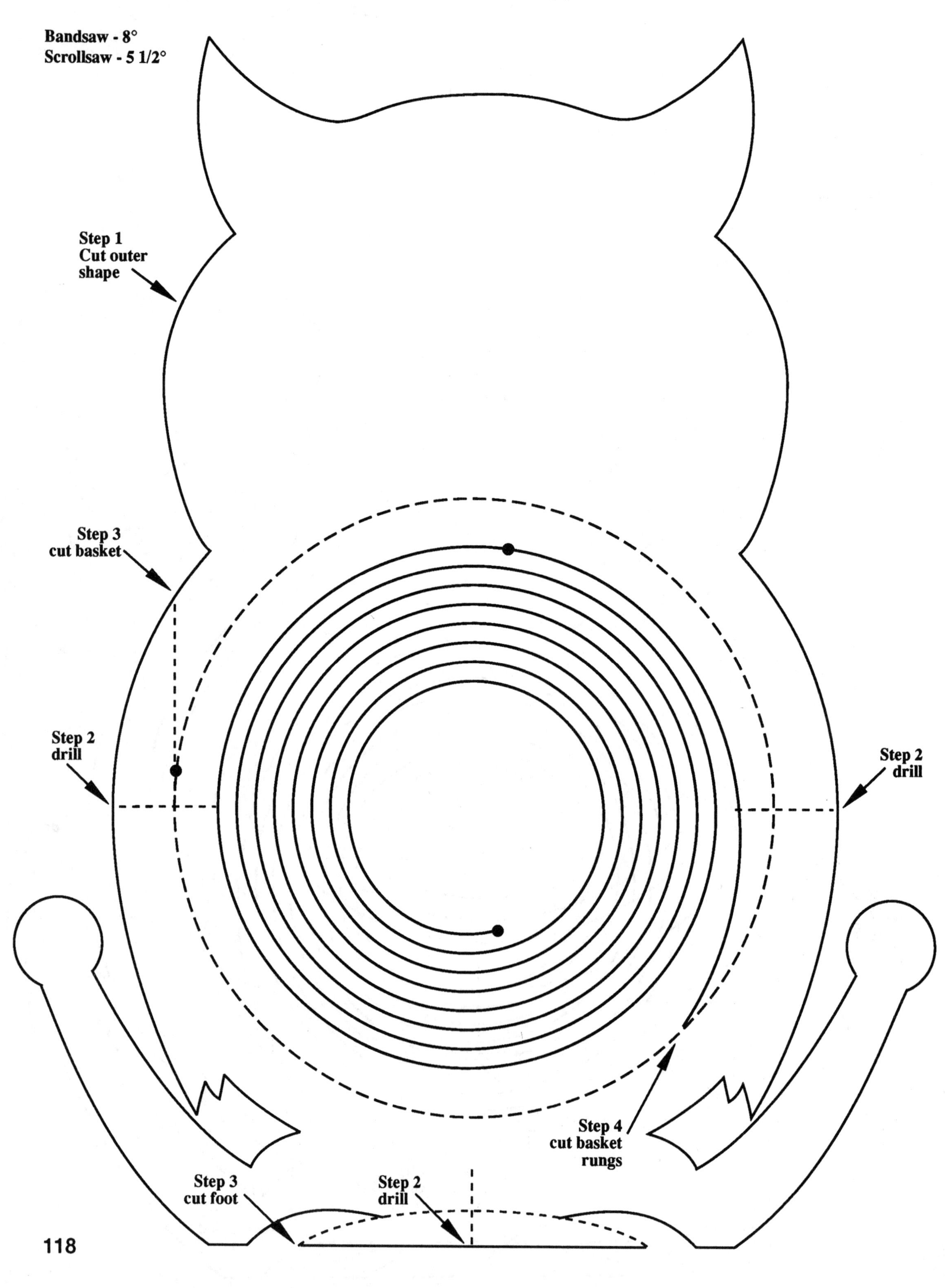
Bandsaw - 8°
Scrollsaw - 5 1/2°
Step 1
Cut outer
shape
Step 3
cut basket
Step 2
drill
Step 2
drill
Step 4
cut basket
rungs
Step 3
cut foot
Step 2
drill

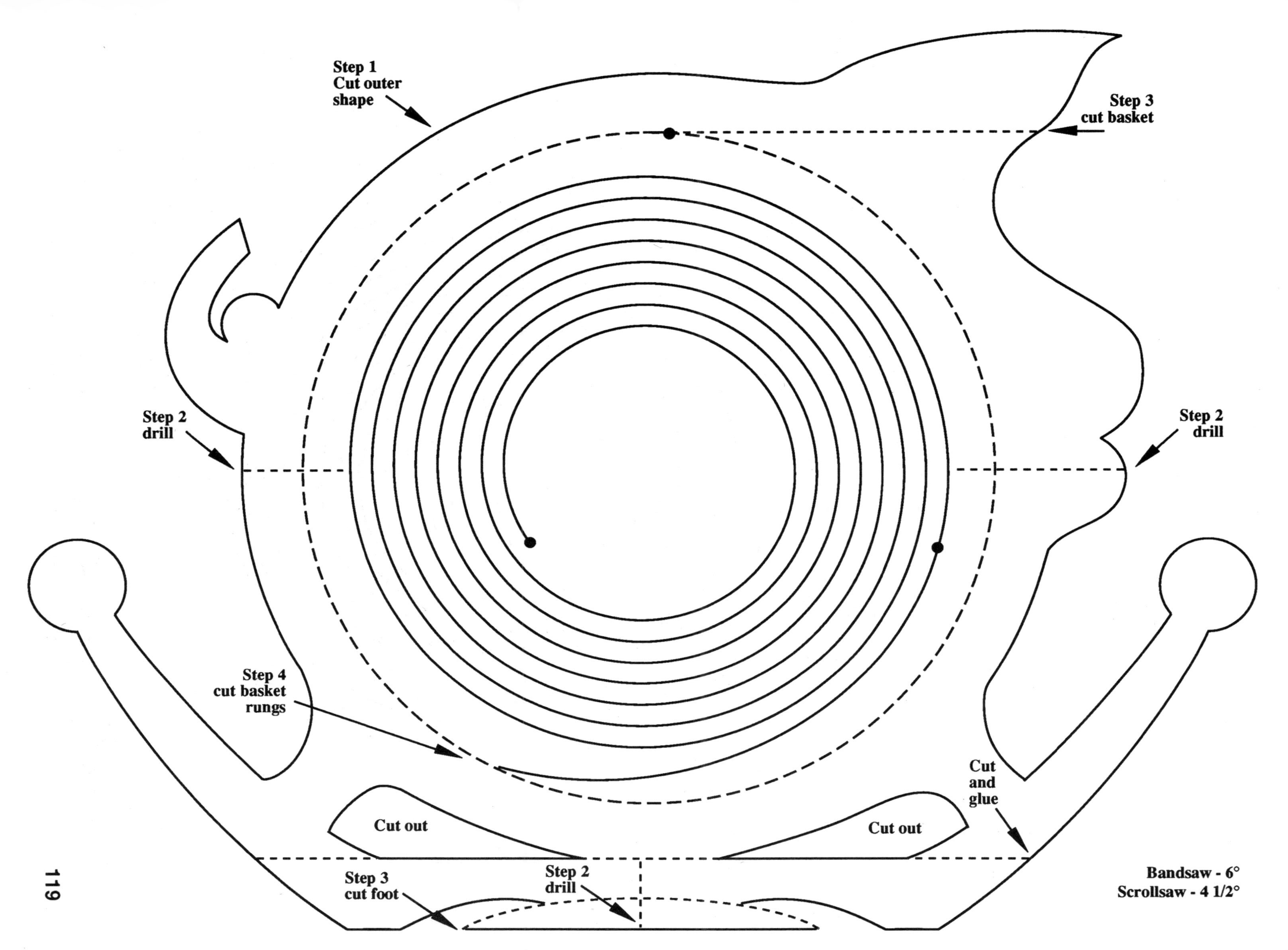

Step 1
Cut outer
shape
Step 3
cut basket
Step 2
drill
Step 2
drill
Step 4
cut basket
rungs
Cut
and
glue
Cut out
Cut out
Step 3
cut foot
Step 2
drill
Bandsaw - 6°
Scrollsaw - 4 1/2°

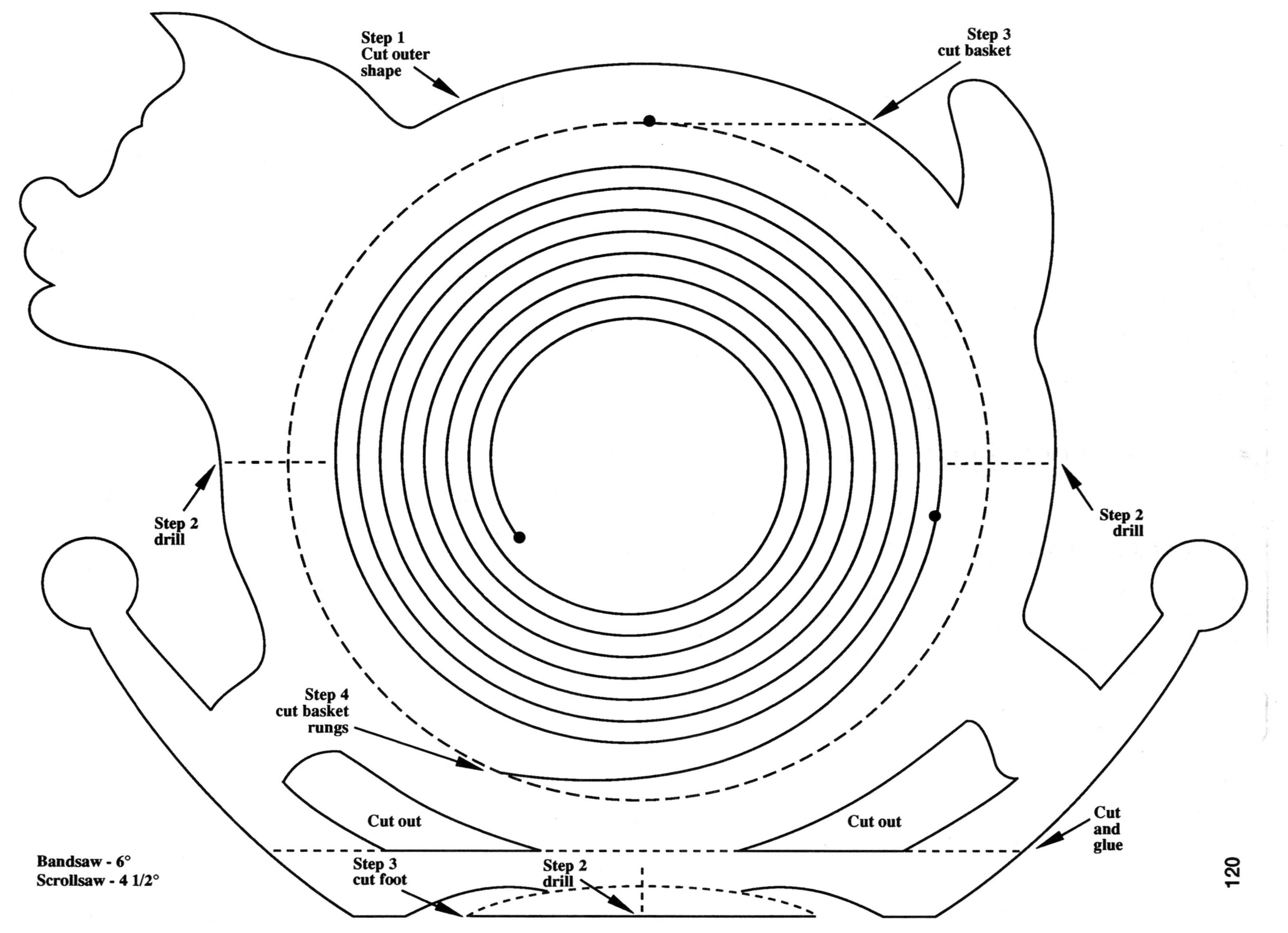
Step 1
Cut outer
shape
Step 3
cut basket
Step 2
drill
Step 2
drill
Step 4
cut basket
rungs
Cut out
Cut out
Cut
and
glue
Bandsaw - 6°
Scrollsaw - 4 1/2°
Step 3
cut foot
Step 2
drill

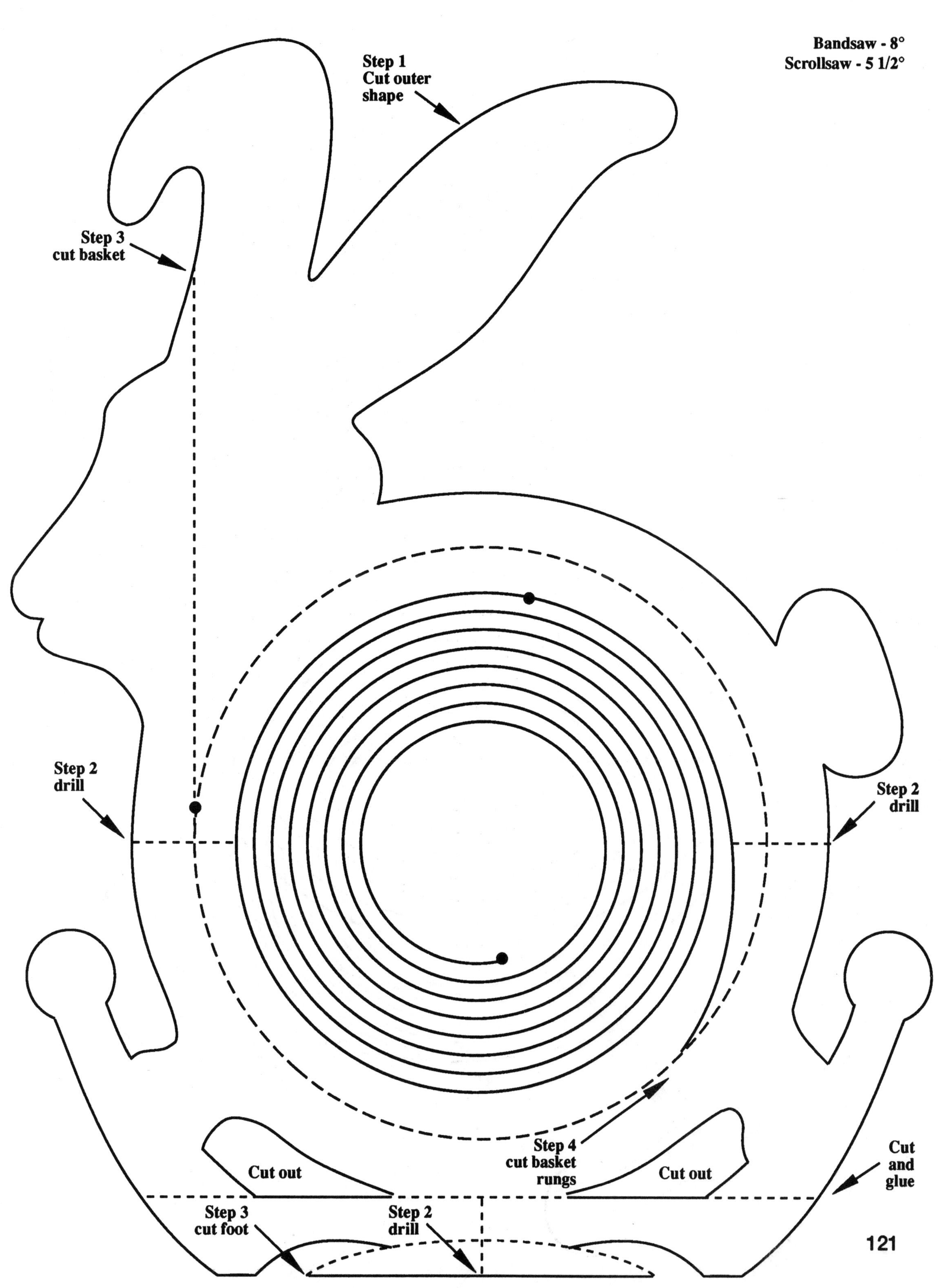

Bandsaw - 8°
Scrollsaw - 5 1/2°
Step 1
Cut outer
shape
Step 3
cut basket
Step 2
drill
Step 2
drill
Step 4
cut basket
rungs
Cut out
Cut out
Cut
and
glue
Step 3
cut foot
Step 2
drill

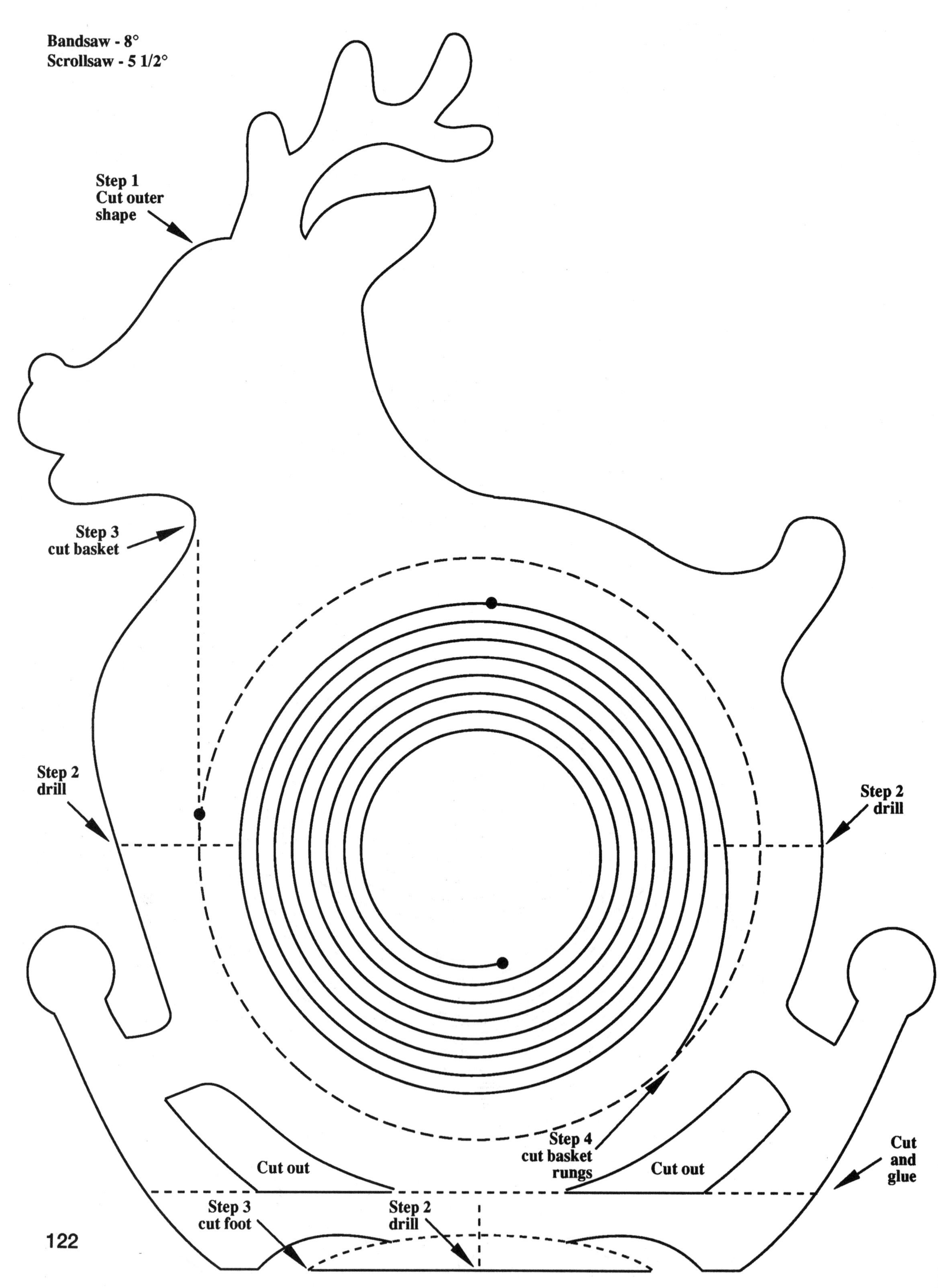

Bandsaw - 8°
Scrollsaw - 5 1/2°
Step 1
Cut outer
shape
Step 3
cut basket
Step 2
drill
Step 2
drill
Step 4
cut basket
rungs
Cut out
Cut out
Cut
and
glue
Step 3
cut foot
Step 2
drill

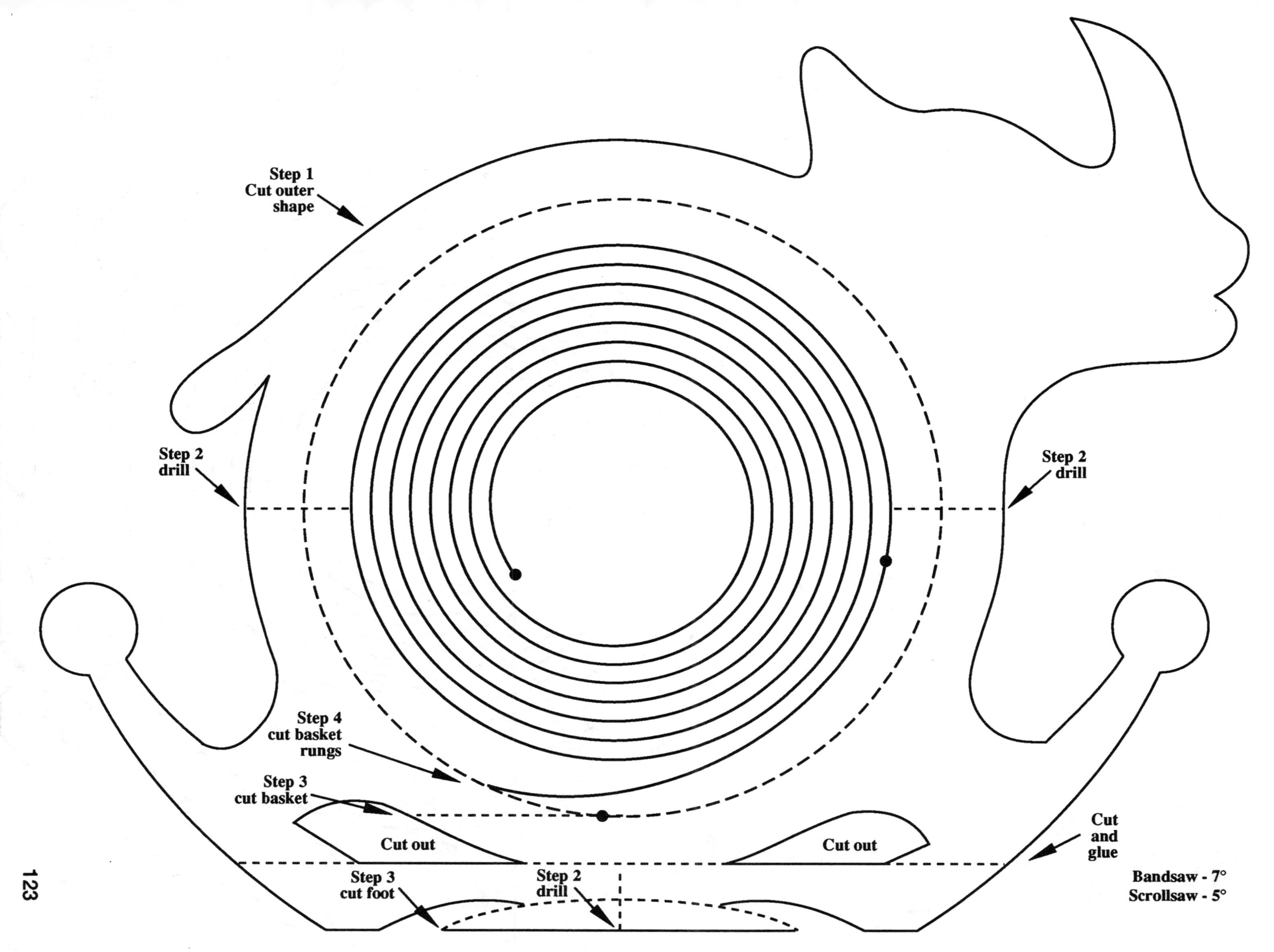
Step 1
Cut outer
shape
Step 2
drill
Step 2
drill
Step 4
cut basket
rungs
Step 3
cut basket
Cut out
Cut out
Cut
and
glue
Step 3
cut foot
Step 2
drill
Bandsaw - 7°
Scrollsaw - 5°

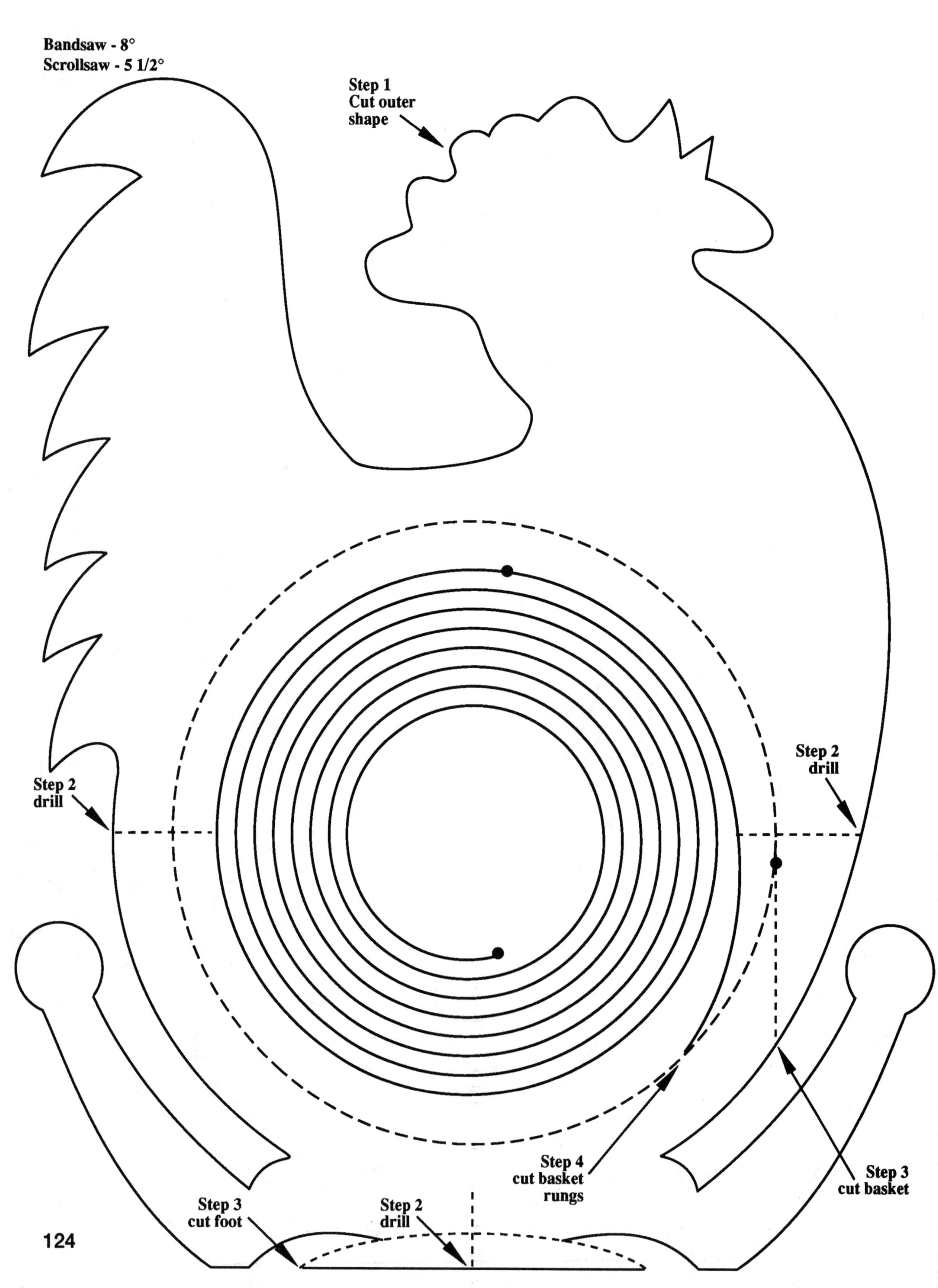
Bandsaw - 8°
Scrollsaw - 5 1/2°
Step 1
Cut outer
shape
Step 2
drill
Step 2
drill
Step 4
cut basket
rungs
Step 3
cut basket
Step 3
cut foot
Step 2
drill

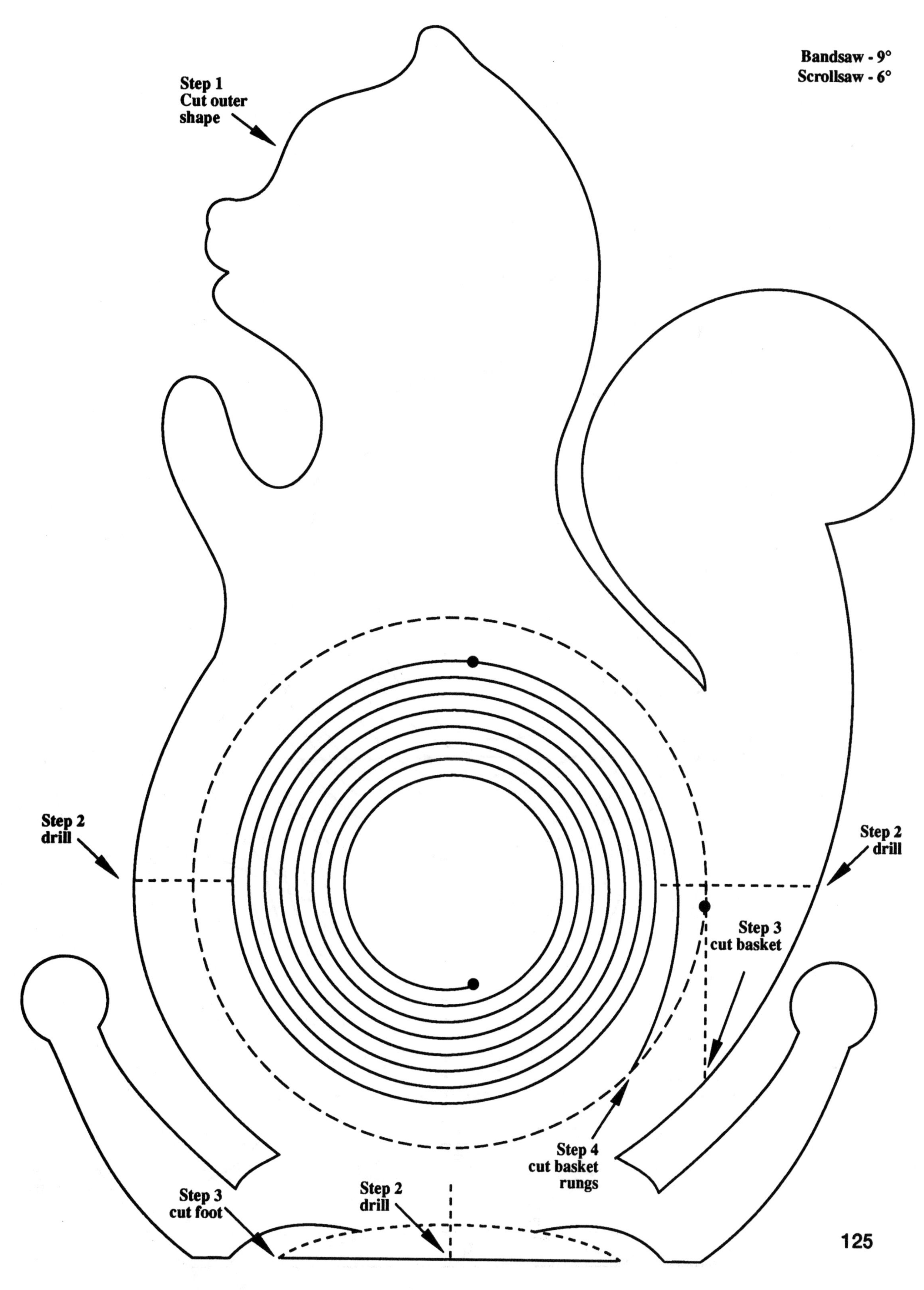
Bandsaw - 9°
Scrollsaw - 6°
Step 1
Cut outer
shape
Step 2
drill
Step 2
drill
Step 3
cut basket
Step 4
cut basket
rungs
Step 3
cut foot
Step 2
drill

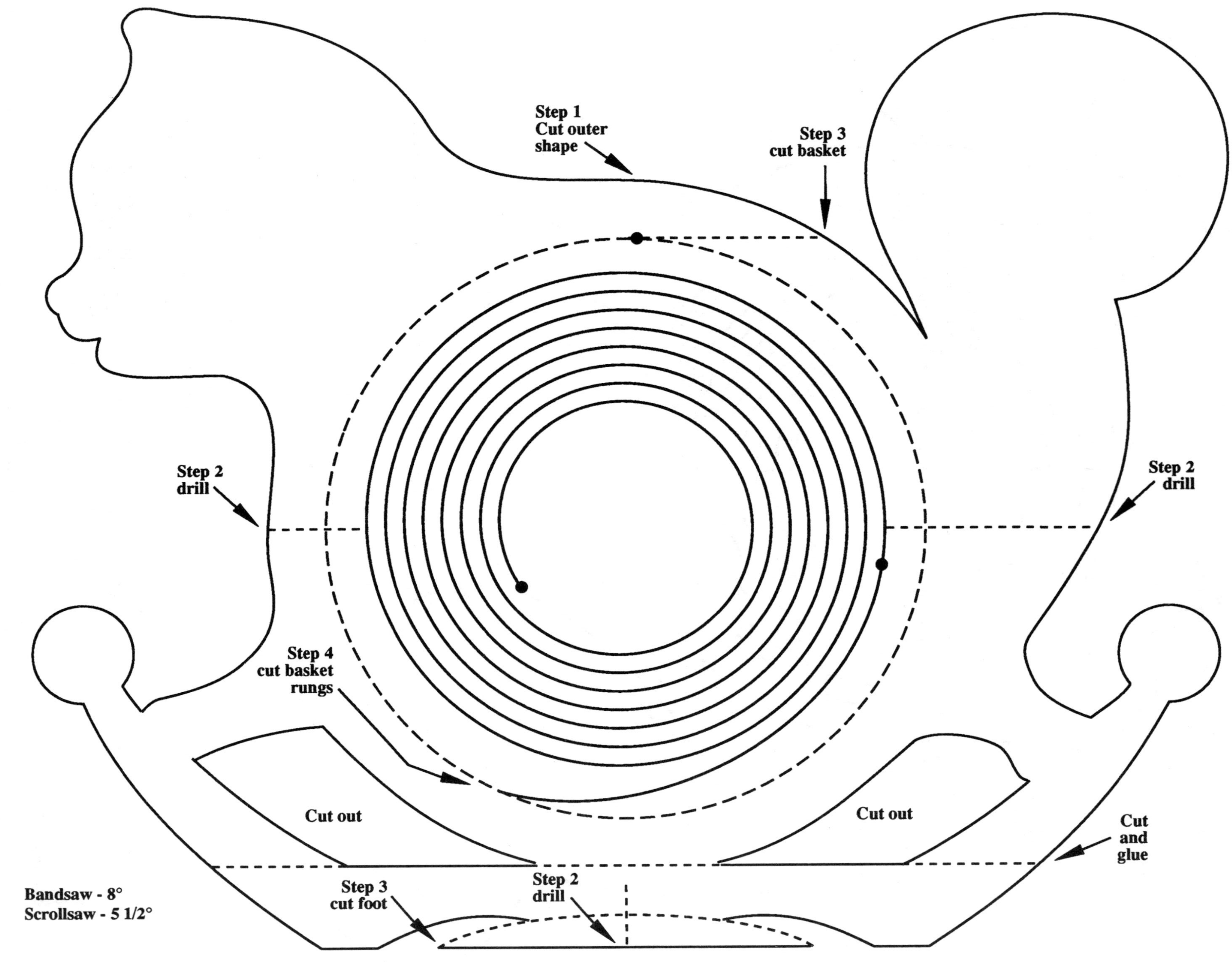
Step 1
Cut outer
shape
Step 3
cut basket
Step 2
drill
Step 2
drill
Step 4
cut basket
rungs
Cut out
Cut out
Cut
and
glue
Step 3
cut foot
Step 2
drill
Bandsaw - 8°
Scrollsaw - 5 1/2°

FREE CATALOG OFFER

Are you interested in more unique designs?

Yes, please add my name to your mailing list for a catalog of more unique ideas.

NAME ____________________

ADDRESS ____________________

CITY ____________________ STATE ______ ZIP ____________

THE BERRY BASKET • PO BOX 925-BK1 • CENTRALIA, WA 98531 • **1-800-206-9009**

Do you have friends who are interested in a catalog of unique ideas?

Yes, please add my friend to your mailing list and send them a catalog of unique ideas.

NAME ____________________

ADDRESS ____________________

CITY ____________________ STATE ______ ZIP ____________

THE BERRY BASKET • PO BOX 925-BK1 • CENTRALIA, WA 98531 • **1-800-206-9009**

WOODWORKING SURVEY

We always appreciate when people take time to write and let us know what they like and what they'd like to see more of. We know more of you would like to do the same, but find it hard to find the time. So here's an opportunity to do just that! It's easy - just grab a pen and mark a box! We'll personally look at every survey returned and use your responses to help design future patterns and projects.

1. My skill level is:
   - ☐ Beginner ☐ Intermediate ☐ Advanced
2. I like to complete projects that are:
   - ☐ Simple ☐ Intermediate ☐ Intricate
3. I prefer projects that require:
   - ☐ Thin material ☐ Thick material (3/4" or more)
   - ☐ Both
4. I feel the amount of instructions/directions pertaining to the patterns/projects in this book are:
   - ☐ Clear and sufficient
   - ☐ Unclear and incomplete
5. My favorite pattern themes are: (mark all that apply)
   - ☐ Wildlife ☐ Religious
   - ☐ Country ☐ Floral
   - ☐ Victorian ☐ Sports
   - ☐ Southwest ☐ Holiday/Celebration
   - ☐ Children's ☐ Other ____________
6. I would like more of the following projects: (mark all that apply)
   - ☐ Clocks ☐ Baskets
   - ☐ Shelves ☐ Mirrors/Picture Frames
   - ☐ Doll Furniture ☐ Plaques
   - ☐ Birdhouses ☐ Other____________

Tape to prepare for mail

Fold here second

The Berry Basket
PO Box 925-BK1
Centralia, WA 98531

Place stamp here

The Berry Basket
PO Box 925-BK1
Centralia, WA 98531

Fold here first